Winner of the Whitbread Award

"How did he do it? How did Seamus Heaney fashion verses, singularly handsome verses that not only capture the somber grandeur and mythic vigor of the Anglo-Saxon original, but also reflect the rhythm and timbre of the English we speak today. . . . This newborn translation makes accessible to everyone the first supremely great poem to be written in the English language."
—Colin Campbell, *Christian Science Monitor*

"Mr. Heaney's translation beats with a recurring pulse, from homely and concrete to elevated and back again. The great battle scenes are rendered with a power and grisly horror both increased and made oddly transparent by a freshness and innocence of diction. . . . In sustaining contrast is the lyricism, quiet yet immediate, of the small passages." —Richard Eder, *New York Times*

"As vivid as a tabloid headline and as visceral as a nightmare. Heaney's own poetic vernacular . . . is the perfect match for the *Beowulf* poet's Anglo-Saxon. Heaney uses this idiom not to modernize the epic but to showcase its surprisingly contemporary feel. . . . As retooled by Heaney, *Beowulf* should easily be good for another millenium." —Malcolm Jones, *Newsweek*

"Heaney's word choices succeed brilliantly in reconstructing a barbaric world. . . . Could well become the classroom standard for the 21st century." —Edward Southern, *Atlanta Journal-Constitution*

"Seamus Heaney's splendid verse translation and bilingual edition of *Beowulf* bring the poem into focus again as a work of the greatest imaginative intensity. . . . *Beowulf* has an elemental grandeur, a ruthless beauty, and an incandescent dignity that belong only to the greatest poetry."
—Edward Hirsch, *Los Angeles Times Book Review*, front-page review

"Heaney's *Beowulf* is a rhythmic masterpiece. He employs a wonderfully malleable 'sprung' or 'broken' tetrameter. . . . Heaney gleefully mixes the stresses, creating a thundering battle of anapests, iambs, amphibrachs and other accents as explosive as Beowulf's brawl with the monster Grendel." —John Mark Eberhart, *Miami Herald*

"Credit for this surge of interest should rest squarely on the marvelous language that Heaney has found to set this old warhorse of a saga running again. . . . Heaney's poetry makes eloquently persuasive the hero's tragic stature. . . . [A] newly burnished treasure." —Paul Gray, *Time*

"Heaney's alliterative translation marches to an ancient beat that drives the poem forward. . . . It's hard to miss [Heaney's] own flair, his grasp of language at once earthy and other-worldly, his bold descriptions and his loud exclamation. *Beowulf* is exciting again." —Deirdre Parker Smith, *Salisbury (N.C.) Post*

"Heaney has transformed *Beowulf* into a hit—a vivid, gripping tale written in an elegant flowing style. . . . Heaney's version is flawless . . . And [his] marvelous introduction . . . is alone worth the price of the book." —Eve Claxton, *Time Out N.Y.*

"How powerful the oldest, most archetypical literary works remain, especially when newly rendered by so accomplished a hand. . . . A new standard for versions of the old epic." —*Booklist*

"*Beowulf* is a fantastic, crackling good yarn. . . . [An] astoundingly warm, briskly paced, blazingly readable reworking. . . . Thanks to Seamus Heaney, [the] tale feels as fresh today as it must have felt all those years ago around the campfire." —Dave Ferman, *Star-Telegram*

"Both casual readers and serious academics should find this new *Beowulf* extremely exciting. A great translation of a great poem must give us glimpses of the original's greatness—but it must have its own particular kind of greatness. And Heaney's does."
—Ron Smith, *Richmond Times-Dispatch*

"Looking back, I wish I had been able to read a translation like Heaney's. It has persuaded me that the poem is indeed a masterpiece."
—D. M. Thomas, *Toronto Globe and Mail*

"[Heaney] has given us a grand, noble, and sorrowful book from a far distant world. To give ourselves up to that world wholly for the length of a concentrated reading can be a spiritual voyage that is profound and unforgettable."
—Peter Neumeyer, *San Diego Union Tribune*

"Heaney's 21-page introduction shines with characteristic clarity and freshness—and should well equip the unfamiliar reader to make a romp, if not a study, of the work itself. . . . [The] translation is utterly enchanting."
—Micheal Pekenham, *The Sun*

"[Heaney] renders the poem in vigorous, fluent lines that read with the directness and ease of good prose. The result is a fresh work, moving and vivid. . . ."
—Fritz Lanham, *Houston Chronicle*

"[A] stunning new translation . . . [that] makes this northern *Gilgamesh* gripping and racy, startlingly contemporary."
—Cynthia L. Haven, *San Francisco Sunday Examiner & Chronicle*

"Heaney is inspired. . . . His introduction [is] itself a profound essay on the poem, and an immediate classic. . . . [A] brilliant millennial *Beowulf*."
—Dan Chiasson, *Boston Book Review*

"An extraordinary accomplishment."   —*Newark Star-Ledger*

"Heaney's Introduction does everything it should. . . . The abiding impression is one of devotion and enthrallment. We end the Introduction sensing that Heaney might have found a great poetic ancestor, and touched hands with him across the centuries. And he has—no question."
   —Andrew Motion, British Poet Laureate, in *The Financial Times*

"Thanks to Seamus Heaney's marvellous recreation—in both senses—this dark and gloomy work finally comes out into the light."   —*The Economist*

"Heaney has turned to *Beowulf*, and the result is magnificent, breathtaking. . . . Heaney has created something imperishable and great that is stainless—stainless, because its force as poetry makes it untouchable by the claw of literalism: it lives singly, as an English language poem."   —James Wood, *The Guardian*

"The translation itself rides boldly through the reefs of scholarship. . . . *Beowulf*, an elegy for heroism and a critique of feud and fratricide, is alive and well."   —Michael Alexander, *The Observer*

"Heaney's excellent translation has the virtue of being both direct and sophisticated, making previous versions look slightly flowery and antique by comparison. His intelligence, fine ear and obvious love of the poem bring *Beowulf* alive as melancholy masterpiece, a complex Christian-pagan lament about duty, glory, loss and transience. . . . Heaney has done it (and us) a great service."

          —Claire Harman, *Evening Standard*

BEOWULF

POETRY

Death of a Naturalist

Door into the Dark

Wintering Out

North

Field Work

Poems 1965–1975

Sweeney Astray: A Version from the Irish

Station Island

The Haw Lantern

Selected Poems 1966–1987

Seeing Things

Sweeney's Flight (with photographs by Rachel Giese)

The Spirit Level

Opened Ground: Selected Poems 1966–1996

CRITICISM

Preoccupations: Selected Prose 1968–1978

The Government of the Tongue

The Redress of Poetry

PLAYS

The Cure at Troy: A Version of Sophocles' Philoctetes

BEOWULF

A NEW VERSE TRANSLATION

SEAMUS HEANEY

W. W. NORTON & COMPANY

New York • London

Library of Congress Cataloging-in-Publication Data
Beowulf. English & English (Old English)
    Beowulf / [translated by] Seamus Heaney. — 1st ed.
        p.   cm.
    Text in English and Old English.
    1. Heroes—Scandinavia—Poetry.   2. Epic poetry, English (Old).
    3. Monsters—Poetry.   4. Dragons—Poetry.   I. Heaney, Seamus.
PE1583.H43   1999
829'.3—dc21   99-23209
    ISBN 0-393-32097-9 pbk.

W. W. Norton & Company, Inc.
500 Fifth Avenue, New York, N.Y. 10110
www.wwnorton.com

W. W. Norton & Company Ltd.
Castle House, 75/76 Wells Street, London W1T 3QT

31 33 35 34 32

The Old English text of the poem is based on Beowulf, with the
Finnesburg Fragment, edited by C. L. Wrenn and W. F. Bolton
(University of Exeter Press, 1988), and is printed here by kind
permission of W. F. Bolton and the University of Exeter Press.

In memory of Ted Hughes

Contents

Introduction

And now this is 'an inheritance'—
Upright, rudimentary, unshiftably planked
In the long ago, yet willable forward

Again and again and again.

BEOWULF: THE POEM

The poem called *Beowulf* was composed sometime between the middle of the seventh and the end of the tenth century of the first millennium, in the language that is to-day called Anglo-Saxon or Old English. It is a heroic narrative, more than three thousand lines long, concerning the deeds of a Scandinavian prince, also called Beowulf, and it stands as one of the foundation works of poetry in English. The fact that the English language has changed so much in the last thousand years means, however, that the poem is now generally read in translation and mostly in English courses at schools and universities. This has contributed to the impression that it was written (as Osip Mandelstam said of *The Divine Comedy*) "on official paper," which is unfortunate, since what we are dealing with is a work of the greatest imaginative vitality, a masterpiece where the structuring of the tale is as elaborate as the beautiful contrivances of its language. Its narrative elements may belong to a previous age but as a work of art it lives in its own continuous present, equal to our knowledge of reality in the present time.

The poem was written in England but the events it describes are set in Scandinavia, in a "once upon a time" that is partly historical. Its hero, Beowulf, is the biggest presence among the warriors in the land of the Geats, a territory situated in what is now southern Sweden, and early in the poem Beowulf crosses the sea to the land of the Danes in order to clear their country of a man-eating monster called Grendel. From this expedition (which involves him in a second contest with Grendel's mother) he returns in triumph and eventually rules for fifty years as king of his homeland. Then a dragon begins to terrorize the countryside and Beowulf must confront it. In a final climactic encounter, he does manage to slay the dragon, but he also meets his own death and enters the legends of his people as a warrior of high renown.

We know about the poem more or less by chance because it exists in one manuscript only. This unique copy (now in the British Library) barely survived a fire in the eighteenth century and was then transcribed and titled, retranscribed and edited, translated and adapted, interpreted and reinterpreted, until it has become canonical. For decades it has been a set book on English syllabuses at university level all over the world. The fact that many English departments require it to be studied in the original continues to generate resistance, most notably at Oxford University, where the pros and cons of the inclusion of part of it as a compulsory element in the English course have been debated regularly in recent years.

For generations of undergraduates, academic study of the poem was often just a matter of construing the meaning, getting a grip on the grammar and vocabulary of Anglo-Saxon, and being able to recognize, translate, and comment upon random extracts which were presented in the examinations. For generations of scholars too the interest had been textual and philological; then there developed a body of research into analogues and sources, a quest for stories and episodes in the folklore and legends of the Nordic peoples which would parallel or foreshadow episodes in *Beowulf*. Scholars were also preoccupied with fixing the exact time and place of the poem's composition, paying minute attention to linguistic, stylistic, and scribal details. More generally, they tried to establish the history and genealogy of the dynasties of Swedes and Geats and Danes to which the poet makes constant allusion; and they devoted themselves to a consideration of the world-view behind the poem, asking to what extent (if at all) the newly Christian understanding of the world which operates in the poet's designing mind displaces him from his imaginative at-homeness in the world of his poem—a pagan Germanic society governed by a heroic code of honour, one where the attainment of a name for warrior-prowess among the living overwhelms any concern about the soul's destiny in the afterlife.

However, when it comes to considering *Beowulf* as a work of literature, there is one publication that stands out. In 1936, the Oxford scholar and teacher J.R.R. Tolkien published an epoch-making paper entitled *"Beowulf:* The Monsters and the Critics" which took for granted the poem's integrity and distinction as a work of art and proceeded to show in what this integrity and distinction inhered. He assumed that the poet had felt his way through the inherited material—the fabulous elements and the traditional accounts of an heroic past—and by a combination of creative intuition and conscious structuring had arrived at a unity of effect and a balanced order. He assumed, in other words, that the *Beowulf* poet was an imaginative writer rather than some kind of back-formation derived from nineteenth-century folklore and philology. Tolkien's brilliant literary treatment changed the way the poem was valued and initiated a new era—and new terms—of appreciation.

It is impossible to attain a full understanding and estimate of *Beowulf* without recourse to this immense body of commentary and elucidation. Nevertheless, readers coming to the poem for the first time are likely to be as delighted as they are discomfited by the strangeness of the names and the immediate lack of known reference points. An English speaker new to *The Iliad* or *The Odyssey* or *The Aeneid* will probably at least have heard of Troy and Helen, or of Penelope and the Cyclops, or of Dido and the golden bough. These epics may be in Greek and Latin, yet the classical heritage has entered the cultural memory enshrined in English so thoroughly that their worlds are more familiar than that of the first native epic, even though it was composed centuries after them. Achilles rings a bell, but not Scyld Scēfing. Ithaca leads the mind in a certain direction, but not Heorot. The Sibyl of Cumae will stir certain associations, but not bad Queen Modthryth. First-time readers of *Beowulf* very quickly rediscover the meaning of the term "the dark ages," and it is in the hope of dispelling some of the puzzlement they are bound to feel that I have added the marginal glosses which appear in the following pages.

Still, in spite of the sensation of being caught between a "shield-wall" of opaque references and a "word-hoard" that is old and strange, such readers are also bound to feel a certain "shock of the new." This is because the poem possesses a mythic potency. Like Shield Sheafson (as Scyld Scēfing is known in this translation), it arrives from somewhere beyond the known bourne of our experience, and having fulfilled its purpose (again like Shield), it passes once more into the beyond. In the intervening time, the poet conjures up a work as remote as Shield's funeral boat borne towards the horizon, as commanding as the horn-pronged gables of King Hrothgar's hall, as solid and dazzling as Beowulf's funeral pyre that is set ablaze at the end. These opening and closing scenes retain a haunting presence in the mind; they are set pieces but they have the life-marking power of certain dreams. They are like the pillars of the gate of horn, through which wise dreams of true art can still be said to pass.

What happens in between is what William Butler Yeats would have called a phantasmagoria. Three agons, three struggles in which the preternatural force-for-evil of the hero's enemies comes springing at him in demonic shapes. Three encounters with what the critical literature and the textbook glossaries call "the monsters." In three archetypal sites of fear: the barricaded night-house, the infested underwater current, and the reptile-haunted rocks of a wilderness. If we think of the poem in this way, its place in world art becomes clearer and more secure. We can conceive of it re-presented and transformed in performance in a *bunraku* theatre in Japan, where the puppetry and the poetry are mutually supportive, a mixture of technicolour spectacle and ritual chant. Or we can equally envisage it as an animated cartoon (and there has been at least one shot at this already), full of mutating graphics and minatory stereophonics. We can avoid, at any rate, the slightly cardboard effect which the word "monster" tends to introduce, and give the poem a fresh chance to sweep "in off the moors, down through the mist bands" of Anglo-Saxon England, forward into the global village of the third millennium.

Nevertheless, the dream element and overall power to haunt come at a certain readerly price. The poem abounds in passages which will leave an unprepared audience bewildered. Just when the narrative seems ready to take another step ahead into the main Beowulf story, it sidesteps. For a moment it is as if we have been channel-surfed into another poem, and at two points in this translation I indicate that we are in fact participating in a poem-within-our-poem not only by the use of italics but by a slight quickening of pace and shortening of metrical rein. The passages occur in lines 883–914 and lines 1070–1158, and on each occasion a minstrel has begun to chant a poem as part of the celebration of Beowulf's achievement. In the former case, the minstrel expresses his praise by telling the story of Sigemund's victory over a dragon, which both parallels Beowulf's triumph over Grendel and prefigures his fatal encounter with the *wyrm* in his old age. In the latter—the most famous of what were once called the "digressions" in the poem, the one dealing with a fight between Danes and Frisians at the stronghold of Finn, the Frisian king— the song the minstrel sings has a less obvious bearing on the immediate situation of the hero, but its import is nevertheless central to both the historical and the imaginative world of the poem.

The "Finnsburg episode" envelops us in a society that is at once honour-bound and blood-stained, presided over by the laws of the blood-feud, where the kin of a person slain are bound to exact a price for the death, either by slaying the killer or by receiving satisfaction in the form of *wergild* (the "man-price"), a legally fixed compensation. The claustrophobic and doom-laden atmosphere of this interlude gives the reader an intense intimation of what *wyrd*, or fate, meant not only to the characters in the Finn story but to those participating in the main action of *Beowulf* itself. All conceive of themselves as hooped within the great wheel of necessity, in thrall to a code of loyalty and bravery, bound to seek glory in the eye of the warrior world. The little nations are grouped around their lord, the greater nations spoil for war and menace the little ones, a lord dies, defencelessness ensues, the enemy strikes, vengeance for the dead becomes an ethic for the living, bloodshed begets further bloodshed, the wheel turns, the generations tread and tread and tread. Which is what I meant above when I said that the import of the Finnsburg passage is central to the historical and imaginative world of the poem as a whole.

One way of reading *Beowulf* is to think of it as three agons in the hero's life, but another way would be to regard it as a poem which contemplates the destinies of three peoples by tracing their interweaving histories in the story of the central character. First we meet the Danes—variously known as the Shieldings (after Shield Sheafson, the founder of their line), the Ingwins, the Spear-Danes, the Bright-Danes, the West-Danes, and so on—a people in the full summer of their power, symbolized by the high hall built by King Hrothgar, one "meant to be a wonder of the world." The threat to this gilded order comes from within, from marshes beyond the pale, from the bottom of the haunted mere where "Cain's clan," in the shape of Grendel and his troll-dam, trawl and scavenge and bide their time. But it also comes from without, from the Heathobards, for example, whom the Danes have defeated in battle and from whom they can therefore expect retaliatory war (see ll. 2020–69).

Beowulf actually predicts this turn of events when he goes back to his own country after saving the Danes (for the time being, at any rate) by staving off the two "reavers from hell." In the hall of his "ring-giver," Hygelac, lord of the Geats, the hero discourses about his adventures in a securely fortified cliff-top enclosure. But this security is only temporary, for it is the destiny of the Geat people to be left lordless in the end. Hygelac's alliances eventually involve him in deadly war with the Swedish king, Ongentheow, and even though he does not personally deliver the fatal stroke (two of his thanes are responsible for this—see ll. 2484–89 and then the lengthier reprise of this incident at ll. 2922–3003), he is known in the poem as "Ongentheow's killer." Hence it comes to pass that after the death of Beowulf, who eventually succeeds Hygelac, the Geats experience a great foreboding and the epic closes in a mood of sombre expectation. A world is passing away, the Swedes and others are massing on the borders to attack, and there is no lord or hero to rally the defence.

The Swedes, therefore, are the third nation whose history and destiny are woven into the narrative, and even though no part of the main action is set in their territory, they and their kings constantly stalk the horizon of dread within which the main protagonists pursue their conflicts and allegiances. The Swedish dimension gradually becomes an important element in the poem's emotional and imaginative geography, a geography which entails, it should be said, no very clear map-sense of the world, more an apprehension of menaced borders, of danger gathering beyond the mere and the marshes, of *mearc-stapas* "prowling the moors, huge marauders / from some other world."

Within these phantasmal boundaries, each lord's hall is an actual and a symbolic refuge. Here is heat and light, rank and ceremony, human solidarity and culture; the *duguð* share the mead-benches with the *geogoð*, the veterans with their tales of warrior kings and hero-saviours from the past rub shoulders with young braves—*þegnas*, *eorlas*, thanes, retainers—keen to win such renown in the future. The prospect of gaining a glorious name in the *wael-raes*, in the rush of battle-slaughter, the pride of defending one's lord and bearing heroic witness to the integrity of the bond between him and his hall-companions—a bond sealed in the *gléo* and *gidd* of peace-time feasting and ring-giving—this is what gave drive and sanction to the Germanic warrior-culture enshrined in *Beowulf*.

Heorot and Hygelac's hall are the hubs of this value system upon which the poem's action turns. But there is another, outer rim of value, a circumference of understanding within which the heroic world is occasionally viewed as from a distance and recognized for what it is, an earlier state of consciousness and culture, one which has not been altogether shed but which has now been comprehended as part of another pattern. And this circumference and pattern arise, of course, from the poet's Christianity and from his perspective as an Englishman looking back at places and legends which his ancestors knew before they made their migration from continental Europe to their new home on the island of the Britons. As a consequence of his doctrinal certitude, which is as composed as it is ardent, the poet can view the story-time of his poem with a certain historical detachment and even censure the ways of those who lived *in illo tempore*:

> Sometimes at pagan shrines they vowed
> offerings to idols, swore oaths
> that the killer of souls might come to their aid
> and save the people. That was their way,
> their heathenish hope; deep in their hearts
> they remembered hell.   (ll. 175–80)

At the same time, as a result of his inherited vernacular culture and the imaginative sympathy which distinguishes him as an artist, the poet can lend the full weight of his rhetorical power to Beowulf as he utters the first principles of the northern warrior's honour-code:

> It is always better
> to avenge dear ones than to indulge in mourning.

For every one of us, living in this world
means waiting for our end. Let whoever can
win glory before death. When a warrior is gone,
that will be his best and only bulwark. (ll. 1384–89)

In an age when "the instability of the human subject" is constantly argued for if not presumed, there should be no problem with a poem which is woven from two such different psychic fabrics. In fact, *Beowulf* perfectly answers the early modern conception of a work of creative imagination as one in which conflicting realities find accommodation within a new order; and this reconciliation occurs, it seems to me, most poignantly and most profoundly in the poem's third section, once the dragon enters the picture and the hero in old age must gather his powers for the final climactic ordeal. From the moment Beowulf advances under the crags, into the comfortless arena bounded by the rock-wall, the reader knows he is one of those "marked by fate." The poetry is imbued with a strong intuition of *wyrd* hovering close, "unknowable but certain," and yet, because it is imagined within a consciousness which has learned to expect that the soul will find an ultimate home "among the steadfast ones," this primal human emotion has been transmuted into something less "zero at the bone," more metaphysically tempered.

A similar transposition from a plane of regard which is, as it were, helmeted and hall-bound to one which sees things in a slightly more heavenly light is discernible in the different ways the poet imagines gold. Gold is a constant element, gleaming solidly in underground vaults, on the breasts of queens or the arms and regalia of warriors on the mead-benches. It is loaded into boats as spoil, handed out in bent bars as hall gifts, buried in the earth as treasure, persisting underground as an affirmation of a people's glorious past and an elegy for it. It pervades the ethos of the poem the way sex pervades consumer culture. And yet the bullion with which Waels's son, Sigemund, weighs down the hold after an earlier dragon-slaying triumph (in the old days, long before Beowulf's time) is a more trustworthy substance than that which is secured behind the walls of Beowulf's barrow. By the end of the poem, gold has suffered a radiation from the Christian vision. It is not that it yet equals riches in the medieval sense of worldly corruption, just that its status as the ore of all value has been put in doubt. It is *lǣne*, transitory, passing from hand to hand, and its changed status is registered as a symptom of the changed world. Once the dragon is disturbed, the melancholy and sense of displacement which pervade the last movement of the poem enter the hoard as a disabling and ominous light. And the dragon himself, as a genius of the older order, is bathed in this light, so that even as he begins to stir, the reader has a premonition that the days of his empery are numbered.

Nevertheless, the dragon has a wonderful inevitability about him and a unique glamour. It is not that the other monsters are lacking in presence and aura; it is more that they remain, for all their power to terrorize, creatures of the physical world. Grendel comes alive in the reader's imagination as a kind of dog-breath in the dark, a fear of collision with some hard-boned and immensely strong android frame, a mixture of Caliban and hoplite. And while his mother too has a definite brute-bearing about her, a creature of slouch and lunge on land if seal-swift in the water, she nevertheless retains a certain non-strangeness. As antagonists of a hero being tested, Grendel and his mother possess an appropriate head-on strength. The poet may need them as figures who do the devil's work, but the poem needs them more as figures who call up and show off Beowulf's physical might and his superb gifts as a warrior. They are the right enemies for a young glory-hunter, instigators of the formal boast, worthy trophies to be carried back from the grim testing-ground— Grendel's arm is ripped off and nailed up, his head severed and paraded in Heorot. It is all consonant with the surge of youth and the compulsion to win fame "as wide as the wind's home, /

as the sea around cliffs," utterly a manifestation of the Germanic heroic code.

Enter then, fifty years later, the dragon. From his dry-stone vault, from a nest where he is heaped in coils around the body-heated gold. Once he is wakened, there is something glorious in the way he manifests himself, a Fourth of July effulgence fire-working its path across the night sky; and yet, because of the centuries he has spent dormant in the tumulus, there is a found-edness as well as a lambency about him. He is at once a stratum of the earth and a streamer in the air, no painted dragon but a fig-ure of real oneiric power, one that can easily survive the preju-dice which arises at the very mention of the word "dragon." Whether in medieval art or in modern Disney cartoons, the dragon can strike us as far less horrific than he is meant to be, but in the final movement of *Beowulf*, he lodges himself in the imagi-nation as *wyrd* rather than *wyrm*, more a destiny than a set of rep-tilian vertebrae.

Grendel and his mother enter Beowulf's life from the outside, accidentally, challenges which in other circumstances he might not have taken up, enemies from whom he might have been dis-tracted or deflected. The dragon, on the other hand, is a given of his home ground, abiding in his underearth as in his understand-ing, waiting for the meeting, the watcher at the ford, the ques-tioner who sits so sly, the "lion-limb," as Gerard Manley Hopkins might have called him, against whom Beowulf's body and soul must measure themselves. Dragon equals shadow-line, the psalmist's valley of the shadow of death, the embodiment of a knowledge deeply ingrained in the species which is the very knowledge of the price to be paid for physical and spiritual sur-vival.

It has often been observed that all the scriptural references in *Beowulf* are to the Old Testament. The poet is more in sympathy with the tragic, waiting, unredeemed phase of things than with any transcendental promise. Beowulf's mood as he gets ready to fight the dragon—who could be read as a projection of Beowulf's own chthonic wisdom refined in the crucible of experience—recalls the mood of other tragic heroes: Oedipus at Colonus, Lear at his "ripeness is all" extremity, Hamlet in the last illuminations of his "prophetic soul":

> no easy bargain
> would be made in that place by any man.
>
> The veteran king sat down on the cliff-top.
> He wished good luck to the Geats who had shared
> his hearth and his gold. He was sad at heart,
> unsettled yet ready, sensing his death.
> His fate hovered near, unknowable but certain.   (ll. 2415–21)

Here the poet attains a level of insight that approaches the visionary. The subjective and the inevitable are in perfect balance, what is solidly established is bathed in an element which is completely sixth-sensed, and indeed the whole slow-motion, constantly self-deferring approach to the hero's death and funeral continues to be like this. Beowulf's soul may not yet have fled "to its destined place among the steadfast ones," but there is already a beyond-the-grave aspect to him, a revenant quality about his resoluteness. This is not just metrical narrative full of anthropological interest and typical heroic-age motifs; it is poetry of a high order, in which passages of great lyric intensity—such as the "Lay of the Last Survivor" (ll. 2247–66) and, even more remarkably, the so-called "Father's Lament" (ll. 2444–62)—rise like emanations from some fissure in the bedrock of the human capacity to endure:

> It was like the misery felt by an old man
> who has lived to see his son's body
> swing on the gallows. He begins to keen
> and weep for his boy, watching the raven
> gloat where he hangs: he can be of no help.

The wisdom of age is worthless to him.
Morning after morning, he wakes to remember
that his child has gone; he has no interest
in living on until another heir
is born in the hall . . .

. . . .

Alone with his longing, he lies down on his bed
and sings a lament; everything seems too large,
the steadings and the fields.

Such passages mark an ultimate stage in poetic attainment; they are the imaginative equivalent of Beowulf's spiritual state at the end, when he tells his men that "doom of battle will bear [their] lord away," in the same way that the sea-journeys so vividly described in lines 210–28 and 1903–24 are the equivalent of his exultant prime.

At these moments of lyric intensity, the keel of the poetry is deeply set in the element of sensation while the mind's lookout sways metrically and far-sightedly in the element of pure comprehension. Which is to say that the elevation of *Beowulf* is always, paradoxically, buoyantly down to earth. And nowhere is this more obviously and memorably the case than in the account of the hero's funeral with which the poem ends. Here the inexorable and the elegiac combine in a description of the funeral pyre being got ready, the body being burnt, and the barrow being constructed—a scene at once immemorial and oddly contemporary. The Geat woman who cries out in dread as the flames consume the body of her dead lord could come straight from a late-twentieth-century news report, from Rwanda or Kosovo; her keen is a nightmare glimpse into the minds of people who have survived traumatic, even monstrous events and who are now being exposed to a comfortless future. We immediately recognize her predicament and the pitch of her grief and find ourselves the better for having them expressed with such adequacy and dignity and unforgiving truth:

On a height they kindled the hugest of all
funeral fires; fumes of woodsmoke
billowed darkly up, the blaze roared
and drowned out their weeping, wind died down
and flames wrought havoc in the hot bone-house,
burning it to the core. They were disconsolate
and wailed aloud for their lord's decease.
A Geat woman too sang out in grief;
with hair bound up, she unburdened herself
of her worst fears, a wild litany
of nightmare and lament: her nation invaded,
enemies on the rampage, bodies in piles,
slavery and abasement. Heaven swallowed the smoke.

(ll. 3143–55)

ABOUT THIS TRANSLATION

When I was an undergraduate at Queen's University, Belfast, I studied *Beowulf* and other Anglo-Saxon poems and developed not only a feel for the language but a fondness for the melancholy and fortitude that characterized the poetry. Consequently, when an invitation to translate the poem arrived from the editors of *The Norton Anthology of English Literature,* I was tempted to try my hand. While I had no great expertise in Old English, I had a strong desire to get back to the first stratum of the language and to "assay the hoard" (l. 2509). This was during the middle years of the 1980s, when I had begun a regular teaching job at Harvard and was opening my ear to the untethered music of some contemporary American poetry. Saying yes to the *Beowulf* commission would be (I argued with myself) a kind of aural antidote, a way of ensuring that my linguistic anchor would stay lodged on the Anglo-Saxon sea-floor. So I undertook to do it.

Very soon, however, I hesitated. It was labour-intensive work, scriptorium-slow. I worked dutifully, like a sixth-former at homework. I would set myself twenty lines a day, write out my glossary of hard words in longhand, try to pick a way through the syntax, get the run of the meaning established in my head, and then hope that the lines could be turned into metrical shape and raised to the power of verse. Often, however, the whole attempt to turn it into modern English seemed to me like trying to bring down a megalith with a toy hammer. What had been so attractive in the first place, the hand-built, rock-sure feel of the thing, began to defeat me. I turned to other work, the commissioning editors did not pursue me, and the project went into abeyance.

Even so, I had an instinct that it should not be let go. An understanding I had worked out for myself concerning my own linguistic and literary origins made me reluctant to abandon the task. I had noticed, for example, that without any conscious intent on my part certain lines in the first poem in my first book conformed to the requirements of Anglo-Saxon metrics. These lines were made up of two balancing halves, each half containing two stressed syllables—"the spade sinks   into gravelly ground: / My father, digging.   I look down"—and in the case of the second line, there was alliteration linking "digging" and "down" across the caesura. Part of me, in other words, had been writing Anglo-Saxon from the start.

This was not surprising, given that the poet who had first formed my ear was Gerard Manley Hopkins. Hopkins was a chip off the Old English block, and the earliest lines I published when I was a student were as much pastiche Anglo-Saxon as they were pastiche Hopkins: "Starling thatch-watches and sudden swallow / Straight breaks to mud-nest, home-rest rafter" and so on. I have written about all this elsewhere and about the relation of my Hopkins ventriloquism to the speech patterns of Ulster—especially as these were caricatured by the poet W. R. Rodgers. Ulster people, according to Rodgers, are "an abrupt people / who like the spiky consonants of speech / and think the soft ones cissy" and get a kick out of "anything that gives or takes attack / like Micks, Teagues, tinkers' gets, Vatican."

Joseph Brodsky once said that poets' biographies are present in the sounds they make and I suppose all I am saying is that I consider *Beowulf* to be part of my voice-right. And yet to persuade myself that I was born into its language and that its language was born into me took a while: for somebody who grew up in the political and cultural conditions of Lord Brookeborough's Northern Ireland, it could hardly have been otherwise.

Sprung from an Irish nationalist background and educated at a Northern Irish Catholic school, I had learned the Irish language and lived within a cultural and ideological frame that regarded it as the language which I should by rights have been speaking but which I had been robbed of. I have also written, for example, about the thrill I experienced when I stumbled upon the word *lachtar* in my Irish-English dictionary and found that this word, which my aunt had always used when speaking of a flock of chicks, was in fact an Irish language word, and, more than that, an Irish word associated in particular with County Derry. Yet here it was, surviving in my aunt's English speech generations after her forebears and mine had ceased to speak Irish. For a long time, therefore, the little word was—to borrow a simile from Joyce—like a rapier point of consciousness pricking me with an awareness of language-loss and cultural dispossession, and tempting me into binary thinking about language. I tended to conceive of English and Irish as adversarial tongues, as either/or conditions rather than both/ands, and this was an attitude which for a long time hampered the development of a more confident and creative way of dealing with the whole vexed question—the question, that is, of the relationship between nationality, language, history, and literary tradition in Ireland.

Luckily, I glimpsed the possibility of release from this kind of cultural determinism early on, in my first arts year at Queen's University, Belfast, when we were lectured on the history of the English language by Professor John Braidwood. Braidwood could not help informing us, for example, that the word "whiskey" is the same word as the Irish and Scots Gaelic word

uisce, meaning water, and that the River Usk in Britain is there-
fore to some extent the River Uisce (or Whiskey); and so in my
mind the stream was suddenly turned into a kind of linguistic
river of rivers issuing from a pristine Celto-British Land of Cock-
aigne, a riverrun of Finnegans Wakespeak pouring out of the
cleft rock of some pre-political, prelapsarian, ur-philological
Big Rock Candy Mountain—and all of this had a wonderfully
sweetening effect upon me. The Irish/English duality, the
Celtic/Saxon antithesis were momentarily collapsed, and in the
resulting etymological eddy a gleam of recognition flashed
through the synapses and I glimpsed an elsewhere of potential
which seemed at the same time to be a somewhere being remem-
bered. The place on the language map where the Usk and the
uisce and the whiskey coincided was definitely a place where the
spirit might find a loophole, an escape route from what John
Montague has called "the partitioned intellect," away into some
unpartitioned linguistic country, a region where one's language
would not be a simple badge of ethnicity or a matter of cultural
preference or official imposition, but an entry into further lan-
guage. And I eventually came upon one of these loopholes in
Beowulf itself.

What happened was that I found in the glossary to C. L.
Wrenn's edition of the poem the Old English word meaning "to
suffer," the word *þolian;* and although at first it looked com-
pletely strange with its thorn symbol instead of the familiar *th,* I
gradually realized that it was not strange at all, for it was the
word that older and less educated people would have used in the
country where I grew up. "They'll just have to learn to thole," my
aunt would say about some family who had suffered an unfore-
seen bereavement. And now suddenly here was "thole" in the
official textual world, mediated through the apparatus of a schol-
arly edition, a little bleeper to remind me that my aunt's lan-
guage was not just a self-enclosed family possession but an
historical heritage, one that involved the journey *þolian* had

made north into Scotland and then across into Ulster with the planters and then across from the planters to the locals who had originally spoken Irish and then farther across again when the Scots Irish emigrated to the American South in the eighteenth century. When I read in John Crowe Ransom the line "Sweet ladies, long may ye bloom, and toughly I hope ye may thole," my heart lifted again, the world widened, something was furthered. The far-flungness of the word, the phenomenological pleasure of finding it variously transformed by Ransom's modernity and *Beowulf*'s venerability made me feel vaguely something for which again I only found the words years later. What I was experiencing as I kept meeting up with *thole* on its multicultural odyssey was the feeling which Osip Mandelstam once defined as a "nostalgia for world culture." And this was a nostalgia I didn't even know I suffered until I experienced its fulfilment in this little epiphany. It was as if, on the analogy of baptism by desire, I had undergone something like illumination by philology. And even though I did not know it at the time, I had by then reached the point where I was ready to translate *Beowulf*. *Polian* had opened my right-of-way.

So, in a sense, the decision to accept Norton's invitation was taken thirty-five years before the invitation was actually issued. But between one's sense of readiness to take on a subject and the actual inscription of the first lines, there is always a problematical hiatus. To put it another way: from the point of view of the writer, words in a poem need what the Polish poet Anna Swir once called "the equivalent of a biological right to life." The erotics of composition are essential to the process, some pre-reflective excitation and orientation, some sense that your own little verse-craft can dock safe and sound at the big quay of the language. And this is as true for translators as it is for poets attempting original work.

It is one thing to find lexical meanings for the words and to have some feel for how the metre might go, but it is quite another thing to find the tuning fork that will give you the note and pitch for the overall music of the work. Without some melody sensed or promised, it is simply impossible for a poet to establish the translator's right-of-way into and through a text. I was therefore lucky to hear this enabling note almost straight away, a familiar local voice, one that had belonged to relatives of my father's, people whom I had once described in a poem as "big voiced Scullions."

I called them "big voiced" because when the men of the family spoke, the words they uttered came across with a weighty distinctness, phonetic units as separate and defined as delph platters displayed on a dresser shelf. A simple sentence such as "We cut the corn to-day" took on immense dignity when one of the Scullions spoke it. They had a kind of Native American solemnity of utterance, as if they were announcing verdicts rather than making small talk. And when I came to ask myself how I wanted *Beowulf* to sound in my version, I realized I wanted it to be speakable by one of those relatives. I therefore tried to frame the famous opening lines in cadences that would have suited their voices, but that still echoed with the sound and sense of the Anglo-Saxon:

Hwaet wē Gār-Dena   in geār-dagum
þēod-cyninga   þrym gefrūnon,
hū ðā æþelingas   ellen fremedon.

Conventional renderings of *hwaet*, the first word of the poem, tend towards the archaic literary, with "lo" and "hark" and "behold" and "attend" and—more colloquially—"listen" being some of the solutions offered previously. But in Hiberno-English Scullionspeak, the particle "so" came naturally to the rescue, because in that idiom "so" operates as an expression which obliterates all previous discourse and narrative, and at the same time functions as an exclamation calling for immediate attention. So, "so" it was:

So. The Spear-Danes in days gone by
and the kings who ruled them had courage and greatness.
We have heard of those princes' heroic campaigns.

I came to the task of translating *Beowulf* with a prejudice in
favour of forthright delivery. I remembered the voice of the poem
as being attractively direct, even though the diction was ornate
and the narrative method at times oblique. What I had always
loved was a kind of foursquareness about the utterance, a feeling
of living inside a constantly indicative mood, in the presence of
an understanding that assumes you share an awareness of the
perilous nature of life and are yet capable of seeing it steadily
and, when necessary, sternly. There is an undeluded quality
about the *Beowulf* poet's sense of the world which gives his lines
immense emotional credibility and allows him to make general
observations about life which are far too grounded in experi-
ence and reticence to be called "moralizing." These so-called
"gnomic" parts of the poem have the cadence and force of earned
wisdom, and their combination of cogency and verity was again
something that I could remember from the speech I heard as a
youngster in the Scullion kitchen. When I translate lines 24–25 as
"Behaviour that's admired / is the path to power among people
everywhere," I am attending as much to the grain of my original
vernacular as to the content of the Anglo-Saxon lines. But then
the evidence suggests that this middle ground between oral tra-
dition and the demands of written practice was also the ground
occupied by the *Beowulf* poet. The style of the poem is hospitable
to the kind of formulaic phrases which are the stock-in-trade of
oral bards, and yet it is marked too by the self-consciousness of
an artist convinced that "we must labour to be beautiful."

In one area, my own labours have been less than thorough-
going. I have not followed the strict metrical rules that bound the
Anglo-Saxon *scop*. I have been guided by the fundamental pat-
tern of four stresses to the line, but I allow myself several trans-
gressions. For example, I don't always employ alliteration, and

sometimes I alliterate only in one half of the line. When these breaches occur, it is because I prefer to let the natural "sound of sense" prevail over the demands of the convention: I have been reluctant to force an artificial shape or an unusual word choice just for the sake of correctness.

In general, the alliteration varies from the shadowy to the substantial, from the properly to the improperly distributed. Substantial and proper are such lines as

The fórtunes of wár   fávoured Hróthgar   (l. 64)
the híghest in the land,   would lénd advíce   (l. 172)
and fínd friéndship   in the Fáther's embráce   (l. 188).

Here the caesura is definite, there are two stresses in each half of the line, and the first stressed syllable of the second half alliterates with the first or the second or both of the stressed syllables in the first half. The main deviation from this is one which other translators have allowed themselves—the freedom, that is, to alliterate on the fourth stressed syllable, a practice which breaks the rule but which nevertheless does bind the line together:

We have héard of those prínces'   heróic campáigns   (l. 3)
and he cróssed óver   into the Lórd's kéeping   (l. 27).

In the course of the translation, such deviations, distortions, syncopations, and extensions do occur; what I was after first and foremost was a narrative line that sounded as if it meant business, and I was prepared to sacrifice other things in pursuit of this directness of utterance.

The appositional nature of the Old English syntax, for example, is somewhat slighted here, as is the *Beowulf* poet's resourcefulness with synonyms and (to a lesser extent) his genius for compound-making, kennings, and all sorts of variation. Usually—as at line 1209, where I render *ȳða ful* as "frothing wave-vat," and line 1523, where *beado-lēoma* becomes "battle-torch"—I try to match the poet's analogy-seeking habit at its most original; and I use all the common coinages for the lord of the nation, variously referred to as "ring-giver," "treasure-giver," "his people's shield" or "shepherd" or "helmet." I have been less faithful, however, to the way the poet rings the changes when it comes to compounds meaning a sword or a spear or a battle or any bloody encounter with foes. Old English abounds in vigorous and evocative and specifically poetic words for these things, but I have tended to follow modern usage and in the main have called a sword a sword.

There was one area, however, where a certain strangeness in the diction came naturally. In those instances where a local Ulster word seemed either poetically or historically right, I felt free to use it. For example, at lines 324 and 2988 I use the word "graith" for "harness" and at 3026 "hoked" for "rooted about" because the local term seemed in each case to have special body and force. Then, for reasons of historical suggestiveness, I have in several instances used the word "bawn" to refer to Hrothgar's hall. In Elizabethan English, bawn (from the Irish *bó-dhún,* a fort for cattle) referred specifically to the fortified dwellings which the English planters built in Ireland to keep the dispossessed natives at bay, so it seemed the proper term to apply to the embattled keep where Hrothgar waits and watches. Indeed, every time I read the lovely interlude that tells of the minstrel singing in Heorot just before the first attacks of Grendel, I cannot help thinking of Edmund Spenser in Kilcolman Castle, reading the early cantos of *The Faerie Queene* to Sir Walter Raleigh, just before the Irish burned the castle and drove Spenser out of Munster back to the Elizabethan court. Putting a bawn into *Beowulf* seems one way for an Irish poet to come to terms with that complex history of conquest and colony, absorption and resistance, integrity and antagonism, a history which has to be clearly acknowledged by all concerned in order to render it ever more "willable forward / Again and again and again."

S.H.

A Note on Names

Old English, like Modern German, contained many compound words, most of which have been lost in Modern English. Most of the names in *Beowulf* are compounds. Hrothgar is a combination of words meaning "glory" and "spear"; the name of his older brother, Heorogar, comes from "army" and "spear"; Hrothgar's sons Hrethric and Hrothmund contain the first elements of their father's name combined, respectively, with *ric* (kingdom, empire, Modern German *Reich*) and *mund* (hand, protection). As in the case of the Danish dynasty, family names often alliterate. Masculine names of the warrior class have military associations. The importance of family and the demands of alliteration frequently lead to the designation of characters by formulas identifying them in terms of relationships. Thus Beowulf is referred to as "son of Ecgtheow" or "kinsman of Hygelac" (his uncle and lord).

The Old English spellings of names are mostly preserved in the translation. A few rules of pronunciation are worth keeping in mind. Initial *H* before *r* was sounded, and so Hrothgar's name alliterates with that of his brother Heorogar. The combination *cg* has the value of *dg* in words like "edge." The first element in the name of Beowulf's father "Ecgtheow" is the same word as "edge," and, by the figure of speech called synecdoche (a part of something stands for the whole), *ecg* stands for *sword* and Ecgtheow means "sword-servant."

Alfred David

BEOWULF

Hwæt wē Gār-Dena   in geār-dagum
þēod-cyninga   þrym gefrūnon,
hū ðā æþelingas   ellen fremedon.
   Oft Scyld Scēfing   sceaþena þrēatum,
monegum mǣgþum   meodo-setla oftēah;
egsode Eorle,   syððan ǣrest wearð
fēasceaft funden;   hē þæs frōfre gebād:
wēox under wolcnum,   weorð-myndum þāh,
oðþæt him æghwylc   þāra ymb-sittendra
ofer hron-rāde   hȳran scolde,
gomban gyldan: þæt wæs gōd cyning!
Ðǣm eafera wæs   æfter cenned
geong in geardum,   þone God sende
folce tō frōfre;   fyren-ðearfe ongeat,
þæt hīe ǣr drugon   aldor-lēase
lange hwīle;   him þæs Līf-frēa,
wuldres Wealdend,   worold-āre forgeaf;
Bēowulf wæs brēme   —blǣd wīde sprang—
Scyldes eafera,   Scede-landum in.
Swā sceal geong guma   gōde gewyrcean,
fromum feoh-giftum   on fæder bearme,
þæt hine on ylde   eft gewunigen

So. The Spear-Danes in days gone by
and the kings who ruled them had courage and greatness.
We have heard of those princes' heroic campaigns.

There was Shield Sheafson, scourge of many tribes,
a wrecker of mead-benches, rampaging among foes.
This terror of the hall-troops had come far.
A foundling to start with, he would flourish later on
as his powers waxed and his worth was proved.
In the end each clan on the outlying coasts
beyond the whale-road had to yield to him
and begin to pay tribute. That was one good king.

Afterwards a boy-child was born to Shield,
a cub in the yard, a comfort sent
by God to that nation. He knew what they had tholed,
the long times and troubles they'd come through
without a leader; so the Lord of Life,
the glorious Almighty, made this man renowned.
Shield had fathered a famous son:
Beow's name was known through the north.
And a young prince must be prudent like that,
giving freely while his father lives
so that afterwards in age when fighting starts

The Danes have legends about their warrior kings. The most famous was Shield Sheafson, who founded the ruling house

10

20

wil-gesīþas,   þonne wīg cume,
lēode gelǣsten;   lof-dǣdum sceal
in mǣgþa gehwǣre   man geþēon.
　　Him ðā Scyld gewāt   tō gescæp-hwīle,
fela-hrōr, fēran   on Frēan wǣre.
Hī hyne þā ætbǣron   tō brimes faroðe,
swǣse gesīþas,   swā hē selfa bæd,
þenden wordum wēold   wine Scyldinga,
lēof land-fruma   lange āhte.
Þǣr æt hȳðe stōd   hringed-stefna,
īsig ond ūt-fūs,   æþelinges fær;
ālēdon þā   lēofne þēoden,
bēaga bryttan   on bearm scipes,
mǣrne be mæste;   þǣr wæs mādma fela
of feor-wegum,   frætwa, gelǣded.
Ne hȳrde ic cȳmlīcor   cēol gegyrwan
hilde-wǣpnum   ond heaðo-wǣdum,
billum ond byrnum;   him on bearme læg
mādma mænigo,   þā him mid scoldon
on flōdes ǣht   feor gewītan.
Nalæs hī hine lǣssan   lācum tēodan,
þēod-gestrēonum,   þon þā dydon,
þe hine æt frumsceafte   forð onsendon
ǣnne ofer ȳðe   umbor-wesende.
Þā gȳt hī him āsetton   segend gyldenne
hēah ofer hēafod,   lēton holm beran,
gēafon on gār-secg;   him wæs geōmor sefa,
murnende mōd.   Men ne cunnon
secgan tō sōðe,   sele-rǣdende,
hæleð under heofenum,   hwā þǣm hlæste onfēng.
Ðā wæs on burgum   Bēowulf Scyldinga,

steadfast companions will stand by him
and hold the line. Behaviour that's admired
is the path to power among people everywhere.

Shield was still thriving when his time came   *Shield's funeral*
and he crossed over into the Lord's keeping.
His warrior band did what he bade them
when he laid down the law among the Danes:
30   they shouldered him out to the sea's flood,
the chief they revered who had long ruled them.
A ring-whorled prow rode in the harbour,
ice-clad, outbound, a craft for a prince.
They stretched their beloved lord in his boat,
laid out by the mast, amidships,
the great ring-giver. Far-fetched treasures
were piled upon him, and precious gear.
I never heard before of a ship so well furbished
with battle tackle, bladed weapons
40   and coats of mail. The massed treasure
was loaded on top of him: it would travel far
on out into the ocean's sway.
They decked his body no less bountifully
with offerings than those first ones did
who cast him away when he was a child
and launched him alone out over the waves.
And they set a gold standard up
high above his head and let him drift
to wind and tide, bewailing him
50   and mourning their loss. No man can tell,
no wise man in hall or weathered veteran
knows for certain who salvaged that load.

Then it fell to Beow to keep the forts.

lēof lēod-cyning, longe þrāge
folcum gefrǣge; fæder ellor hwearf,
aldor of earde. Oþþæt him eft onwōc
hēah Healfdene; hēold, þenden lifde,
gamol ond gūð-rēouw, glæde Scyldingas.
Đǣm fēower bearn forð-gerīmed
in worold wōcun: weoroda rǣswan,
Heorogār, ond Hrōðgār ond Hālga til;
hȳrde ic þæt . . . . . wæs Onelan cwēn,
Heaðo-Scilfingas heals-gebedda.

    Þā wæs Hrōðgāre here-spēd gyfen,
wīges weorð-mynd, þæt him his wine-māgas
georne hȳrdon, oððþæt sēo geogoð gewēox
mago-driht micel. Him on mōd be-arn
þæt heal-reced hātan wolde,
medo-ærn micel men gewyrcean,
þonne yldo bearn ǣfre gefrūnon,
ond þǣr on innan eall gedǣlan
geongum ond ealdum, swylc him God sealde,
būton folc-scare ond feorum gumena.
Đā ic wīde gefrægn weorc gebannan
manigre mǣgþe geond þisne middan-geard,
folc-stede frætwan. Him on fyrste gelomp,
ǣdre mid yldum, þæt hit wearð eal-gearo,
heal-ærna mǣst; scōp him Heort naman,
sē þe his wordes geweald wīde hæfde.
Hē bēot ne ālēh, bēagas dǣlde,
sinc æt symle. Sele hlīfade
hēah ond horn-gēap, heaðo-wylma bād,
lāðan līges; ne wæs hit lenge þā gēn,
þæt se ecg-hete āþum-swerian
æfter wæl-nīðe wæcnan scolde.

He was well regarded and ruled the Danes
for a long time after his father took leave
of his life on earth. And then his heir,
the great Halfdane, held sway
for as long as he lived, their elder and warlord.
He was four times a father, this fighter prince:
one by one they entered the world,
Heorogar, Hrothgar, the good Halga
and a daughter, I have heard, who was Onela's queen,
a balm in bed to the battle-scarred Swede.

The fortunes of war favoured Hrothgar.
Friends and kinsmen flocked to his ranks,
young followers, a force that grew
to be a mighty army. So his mind turned
to hall-building: he handed down orders
for men to work on a great mead-hall
meant to be a wonder of the world forever;
it would be his throne-room and there he would dispense
his God-given goods to young and old—
but not the common land or people's lives.
Far and wide through the world, I have heard,
orders for work to adorn that wallstead
were sent to many peoples. And soon it stood there,
finished and ready, in full view,
the hall of halls. Heorot was the name
he had settled on it, whose utterance was law.
Nor did he renege, but doled out rings
and torques at the table. The hall towered,
its gables wide and high and awaiting
a barbarous burning. That doom abided,
but in time it would come: the killer instinct
unleashed among in-laws, the blood-lust rampant.

60

70

80

Shield's heirs: his son Beow succeeded by Halfdane, Halfdane by Hrothgar

King Hrothgar builds Heorot Hall

Ða se ellen-gǣst   earfoðlīce
þrāge geþolode,   sē þe in þȳstrum bād,
þæt hē dōgora gehwām   drēam gehȳrde
hlūdne in healle;   þǣr wæs hearpan swēg,
swutol sang scopes.   Sægde sē þe cūþe
frumsceaft fīra   feorran reccan,
cwæð þæt se Ælmihtiga   eorðan worhte,
wlite-beorhtne wang,   swā wæter bebūgeð:
gesette sige-hrēþig   sunnan ond mōnan
lēoman tō lēohte   land-būendum,
ond gefrætwade   foldan scēatas
leomum ond lēafum;   līf ēac gesceōp
cynna gehwylcum,   þāra ðe cwice hwyrfaþ.
Swā ðā driht-guman   drēamum lifdon,
ēadiglīce,   oððæt ān ongan
fyrene fremman   fēond on helle.
Wæs se grimma gæst   Grendel hāten,
mǣre mearc-stapa,   sē þe mōras hēold,
fen ond fæsten;   fīfel-cynnes eard
won-sǣlī wer   weardode hwīle,
siþðan him Scyppend   forscrifen hæfde
in Caines cynne—   þone cwealm gewræc
ēce Drihten,   þæs þe hē Ābel slōg.
Ne gefeah hē þǣre fǣhðe,   ac hē hine feor forwræc,
Metod for þȳ māne,   man-cynne fram.
Þanon untȳdras   ealle onwōcon,
eotenas ond ylfe   ond orcnēas,
swylce gīgantas,   þā wið Gode wunnon
lange þrāge;   hē him ðæs lēan forgeald.
Gewāt ðā nēosian,   syþðan niht becōm,
hēan hūses,   hū hit Hring-Dene

Then a powerful demon, a prowler through the dark,
nursed a hard grievance. It harrowed him
to hear the din of the loud banquet
every day in the hall, the harp being struck
and the clear song of a skilled poet
telling with mastery of man's beginnings,
how the Almighty had made the earth
a gleaming plain girdled with waters;
in His splendour He set the sun and the moon
to be earth's lamplight, lanterns for men,
and filled the broad lap of the world
with branches and leaves; and quickened life
in every other thing that moved.

So times were pleasant for the people there
until finally one, a fiend out of hell,
began to work his evil in the world.
Grendel was the name of this grim demon
haunting the marches, marauding round the heath
and the desolate fens; he had dwelt for a time
in misery among the banished monsters,
Cain's clan, whom the Creator had outlawed
and condemned as outcasts. For the killing of Abel
the Eternal Lord had exacted a price:
Cain got no good from committing that murder
because the Almighty made him anathema
and out of the curse of his exile there sprang
ogres and elves and evil phantoms
and the giants too who strove with God
time and again until He gave them their reward.

So, after nightfall, Grendel set out
for the lofty house, to see how the Ring-Danes

æfter bēor-þege   gebūn hæfdon;
fand þā ðǣr inne   æþelinga gedriht
swefan æfter symble—   sorge ne cūðon,
wonsceaft wera.   Wiht unhǣlo,
grim ond grǣdig,   gearo sōna wæs,
rēoc ond rēþe,   ond on ræste genam
þrītig þegna;   þanon eft gewāt
hūðe hrēmig   tō hām faran,
mid þǣre wæl-fylle   wīca nēosan.

    Ðā wæs on ūhtan   mid ǣr-dæge
Grendles gūð-cræft   gumum undyrne;
þā wæs æfter wiste   wōp up āhafen,
micel morgen-swēg.   Mǣre þēoden,
æþeling ǣr-gōd,   unblīðe sæt,
þolode ðrȳð-swȳð,   þegn-sorge drēah,
syðþan hīe þæs lāðan   lāst scēawedon
wergan gāstes.   Wæs þæt gewin tō strang,
lāð ond longsum.   Næs hit lengra fyrst,
ac ymb āne niht   eft gefremede
morð-beala māre   ond nō mearn fore,
fǣhðe ond fyrene;   wæs tō fæst on þām.
Þā wæs eāð-fynde   þe him elles hwǣr
gerūmlīcor   ræste sōhte,
bed æfter būrum,   ðā him gebēacnod wæs,
gesægd sōðlīce   sweotolan tācne
heal-ðegnes hete;   hēold hyne syðþan
fyr ond fæstor   sē þǣm fēonde ætwand.

    Swā rīxode   ond wið rihte wan
āna wið eallum,   oðþæt īdel stōd
hūsa sēlest.   Wæs sēo hwīl micel:
twelf wintra tīd   torn geþolode

were settling into it after their drink,
and there he came upon them, a company of the best
asleep from their feasting, insensible to pain
120 and human sorrow. Suddenly then
the God-cursed brute was creating havoc:
greedy and grim, he grabbed thirty men
from their resting places and rushed to his lair,
flushed up and inflamed from the raid,
blundering back with the butchered corpses.

Then as dawn brightened and the day broke
Grendel's powers of destruction were plain:
their wassail was over, they wept to heaven
and mourned under morning. Their mighty prince,
130 the storied leader, sat stricken and helpless,
humiliated by the loss of his guard,
bewildered and stunned, staring aghast
at the demon's trail, in deep distress.
He was numb with grief, but got no respite
for one night later merciless Grendel
struck again with more gruesome murders.
Malignant by nature, he never showed remorse.
It was easy then to meet with a man
shifting himself to a safer distance
140 to bed in the bothies, for who could be blind
to the evidence of his eyes, the obviousness
of that hall-watcher's hate? Whoever escaped
kept a weather-eye open and moved away.

So Grendel ruled in defiance of right,
one against all, until the greatest house
in the world stood empty, a deserted wallstead.
For twelve winters, seasons of woe,

King Hrothgar's
distress and
helplessness

wine Scyldinga,   wēana gehwelcne,
sīdra sorga;   forðām secgum wearð,
ylda bearnum,   undyrne cūð,
gyddum geōmore,   þætte Grendel wan
hwīle wið Hrōþgār,   hete-nīðas wæg,
fyrene ond fǣhðe   fela missēra,
singāle sæce;   sibbe ne wolde
wið manna hwone   mægenes Deniga,
feorh-bealo feorran,   fēa þingian,
nē þǣr nǣnig witena   wēnan þorfte
beorhtre bōte   tō banan folmum;
ac se ǣglǣca   ēhtende wæs,
deorc dēaþ-scūa   duguþe ond geogoþe,
seomade ond syrede;   sin-nihte hēold
mistige mōras;   men ne cunnon
hwyder hel-rūnan   hwyrftum scrīþað.
    Swā fela fyrena   fēond man-cynnes,
atol ān-gengea,   oft gefremede,
heardra hȳnða;   Heorot eardode,
sinc-fāge sel   sweartum nihtum;
nō hē þone gif-stōl   grētan mōste,
māþðum for Metode,   nē his myne wisse.
    Þæt wæs wrǣc micel   wine Scyldinga,
mōdes brecða.   Monig oft gesæt
rīce tō rūne,   rǣd eahtedon,
hwæt swīð-ferhðum   sēlest wǣre
wið fǣr-gryrum   tō gefremmanne.
Hwīlum hīe gehēton   æt hærg-trafum
wīg-weorþunga,   wordum bǣdon,
þæt him gāst-bona   gēoce gefremede
wið þēod-þrēaum.   Swylc wæs þēaw hyra,

150

160

170

the lord of the Shieldings suffered under
his load of sorrow; and so, before long,
150 the news was known over the whole world.
Sad lays were sung about the beset king,
the vicious raids and ravages of Grendel,
his long and unrelenting feud,
nothing but war; how he would never
parley or make peace with any Dane
nor stop his death-dealing nor pay the death-price.
No counsellor could ever expect
fair reparation from those rabid hands.
All were endangered; young and old
160 were hunted down by that dark death-shadow
who lurked and swooped in the long nights
on the misty moors; nobody knows
where these reavers from hell roam on their errands.

So Grendel waged his lonely war,
inflicting constant cruelties on the people,
atrocious hurt. He took over Heorot,
haunted the glittering hall after dark,
but the throne itself, the treasure-seat,
he was kept from approaching; he was the Lord's outcast.

170 These were hard times, heart-breaking
for the prince of the Shieldings; powerful counsellors,
the highest in the land, would lend advice,
plotting how best the bold defenders
might resist and beat off sudden attacks.
Sometimes at pagan shrines they vowed
offerings to idols, swore oaths
that the killer of souls might come to their aid
and save the people. That was their way,

The Danes, hard-pressed, turn for help to heathen gods

hǣþenra hyht;   helle gemundon
in mōd-sefan,   Metod hīe ne cūþon,
dǣda Dēmend,   ne wiston hīe Drihten God
nē hīe hūru heofena Helm   herian ne cūþon,
wuldres Waldend.   Wā bið þǣm ðe sceal
þurh slīðne nīð   sāwle bescūfan
in fȳres fæþm,   frōfre ne wēnan,
wihte gewendan!   Wēl bið þǣm þe mōt
æfter dēað-dæge   Drihten sēcean
ond tō Fæder fæþmum   freoðo wilnian!

  Swā ðā mǣl-ceare   maga Healfdenes
singāla sēað;   ne mihte snotor hæleð
wēan onwendan;   wæs þæt gewin tō swȳð,
lāþ ond longsum,   þe on ðā lēode becōm,
nȳd-wracu nīþ-grim,   niht-bealwa mǣst.

  Þæt fram hām gefrægn   Higelāces þegn,
gōd mid Gēatum,   Grendles dǣda;
sē wæs mon-cynnes   mægenes strengest
on þǣm dæge   þysses līfes,
æþele ond ēacen.   Hēt him ȳð-lidan
gōdne gegyrwan;   cwæð, hē gūð-cyning
ofer swan-rāde   sēcean wolde,
mǣrne þēoden,   þā him wæs manna þearf.
Ðone sīð-fæt him   snotere ceorlas
lȳt-hwōn lōgon,   þēah hē him lēof wǣre;
hwetton hige-rōfne,   hǣl scēawedon.
Hæfde se gōda   Gēata lēoda
cempan gecorone,   þāra þe hē cēnoste
findan mihte;   fīf-tȳna sum
sund-wudu sōhte;   secg wīsade,
lagu-cræftig mon,   land-gemyrcu.

their heathenish hope; deep in their hearts
180   they remembered hell. The Almighty Judge
of good deeds and bad, the Lord God,
Head of the Heavens and High King of the World,
was unknown to them. Oh, cursed is he
who in time of trouble has to thrust his soul
in the fire's embrace, forfeiting help;
he has nowhere to turn. But blessed is he
who after death can approach the Lord
and find friendship in the Father's embrace.

So that troubled time continued, woe
190   that never stopped, steady affliction
for Halfdane's son, too hard an ordeal.
There was panic after dark, people endured
raids in the night, riven by the terror.

When he heard about Grendel, Hygelac's thane
was on home ground, over in Geatland.
There was no one else like him alive.
In his day, he was the mightiest man on earth,
high-born and powerful. He ordered a boat
that would ply the waves. He announced his plan:
200   to sail the swan's road and search out that king,
the famous prince who needed defenders.
Nobody tried to keep him from going,
no elder denied him, dear as he was to them.
Instead, they inspected omens and spurred
his ambition to go, whilst he moved about
like the leader he was, enlisting men,
the best he could find; with fourteen others
the warrior boarded the boat as captain,
a canny pilot along coast and currents.

*At the court of King
Hygelac, a Geat
warrior prepares to
help Hrothgar*

Fyrst forð gewāt;   flota wæs on ȳðum,
bāt under beorge.   Beornas gearwe
on stefn stigon—   strēamas wundon,
sund wið sande;   secgas bǣron
on bearm nacan   beorhte frætwe,
gūð-searo geatolīc;   guman ūt scufon,
weras on wil-sīð   wudu bundenne.
Gewāt þā ofer wǣg-holm,   winde gefȳsed,
flota fāmī-heals,   fugle gelīcost,
oðþæt ymb ān-tīd   ōþres dōgores
wunden-stefna   gewaden hæfde,
þæt ðā līðende   land gesāwon,
brim-clifu blīcan,   beorgas stēape,
sīde sǣ-næssas;   þā wæs sund liden,
ēo-letes æt ende.   Þanon up hraðe
Wedera lēode   on wang stigon,
sǣ-wudu sǣldon   —syrcan hrysedon,
gūð-gewǣdo;   Gode þancedon,
þæs þe him ȳþ-lāde   ēaðe wurdon.
   Þā of wealle geseah   weard Scildinga,
sē þe holm-clifu   healdan scolde,
beran ofer bolcan   beorhte randas,
fyrd-searu fūslicu;   hine fyrwyt bræc
mōd-gehygdum,   hwæt þā men wǣron.
Gewāt him þā tō waroðe   wicge rīdan
þegn Hrōðgāres,   þrymmum cwehte
mægen-wudu mundum,   meþel-wordum frægn:
   "Hwæt syndon gē   searo-hæbbendra,
byrnum werede,   þe þus brontne cēol
ofer lagu-strǣte   lǣdan cwōmon,
hider ofer holmas?   Ic hwīle wæs

| 210 | Time went by, the boat was on water, | *The hero and his troop sail from the land of the Geats* |

210 Time went by, the boat was on water,
    in close under the cliffs.
    Men climbed eagerly up the gangplank,
    sand churned in surf, warriors loaded
    a cargo of weapons, shining war-gear
    in the vessel's hold, then heaved out,
    away with a will in their wood-wreathed ship.
    Over the waves, with the wind behind her
    and foam at her neck, she flew like a bird
    until her curved prow had covered the distance
220 and on the following day, at the due hour,
    those seafarers sighted land,
    sunlit cliffs, sheer crags
    and looming headlands, the landfall they sought.
    It was the end of their voyage and the Geats vaulted
    over the side, out on to the sand,
    and moored their ship. There was a clash of mail
    and a thresh of gear. They thanked God
    for that easy crossing on a calm sea.

    When the watchman on the wall, the Shieldings' lookout
230 whose job it was to guard the sea-cliffs,
    saw shields glittering on the gangplank
    and battle-equipment being unloaded
    he had to find out who and what
    the arrivals were. So he rode to the shore,
    this horseman of Hrothgar's, and challenged them
    in formal terms, flourishing his spear:

    "What kind of men are you who arrive
    rigged out for combat in coats of mail,
    sailing here over the sea-lanes
240 in your steep-hulled boat? I have been stationed

The hero and his troop sail from the land of the Geats

The Danish coast-guard challenges the outsiders

ende-sæta, æg-wearde hēold,
þē on land Dena lāðra nǣnig
mid scip-herge sceðþan ne meahte.
Nō hēr cūðlīcor cuman ongunnon
lind-hæbbende; nē gē lēafnes-word
gūð-fremmendra gearwe ne wisson,
māga gemēdu. Nǣfre ic māran geseah
eorla ofer eorþan, ðonne is ēower sum,
secg on searwum; nis þæt seld-guma,
250 wǣpnum geweorðad; nǣfre him his wlite lēoge,
ǣnlīc ansȳn. Nū ic ēower sceal
frum-cyn witan, ǣr gē fyr heonan
lēas-scēaweras on land Dena
furþur fēran. Nū gē feor-būend,
mere-līðende, mīnne gehȳrað
ānfealdne geþōht; ofost is sēlest
tō gecȳðanne hwanan ēowre cyme syndon."
    Him se yldesta andswarode,
werodes wīsa, word-hord onlēac:
260 "Wē synt gum-cynnes Gēata lēode
ond Higelāces heorð-genēatas;
wæs mīn fæder folcum gecȳþed,
æþele ord-fruma Ecgþēow hāten,—
gebād wintra worn, ǣr hē on weg hwurfe,
gamol of geardum; hine gearwe geman
witena wēl-hwylc wīde geond eorþan.
Wē þurh holdne hige hlāford þīnne,
sunu Healfdenes, sēcean cwōmon,
lēod-gebyrgean; wes þū ūs lārena gōd!
270 Habbað wē tō þǣm mǣran micel ǣrende,
Deniga frēan; ne sceal þǣr dyrne sum
wesan, þæs ic wēne. Þū wāst—gif hit is,

as lookout on this coast for a long time.
My job is to watch the waves for raiders,
any danger to the Danish shore.
Never before has a force under arms
disembarked so openly—not bothering to ask
if the sentries allowed them safe passage
or the clan had consented. Nor have I seen
a mightier man-at-arms on this earth
than the one standing here: unless I am mistaken,
250   he is truly noble. This is no mere
hanger-on in a hero's armour.
So now, before you fare inland
as interlopers, I have to be informed
about who you are and where you hail from.
Outsiders from across the water,
I say it again: the sooner you tell
where you come from and why, the better."

The leader of the troop unlocked his word-hoard;
the distinguished one delivered this answer:
260   "We belong by birth to the Geat people
and owe allegiance to Lord Hygelac.
In his day, my father was a famous man,
a noble warrior-lord named Ecgtheow.
He outlasted many a long winter
and went on his way. All over the world
men wise in counsel continue to remember him.
We come in good faith to find your lord
and nation's shield, the son of Halfdane.
Give us the right advice and direction.
270   We have arrived here on a great errand
to the lord of the Danes, and I believe therefore
there should be nothing hidden or withheld between us.

The Geat hero announces himself and explains his mission

swā wē sōþlīce   secgan hȳrdon—
þæt mid Scyldingum   sceaðona ic nāt hwylc,
dēogol dǣd-hata,   deorcum nihtum
ēaweð þurh egsan   uncūðne nīð,
hȳnðu ond hrā-fyl.   Ic þæs Hrōðgār mæg
þurh rūmne sefan   rǣd gelǣran,
hū hē frōd ond gōd   fēond oferswȳðeþ—
gyf him edwenden   ǣfre scolde
bealuwa bisigu,   bōt eft cuman—
ond þā cear-wylmas   cōlran wurðaþ;
oððe ā syþðan   earfoð-þrāge,
þrēa-nȳd þolað,   þenden þǣr wunað
on hēah-stede   hūsa sēlest."

    Weard maþelode,   ðǣr on wicge sæt,
ombeht unforht;   "Ǣghwæþres sceal
scearp scyld-wiga   gescād witan,
worda ond worca,   sē þe wēl þenceð.
Ic þæt gehȳre,   þæt þis is hold weorod
frēan Scyldinga.   Gewītaþ forð beran
wǣpen ond gewǣdu;   ic ēow wīsige:
swylce ic magu-þegnas   mīne hāte
wið fēonda gehwone   flotan ēowerne,
nīw-tyrwydne   nacan on sande
ārum healdan,   oþðæt eft byreð
ofer lagu-strēamas   lēofne mannan
wudu wunden-hals   tō Weder-mearce:
gōd-fremmendra   swylcum gifeþe bið,
þæt þone hilde-rǣs   hāl gedīgeð."

    Gewiton him þā fēran.   Flota stille bād,
seomode on sāle   sīd-fæþmed scip,
on ancre fæst.   Eofor-līc scionon

280

290

300

So tell us if what we have heard is true
about this threat, whatever it is,
this danger abroad in the dark nights,
this corpse-maker mongering death
in the Shieldings' country. I come to proffer
my wholehearted help and counsel.
I can show the wise Hrothgar a way
280   to defeat his enemy and find respite—
if any respite is to reach him, ever.
I can calm the turmoil and terror in his mind.
Otherwise, he must endure woes
and live with grief for as long as his hall
stands at the horizon, on its high ground."

Undaunted, sitting astride his horse,
the coast-guard answered, "Anyone with gumption
and a sharp mind will take the measure
of two things: what's said and what's done.
290   I believe what you have told me: that you are a troop
loyal to our king. So come ahead
with your arms and your gear, and I will guide you.
What's more, I'll order my own comrades
on their word of honour to watch your boat
down there on the strand—keep her safe
in her fresh tar, until the time comes
for her curved prow to preen on the waves
and bear this hero back to Geatland.
May one so valiant and venturesome
300   come unharmed through the clash of battle."

So they went on their way. The ship rode the water,
broad-beamed, bound by its hawser
and anchored fast. Boar-shapes flashed

*The coast-guard
allows the Geats to
pass*

ofer hlēor-bergan: gehroden golde,
fāh ond fȳ-heard,   ferh wearde hēold:
gūþ-mōd grummon.   Guman ōnetton,
sigon ætsomne,   oþþæt hȳ sæl timbred,
geatolīc ond gold-fāh   ongyton mihton;
þæt wæs fore-mǣrost   fold-būendum
receda under roderum,   on þǣm se rīca bād;
līxte se lēoma   ofer landa fela.
Him þā hilde-dēor   hof mōdigra
torht getǣhte,   þæt hīe him tō mihton
gegnum gangan;   gūð-beorna sum
wicg gewende,   word æfter cwæð:
"Mǣl is mē tō fēran.   Fæder al-walda
mid ār-stafum   ēowic gehealde
sīða gesunde!   Ic tō sǣ wille,
wið wrāð werod   wearde healdan."
     Strǣt wæs stān-fāh,   stīg wīsode
gumum ætgædere.   Gūð-byrne scān,
heard, hond-locen,   hring-īren scīr
song in searwum.   Þā hī tō sele furðum
in hyra gryre-geatwum   gangan cwōmon,
setton sǣ-mēþe   sīde scyldas,
rondas regn-hearde,   wið þæs recedes weal;
bugon þā tō bence,   byrnan hringdon,
gūð-searo gumena.   Gāras stōdon,
sǣ-manna searo,   samod ætgædere,
æsc-holt ufan grǣg;   wæs sē īren-þrēat
wǣpnum gewurþad.   Þā ðǣr wlonc hæleð
ōret-mecgas   æfter æþelum frægn:
     "Hwanon ferigeað gē   fǣtte scyldas,
grǣge syrcan   ond grīm-helmas,

above their cheek-guards, the brightly forged
work of goldsmiths, watching over
those stern-faced men. They marched in step,
hurrying on till the timbered hall
rose before them, radiant with gold.
Nobody on earth knew of another
310   building like it. Majesty lodged there,
its light shone over many lands.
So their gallant escort guided them
to that dazzling stronghold and indicated
the shortest way to it; then the noble warrior
wheeled on his horse and spoke these words:
"It is time for me to go. May the Almighty
Father keep you and in His kindness
watch over your exploits. I'm away to the sea,
back on alert against enemy raiders."

320   It was a paved track, a path that kept them
in marching order. Their mail-shirts glinted,
hard and hand-linked; the high-gloss iron
of their armour rang. So they duly arrived
in their grim war-graith and gear at the hall,
and, weary from the sea, stacked wide shields
of the toughest hardwood against the wall,
then collapsed on the benches; battle-dress
and weapons clashed. They collected their spears
in a seafarers' stook, a stand of greyish
330   tapering ash. And the troops themselves
were as good as their weapons.
                    Then a proud warrior
questioned the men concerning their origins:
"Where do you come from, carrying these
decorated shields and shirts of mail,

*They arrive at
Heorot*

here-sceafta hēap?   Ic eom Hrōðgāres
ār ond ombiht.   Ne seah ic elþēodige
þus manige men   mōdiglīcran.
Wēn' ic þæt gē for wlenco,   nalles for wræc-sīðum,
ac for hige-þrymmum   Hrōðgār sōhton."
Him þā ellen-rōf   andswarode,
wlanc Wedera lēod,   word æfter spræc,
heard under helme: "Wē synt Higelāces
bēod-genēatas;   Bēowulf is mīn nama.
Wille ic āsecgan   sunu Healfdenes,
mærum þēodne   mīn ærende,
aldre þīnum,   gif hē ūs geunnan wile,
þæt wē hine swā gōdne   grētan mōton."
Wulfgār maþelode: þæt wæs Wendla lēod,
wæs his mōd-sefa   manegum gecȳðed,
wīg ond wīsdōm: "Ic þæs wine Deniga
frēan Scildinga   frīnan wille,
bēaga bryttan,   swā þū bēna eart,
þēoden mærne,   ymb þīnne sīð,
ond þē þā andsware   ædre gecȳðan,
ðe mē se gōda   āgifan þenceð."

    Hwearf þā hrædlīce,   þær Hrōðgār sæt,
eald ond unhār   mid his eorla gedriht;
ēode ellen-rōf,   þæt hē for eaxlum gestōd
Deniga frēan: cūþe hē duguðe þēaw.
Wulfgār maðelode   tō his wine-drihtne:
    "Hēr syndon geferede,   feorran cumene
ofer geofenes begang   Gēata lēode;
þone yldestan   ōret-mecgas

these cheek-hinged helmets and javelins?
I am Hrothgar's herald and officer.
I have never seen so impressive or large
an assembly of strangers. Stoutness of heart,
bravery not banishment, must have brought you to
    Hrothgar."

340 The man whose name was known for courage,
the Geat leader, resolute in his helmet,
answered in return: "We are retainers
from Hygelac's band. Beowulf is my name.
If your lord and master, the most renowned
son of Halfdane, will hear me out
and graciously allow me to greet him in person,
I am ready and willing to report my errand."

Beowulf announces
his name

Wulfgar replied, a Wendel chief
renowned as a warrior, well known for his wisdom
350 and the temper of his mind: "I will take this message,
in accordance with your wish, to our noble king,
our dear lord, friend of the Danes,
the giver of rings. I will go and ask him
about your coming here, then hurry back
with whatever reply it pleases him to give."

Formalities are
observed

With that he turned to where Hrothgar sat,
an old man among retainers;
the valiant follower stood four-square
in front of his king: he knew the courtesies.
360 Wulfgar addressed his dear lord:
"People from Geatland have put ashore.
They have sailed far over the wide sea.
They call the chief in charge of their band

Bēowulf nemnað;   hȳ bēnan synt,
þæt hīe, þēoden mīn,   wið þē mōton
wordum wrixlan.   Nō ðū him wearne getēoh
ðīnra gegn-cwida,   glæd-man Hrōðgār:
hȳ on wīg-getāwum   wyrðe þinceað
eorla geæhtlan;   hūru se aldor dēah,
sē þǣm heaðo-rincum   hider wīsade."
     Hrōðgār maþelode,   helm Scyldinga:
"Ic hine cūðe   cniht-wesende;
wæs his eald-fæder   Ecgþēo hāten,
ðǣm tō hām forgeaf   Hrēþel Gēata
āngan dohtor;   is his eafora nū
heard hēr cumen,   sōhte holdne wine.
Ðonne sægdon þæt   sǣ-līþende,
þā ðe gif-sceattas   Gēata fyredon
þyder tō þance,   þæt hē þrītiges
manna mægen-cræft   on his mund-gripe,
heaþo-rōf hæbbe.   Hine hālig God
for ār-stafum   ūs onsende
tō West-Denum,   þæs ic wēn hæbbe,
wið Grendles gryre.   Ic þǣm gōdan sceal
for his mōd-þræce   mādmas bēodan.
Bēo ðū on ofeste,   hāt in gān,
sēon sibbe-gedriht   samod ætgædere;
gesaga him ēac wordum   þæt hīe sint wil-cuman
Deniga lēodum!"   Þā tō dura healle
Wulfgār ēode,   word inne ābēad:
Ēow hēt secgan   sige-drihten mīn,
aldor Ēast-Dena,   þæt hē ēower æþelu can:
ond gē him syndon   ofer sǣ-wylmas,
heard-hicgende,   hider wil-cuman.

by the name of Beowulf. They beg, my lord,
an audience with you, exchange of words
and formal greeting. Most gracious Hrothgar,
do not refuse them, but grant them a reply.
From their arms and appointment, they appear well born
and worthy of respect, especially the one
370   who has led them this far: he is formidable indeed."

Hrothgar, protector of Shieldings, replied: *Hrothgar recognizes*
"I used to know him when he was a young boy.   *Beowulf's name and*
His father before him was called Ecgtheow.   *approves his arrival*
Hrethel the Geat gave Ecgtheow
his daughter in marriage. This man is their son,
here to follow up an old friendship.
A crew of seamen who sailed for me once
with a gift-cargo across to Geatland
returned with marvellous tales about him:
380   a thane, they declared, with the strength of thirty
in the grip of each hand. Now Holy God
has, in His goodness, guided him here
to the West-Danes, to defend us from Grendel.
This is my hope; and for his heroism
I will recompense him with a rich treasure.
Go immediately, bid him and the Geats
he has in attendance to assemble and enter.
Say, moreover, when you speak to them,
they are welcome to Denmark."
                                   At the door of the hall,
390   Wulfgar duly delivered the message:
"My lord, the conquering king of the Danes,
bids me announce that he knows your ancestry;
also that he welcomes you here to Heorot
and salutes your arrival from across the sea.

Nū gē mōton gangan   in ēowrum gūð-getāwum,
under here-grīman,   Hrōðgār gesēon;
lætað hilde-bord   hēr onbīdan,
wudu, wæl-sceaftas,   worda geþinges."
    Ārās þā se rīca,   ymb hine rinc manig,
prȳðlīc þegna hēap;   sume þær bidon,
heaðo-rēaf hēoldon,   swā him se hearda bebēad.
Snyredon ætsomne,   þā secg wīsode,
under Heorotes hrōf;   ēode hilde-dēor,
heard under helme,   þæt hē on hēoðe gestōd.
Bēowulf maðelode   —on him byrne scān,
searo-net seowed   smiþes orþancum
    "Wæs þū, Hrōðgār, hāl!   Ic eom Higelāces
mæg ond mago-ðegn;   hæbbe ic mærða fela
ongunnen on geogoþe.   Mē wearð Grendles þing
on mīnre ēþel-tyrf   undyrne cūð;
secgað sæ-līðend,   þæt þæs sele stande,
reced sēlesta,   rinca gehwylcum
īdel ond unnyt,   siððan æfen-lēoht
under heofenes hādor   beholen weorþeð.
Þā mē þæt gelærdon   lēode mīne,
þā sēlestan,   snotere ceorlas,
þēoden Hrōðgār,   þæt ic þē sōhte,
forþan hīe mægenes cræft   mīne cūþon:
selfe ofersāwon,   ðā ic of searwum cwōm,
fāh from fēondum,   þær ic fīfe geband,
ȳðde eotena cyn,   ond on ȳðum slōg
niceras nihtes,   nearo-þearfe drēah,
wræc Wedera nīð   —wēan āhsodon—
forgrand gramum: ond nū wið Grendel sceal,
wið þām āglæcan   āna gehēgan
ðing wið þyrse.   Ic þē nū ðā,

You are free now to move forward
to meet Hrothgar, in helmets and armour,
but shields must stay here and spears be stacked
until the outcome of the audience is clear."

The hero arose, surrounded closely
by his powerful thanes. A party remained
under orders to keep watch on the arms;
the rest proceeded, led by their prince
under Heorot's roof. And standing on the hearth
in webbed links that the smith had woven,
the fine-forged mesh of his gleaming mail-shirt,
resolute in his helmet, Beowulf spoke:
"Greetings to Hrothgar. I am Hygelac's kinsman,
one of his hall-troop. When I was younger,
I had great triumphs. Then news of Grendel,
hard to ignore, reached me at home:
sailors brought stories of the plight you suffer
in this legendary hall, how it lies deserted,
empty and useless once the evening light
hides itself under heaven's dome.
So every elder and experienced councilman
among my people supported my resolve
to come here to you, King Hrothgar,
because all knew of my awesome strength.
They had seen me boltered in the blood of enemies
when I battled and bound five beasts,
raided a troll-nest and in the night-sea
slaughtered sea-brutes. I have suffered extremes
and avenged the Geats (their enemies brought it
upon themselves, I devastated them).
Now I mean to be a match for Grendel,
settle the outcome in single combat.

Beowulf enters
Heorot. He gives an
account of his heroic
exploits

He declares he will
fight Grendel

brego Beorht-Dena,   biddan wille,
eodor Scyldinga,   ānre bēne:
þæt ðū mē ne forwyrne,   wīgendra hlēo,
frēo-wine folca,   nū ic þus feorran cōm,
þæt ic mōte āna   ond mīnra eorla gedryht,
þes hearda hēap,   Heorot fǣlsian.
Hæbbe ic ēac geāhsod,   þæt se ǣglǣca
for his won-hȳdum   wǣpna ne recceð.
Ic þæt þonne forhicge,   swā mē Higelāc sīe,
mīn mon-drihten,   mōdes blīðe,
þæt ic sweord bere   oþðe sīdne scyld,
geolo-rand tō gūþe;   ac ic mid grāpe sceal
fōn wið fēonde   ond ymb feorh sacan,
lāð wið lāþum;   ðǣr gelȳfan sceal
Dryhtnes dōme   sē þe hine dēað nimeð.
Wēn' ic þæt hē wille,   gif hē wealdan mōt,
in þǣm gūð-sele   Gēotena lēode
etan unforhte,   swā hē oft dyde,
mægen hrēð-manna.   Nā þū mīnne þearft
hafalan hȳdan,   ac hē mē habban wile
drēore fāhne,   gif mec dēað nimeð;
byreð blōdig wæl,   byrgean þenceð,
eteð ān-genga   unmurnlīce,
mearcað mōr-hopu;   nō ðū ymb mīnes ne þearft
līces feorme   leng sorgian.
Onsend Higelāce,   gif mec hild nime,
beadu-scrūda betst,   þæt mīne brēost wereð,
hrægla sēlest;   þæt is Hrǣdlan lāf,
Wēlandes geweorc.   Gǣð ā wyrd swā hīo scel!"
    Hrōðgār maþelode,   helm Scyldinga:
"For were-fyhtum þū,   wine mīn Bēowulf,
ond for ār-stafum   ūsic sōhtest.

And so, my request, O king of Bright-Danes,
dear prince of the Shieldings, friend of the people
and their ring of defence, my one request
430 is that you won't refuse me, who have come this far,
the privilege of purifying Heorot,
with my own men to help me, and nobody else.
I have heard moreover that the monster scorns
in his reckless way to use weapons;
therefore, to heighten Hygelac's fame
and gladden his heart, I hereby renounce
sword and the shelter of the broad shield,
the heavy war-board: hand-to-hand
is how it will be, a life-and-death
440 fight with the fiend. Whichever one death fells
must deem it a just judgement by God.
If Grendel wins, it will be a gruesome day;
he will glut himself on the Geats in the war-hall,
swoop without fear on that flower of manhood
as on others before. Then my face won't be there
to be covered in death: he will carry me away
as he goes to ground, gorged and bloodied;
he will run gloating with my raw corpse
and feed on it alone, in a cruel frenzy,
450 fouling his moor-nest. No need then
to lament for long or lay out my body:
if the battle takes me, send back
this breast-webbing that Weland fashioned
and Hrethel gave me, to Lord Hygelac.
Fate goes ever as fate must."

Hrothgar, the helmet of Shieldings, spoke:
"Beowulf, my friend, you have travelled here
to favour us with help and to fight for us.

Hrothgar recollects a friendship and tells of Grendel's raids

Geslōh þīn fæder   fæhðe mæste,
460 wearþ hē Heaþolāfe   tō hand-bonan
mid Wilfingum;   ðā hine wāra cyn
for here-brōgan   habban ne mihte.
Þanon hē gesōhte   Sūð-Dena folc
ofer ȳða gewealc,   Ār-Scyldinga;
ðā ic furþum wēold   folce Deniga
ond on geogoðe hēold   grimme-rīce,
hord-burh hæleþa;   ðā wæs Heregār dēad,
mīn yldra mæg   unlifigende,
bearn Healfdenes;   sē wæs betera ðonne ic!
470 Siððan þā fæhðe   fēo þingode;
sende ic Wylfingum   ofer wæteres hrycg
ealde mādmas;   hē mē āþas swōr.
Sorh is mē tō secganne   on sefan mīnum
gumena ǣngum,   hwæt mē Grendel hafað
hȳnðo on Heorote   mid his hete-þancum,
fǣr-nīða gefremed;   is mīn flet-werod,
wīg-hēap gewanod;   hīe wyrd forswēop
on Grendles gryre.   God ēaþe mæg
þone dol-sceaðan   dǣda getwǣfan!
480 Ful oft gebēotedon   bēore druncne
ofer ealo-wǣge   ōret-mecgas,
þæt hīe in bēor-sele   bīdan woldon
Grendles gūþe   mid gryrum ecga.
Ðonne wæs þēos medo-heal   on morgen-tīd,
driht-sele drēor-fāh,   þonne dæg līxte,
eal benc-þelu   blōde bestȳmed,
heall heoru-drēore;   āhte ic holdra þȳ lǣs
dēorre duguðe,   þē þā dēað fornam.

There was a feud one time, begun by your father.
460   With his own hands he had killed Heatholaf,
who was a Wulfing; so war was looming
and his people, in fear of it, forced him to leave.
He came away then over rolling waves
to the South-Danes here, the sons of honour.
I was then in the first flush of kingship,
establishing my sway over all the rich strongholds
of this heroic land. Heorogar,
my older brother and the better man,
also a son of Halfdane's, had died.
470   Finally I healed the feud by paying:
I shipped a treasure-trove to the Wulfings
and Ecgtheow acknowledged me with oaths of allegiance.

"It bothers me to have to burden anyone
with all the grief Grendel has caused
and the havoc he has wreaked upon us in Heorot,
our humiliations. My household-guard
are on the wane, fate sweeps them away
into Grendel's clutches—
                              but God can easily
halt these raids and harrowing attacks!

480   "Time and again, when the goblets passed
and seasoned fighters got flushed with beer
they would pledge themselves to protect Heorot
and wait for Grendel with whetted swords.
But when dawn broke and day crept in
over each empty, blood-spattered bench,
the floor of the mead-hall where they had feasted
would be slick with slaughter. And so they died,
faithful retainers, and my following dwindled.

Site nū tō symle,   ond on sǣl meoto
490 sige hrēð-secga,   swā þīn sefa hwette!”
     Þā wæs Gēat-mæcgum   geador ætsomne
on bēor-sele   benc gerȳmed;
þǣr swīð-ferhþe   sittan ēodon,
þrȳðum dealle;   þegn nytte behēold,
sē þe on handa bær   hroden ealo-wǣge,
scencte scīr-wered;   scop hwīlum sang
hādor on Heorote;   þǣr wæs hæleða drēam,
duguð unlȳtel   Dena ond Wedera.
     Unferð maþelode,   Ecglāfes bearn,
500 þe æt fōtum sæt   frēan Scyldinga,
onband beadu-rūne: wæs him Bēowulfes sīð,
mōdges mere-faran,   micel æfþunca,
forþon þe hē ne ūþe,   þæt ænig ōðer man
ǣfre mǣrða þon mā   middan-geardes
gehēdde under heofenum   þonne hē sylfa:
“Eart þū sē Bēowulf,   sē þe wið Brecan wunne,
on sīdne sǣ   ymb sund flite,
ðǣr git for wlence   wada cunnedon
ond for dol-gilpe   on dēop wæter
510 aldrum nēþdon?   Nē inc ænig mon,
nē lēof nē lāð,   belēan mihte
sorh-fullne sīð,   þā git on sund rēon;
þǣr git ēagor-strēam   earmum þehton,
mǣton mere-strǣta,   mundum brugdon,
glidon ofer gār-secg.   Geofon ȳþum wēol,
wintrys wylmum;   git on wæteres ǣht
seofon niht swuncon;   hē þē æt sunde oferflāt,
hæfde māre mægen;   þā hine on morgen-tīd
on Heaþo-Rǣmes   holm up ætbær.

"Now take your place at the table, relish
490   the triumph of heroes to your heart's content."

Then a bench was cleared in that banquet hall

A feast in Heorot

so the Geats could have room to be together
and the party sat, proud in their bearing,
strong and stalwart. An attendant stood by
with a decorated pitcher, pouring bright
helpings of mead. And the minstrel sang,
filling Heorot with his head-clearing voice,
gladdening that great rally of Geats and Danes.

From where he crouched at the king's feet,
500   Unferth, a son of Ecglaf's, spoke

Unferth strikes a discordant note

contrary words. Beowulf's coming,
his sea-braving, made him sick with envy:
he could not brook or abide the fact
that anyone else alive under heaven
might enjoy greater regard than he did:
"Are you the Beowulf who took on Breca

Unferth's version of a swimming contest

in a swimming match on the open sea,
risking the water just to prove that you could win?
It was sheer vanity made you venture out
510   on the main deep. And no matter who tried,
friend or foe, to deflect the pair of you,
neither would back down: the sea-test obsessed you.
You waded in, embracing water,
taking its measure, mastering currents,
riding on the swell. The ocean swayed,
winter went wild in the waves, but you vied
for seven nights; and then he outswam you,
came ashore the stronger contender.
He was cast up safe and sound one morning

Đonon hē gesōhte   swǣsne ēðel,
lēof his lēodum,   lond Brondinga,
freoðo-burh fægere,   þǣr hē folc āhte,
burh ond bēagas.   Bēot eal wið þē
sunu Bēanstānes   sōðe gelǣste.
Đonne wēne ic tō þē   wyrsan geþingea,
ðēah þū heaðo-rǣsa   gehwǣr dohte,
grimre gūðe,   gif þū Grendles dearst
niht-longne fyrst   nēan bīdan."

   Bēowulf maþelode,   bearn Ecgþēowes:
"Hwæt þū worn fela,   wine mīn Unferð,
bēore druncen   ymb Brecan sprǣce,
sǣgdest from his sīðe!   Sōð ic talige
þæt ic mere-strengo   māran āhte,
earfeþo on ȳþum,   ðonne ǣnig ōþer man.
Wit þæt gecwǣdon   cniht-wesende
ond gebēotedon   —wǣron bēgen þā gīt
on geogoð-fēore—   þæt wit on gār-secg ūt
aldrum nēðdon;   ond þæt geæfndon swā.
Hæfdon swurd nacod,   þā wit on sund rēon,
heard on handa;   wit unc wið hron-fixas
werian þōhton;   nō hē wiht fram mē
flōd-ȳþum feor   flēotan meahte,
hraþor on holme,   nō ic fram him wolde.
Dā wit ætsomne   on sǣ wǣron
fīf nihta fyrst,   oþþæt unc flōd tōdrāf,
wado weallende,   wedera cealdost,
nīpende niht,   ond norþan-wind
heaðo-grim ondhwearf.   Hrēo wǣron ȳþa,
wæs mere-fixa   mōd onhrēred.
Þǣr mē wið lāðum   līc-syrce mīn,
heard, hond-locen,   helpe gefremede,

among the Heathoreams, then made his way
to where he belonged in Bronding country,
home again, sure of his ground
in strongroom and bawn. So Breca made good
his boast upon you and was proved right.
No matter, therefore, how you may have fared
in every bout and battle until now,
this time you'll be worsted; no one has ever
outlasted an entire night against Grendel."

Beowulf, Ecgtheow's son, replied:

"Well, friend Unferth, you have had your say
about Breca and me. But it was mostly beer
that was doing the talking. The truth is this:
when the going was heavy in those high waves,
I was the strongest swimmer of all.
We'd been children together and we grew up
daring ourselves to outdo each other,
boasting and urging each other to risk
our lives on the sea. And so it turned out.
Each of us swam holding a sword,

a naked, hard-proofed blade for protection
against the whale-beasts. But Breca could never
move out farther or faster from me
than I could manage to move from him.
Shoulder to shoulder, we struggled on
for five nights, until the long flow
and pitch of the waves, the perishing cold,
night falling and winds from the north
drove us apart. The deep boiled up
and its wallowing sent the sea-brutes wild.

My armour helped me to hold out;
my hard-ringed chain-mail, hand-forged and linked,

Beowulf corrects Unferth

beado-hrægl brōden   on brēostum læg
golde gegyrwed.   Mē tō grunde tēah
fāh fēond-scaða,   fæste hæfde
grim on grāpe;   hwæþre mē gyfeþe wearð,
þæt ic āglǣcan   orde gerǣhte,
hilde-bille;   heaþo-rǣs fornam
mihtig mere-dēor   þurh mīne hand.

  "Swā mec gelōme   lāðo-getēonan
þrēatedon þearle;   ic him þēnode
dēoran sweorde,   swā hit gedēfe wæs.
Næs hīe ðǣre fylle   gefēan hæfdon,
mān-fordǣdlan,   þæt hīe mē þēgon,
symbel ymbsǣton   sǣ-grunde nēah;
ac on mergenne   mēcum wunde
be ȳð-lāfe   uppe lǣgon,
sweordum āswefede,   þæt syðþan nā
ymb brontne ford   brim-līðende
lāde ne letton.   Lēoht ēastan cōm,
beorht bēacen Godes;   brimu swaþredon
þæt ic sǣ-nǣssas   gesēon mihte,
windige weallas.   Wyrd oft nereð
unfǣgne eorl,   þonne his ellen dēah.
Hwæþere mē gesǣlde,   þæt ic mid sweorde ofslōh
niceras nigene.   Nō ic on niht gefrægn
under heofones hwealf   heardran feohtan,
nē on ēg-strēamum   earmran mannon.
Hwæþere ic fāra feng   fēore gedīgde,
sīþes wērig.   Ðā mec sǣ oþbær,
flōd æfter faroðe   on Finna land,
wadu weallendu.   Nō ic wiht fram þē
swylcra searo-nīða   secgan hȳrde,

560

570

580

a fine, close-fitting filigree of gold,
kept me safe when some ocean creature
pulled me to the bottom. Pinioned fast
and swathed in its grip, I was granted one
final chance: my sword plunged
and the ordeal was over. Through my own hands,
the fury of battle had finished off the sea-beast.

"Time and again, foul things attacked me,
560   lurking and stalking, but I lashed out,
gave as good as I got with my sword.
My flesh was not for feasting on,
there would be no monsters gnawing and gloating
over their banquet at the bottom of the sea.
Instead, in the morning, mangled and sleeping
the sleep of the sword, they slopped and floated
like the ocean's leavings. From now on
sailors would be safe, the deep-sea raids
were over for good. Light came from the east,
570   bright guarantee of God, and the waves
went quiet; I could see headlands
and buffeted cliffs. Often, for undaunted courage,
fate spares the man it has not already marked.
However it occurred, my sword had killed
nine sea-monsters. Such night-dangers
and hard ordeals I have never heard of
nor of a man more desolate in surging waves.
But worn out as I was, I survived,
came through with my life. The ocean lifted
580   and laid me ashore, I landed safe
on the coast of Finland.
                         Now I cannot recall
any fight you entered, Unferth,

Beowulf tells of his
ordeal in the sea

billa brōgan.　Breca nǣfre gīt
æt heaðo-lāce,　nē gehwæþer incer,
swā dēorlīce　dǣd gefremede
fāgum sweordum　—nō ic þæs fela gylpe—
þēah ðū þīnum brōðrum　tō banan wurde,
hēafod-mǣgum;　þæs þū in helle scealt
werhðo drēogan,　þēah þīn wit duge.
590 Secge ic þē tō sōðe,　sunu Ecglāfes,
þæt nǣfre Grendel swā fela　gryra gefremede,
atol ǣglǣca　ealdre þīnum,
hȳnðo on Heorote,　gif þīn hige wǣre,
sefa swā searo-grim,　swā þū self talast;
ac hē hafað onfunden,　þæt hē þā fǣhðe ne þearf,
atole ecg-þræce　ēower lēode
swīðe onsittan,　Sige-Scyldinga.
Nymeð nȳd-bāde,　nǣnegum ārað
lēode Deniga,　ac hē lust wigeð,
600 swefeð ond sendeþ,　secce ne wēneþ
tō Gār-Denum.　Ac ic him Gēata sceal
eafoð ond ellen　ungeāra nū,
gūþe gebēodan.　Gǣþ eft sē þe mōt
tō medo mōdig,　siþþan morgen-lēoht
ofer ylda bearn　ōþres dōgores,
sunne swegl-wered　sūþan scīneð!"
　　Þā wæs on sālum　sinces brytta,
gamol-feax ond gūð-rōf;　gēoce gelȳfde
brego Beorht-Dena,　gehȳrde on Bēowulfe
610 folces hyrde　fæst-rǣdne geþōht.
Ðǣr wæs hæleþa hleahtor,　hlyn swynsode,
word wǣron wynsume.　Ēode Wealhþēow forð,
cwēn Hrōðgāres,　cynna gemyndig;
grētte gold-hroden　guman on healle,

that bears comparison. I don't boast when I say
that neither you nor Breca were ever much
celebrated for swordsmanship
or for facing danger on the field of battle.
You killed your own kith and kin,
so for all your cleverness and quick tongue,
you will suffer damnation in the depths of hell.
590   The fact is, Unferth, if you were truly
as keen or courageous as you claim to be
Grendel would never have got away with
such unchecked atrocity, attacks on your king,
havoc in Heorot and horrors everywhere.
But he knows he need never be in dread
of your blade making a mizzle of his blood
or of vengeance arriving ever from this quarter—
from the Victory-Shieldings, the shoulderers of the spear.
He knows he can trample down you Danes
600   to his heart's content, humiliate and murder
without fear of reprisal. But he will find me different.
I will show him how Geats shape to kill
in the heat of battle. Then whoever wants to
may go bravely to mead, when morning light,
scarfed in sun-dazzle, shines forth from the south
and brings another daybreak to the world."

*Unferth rebuked.
Beowulf reaffirms his
determination to
defeat Grendel*

Then the grey-haired treasure-giver was glad;
far-famed in battle, the prince of Bright-Danes
and keeper of his people counted on Beowulf,
610   on the warrior's steadfastness and his word.
So the laughter started, the din got louder
and the crowd was happy. Wealhtheow came in,
Hrothgar's queen, observing the courtesies.
Adorned in her gold, she graciously saluted

*Wealhtheow,
Hrothgar's queen,
graces the banquet*

ond þā frēolic wīf   ful gesealde
ǣrest Ēast-Dena   ēþel-wearde;
bæd hine blīðne   æt þǣre bēor-þege,
lēodum lēofne;   hē on lust geþeah
symbel ond sele-ful,   sige-rōf kyning.
620 Ymb-ēode þā   ides Helminga
duguþe ond geogoþe   dæl ǣghwylcne,
sinc-fato sealde,   oþþæt sǣl ālamp,
þæt hīo Bēowulfe,   bēag-hroden cwēn
mōde geþungen,   medo-ful ætbær.
Grētte Gēata lēod,   gode þancode
wīs-fæst wordum,   þæs ðe hire se willa gelamp,
þæt hēo on ǣnigne   eorl gelȳfde
fyrena frōfre.   Hē þæt ful geþeah,
wæl-rēow wiga,   æt Wealhþēon,
630 ond þā gyddode   gūþe gefȳsed;
Bēowulf maþelode,   bearn Ecgþēowes:
"Ic þæt hogode,   þā ic on holm gestāh,
sǣ-bāt gesæt   mid mīnra secga gedriht,
þæt ic ānunga   ēowra lēoda
willan geworhte,   oþðe on wæl crunge,
fēond-grāpum fæst.   Ic gefremman sceal
eorlīc ellen,   oþðe ende-dæg
on þisse meodu-healle   mīnne gebīdan."
Ðām wīfe þā word   wēl līcodon,
640 gilp-cwide Gēates;   ēode gold-hroden
frēolicu folc-cwēn   tō hire frēan sittan.
    Þā wæs eft swā ǣr   inne on healle
þrȳð-word sprecen,   ðēod on sǣlum,
sige-folca swēg,   oþþæt semninga

the men in hall, then handed the cup
first to Hrothgar, their homeland's guardian,
urging him to drink deep and enjoy it
because he was dear to them. And he drank it down
like the warlord he was, with festive cheer.
So the Helming woman went on her rounds,
queenly and dignified, decked out in rings,
offering the goblet to all ranks,
treating the household and the assembled troop
until it was Beowulf's turn to take it from her hand.
With measured words she welcomed the Geat
and thanked God for granting her wish
that a deliverer she could believe in would arrive
to ease their afflictions. He accepted the cup,
a daunting man, dangerous in action
and eager for it always. He addressed Wealhtheow;
Beowulf, son of Ecgtheow, said:

"I had a fixed purpose when I put to sea.
As I sat in the boat with my band of men,
I meant to perform to the uttermost
what your people wanted or perish in the attempt,
in the fiend's clutches. And I shall fulfil that purpose,
prove myself with a proud deed
or meet my death here in the mead-hall."

This formal boast by Beowulf the Geat
pleased the lady well and she went to sit
by Hrothgar, regal and arrayed with gold.

Then it was like old times in the echoing hall,
proud talk and the people happy,
loud and excited; until soon enough

Beowulf's formal boast

Hrothgar leaves Heorot in Beowulf's keeping

sunu Healfdenes   sēcean wolde
æfen-ræste.   Wiste þǣm āhlǣcan
tō þǣm hēah-sele   hilde geþinged,
siððan hīe sunnan lēoht   gesēon meahton,
oþ ðe nīpende   niht ofer ealle,
scadu-helma gesceapu   scrīðan cwōman
wan under wolcnum.   Werod eall ārās.
Gegrētte þā   guma ōþerne,
Hrōðgār Bēowulf,   ond him hǣl ābēad,
wīn-ærnes geweald,   ond þæt word ācwæð:
"Nǣfre ic ǣnegum men   ǣr ālȳfde,
siþðan ic hond ond rond   hebban mihte,
ðrȳþ-ærn Dena   būton þē nū ðā.
Hafa nū ond geheald   husa sēlest:
gemyne mǣrþo,   mægen-ellen cȳð,
waca wið wrāþum!   Ne bið þē wilna gād
gif þū þæt ellen-weorc   aldre gedīgest."
      Đā him Hrōþgār gewāt   mid his hæleþa gedryht,
eodur Scyldinga   ūt of healle;
wolde wīg-fruma   Wealhþēo sēcan,
cwēn tō gebeddan.   Hæfde kyning-wuldor
Grendle tōgēanes,   swā guman gefrungon,
sele-weard āseted;   sundor-nytte behēold
ymb aldor Dena,   eoton-weard' ābēad.
Hūru Gēata lēod   georne truwode
mōdgan mægnes,   Metodes hyldo.
Đā hē him of dyde   īsern-byrnan,
helm of hafelan,   sealde his hyrsted sweord,
īrena cyst   ombiht-þegne,
ond gehealdan hēt   hilde-geatwe.
Gespræc þā se gōda   gylp-worda sum,
Bēowulf Gēata,   ǣr hē on bed stige:

Halfdane's heir had to be away
to his night's rest. He realized
that the demon was going to descend on the hall,
that he had plotted all day, from dawn-light
until darkness gathered again over the world
650 and stealthy night-shapes came stealing forth
under the cloud-murk. The company stood
as the two leaders took leave of each other:
Hrothgar wished Beowulf health and good luck,
named him hall-warden and announced as follows:
"Never, since my hand could hold a shield
have I entrusted or given control
of the Danes' hall to anyone but you.
Ward and guard it, for it is the greatest of houses.
Be on your mettle now, keep in mind your fame,
660 beware of the enemy. There's nothing you wish for
that won't be yours if you win through alive."

Hrothgar departed then with his house-guard.
The lord of the Shieldings, their shelter in war,
left the mead-hall to lie with Wealhtheow,
his queen and bedmate. The King of Glory
(as people learned) had posted a lookout
who was a match for Grendel, a guard against monsters,
special protection to the Danish prince.
And the Geat placed complete trust
670 in his strength of limb and the Lord's favour.
He began to remove his iron breast-mail,
took off the helmet and handed his attendant
the patterned sword, a smith's masterpiece,
ordering him to keep the equipment guarded.
And before he bedded down, Beowulf,
that prince of goodness, proudly asserted:

*Beowulf renounces
the use of weapons*

"Nō ic mē an here-wæsmun   hnāgran talige
gūþ-geweorca   þonne Grendel hine;
forþan ic hine sweorde   swebban nelle,
aldre benēotan,   þēah ic eal mæge.
Nāt hē þāra gōda,   þæt hē mē ongēan slēa,
rand gehēawe,   þēah ðe hē rōf sīe
nīþ-geweorca: ac wit on niht sculon
secge ofersittan,   gif hē gesēcean dear
wīg ofer wǣpen: ond siþðan wītig God
on swā hwæþere hond,   hālig Dryhten,
mǣrðo dēme,   swā him gemet þince."
Hylde hine þā heaþo-dēor,   hlēor-bolster onfēng
eorles andwlitan,   ond hine ymb monig
snellīc sǣ-rinc   sele-reste gebēah.
Nænig heora þōhte,   þæt hē þanon scolde
eft eard-lufan   ǣfre gesēcean,
folc oþðe frēo-burh,   þǣr hē āfēded wæs;
ac hīe hæfdon gefrūnen,   þæt hīe ǣr tō fela micles
in þǣm wīn-sele   wæl-dēað fornam,
Denigea lēode.   Ac him Dryhten forgeaf
wīg-spēda gewiofu,   Wedera lēodum,
frōfor ond fultum,   þæt hīe fēond heora
ðurh ānes cræft   ealle ofercōmon,
selfes mihtum.   Sōð is gecȳþed,
þæt mihtig God   manna cynnes
weold wīde-ferhð.   Cōm on wanre niht
scrīðan sceadu-genga;   scēotend swǣfon,
þā þæt horn-reced   healdan scoldon,
ealle būton ānum.   Þæt wæs yldum cūþ,
þæt hīe ne mōste,   þā Metod nolde,
se syn-scaþa   under sceadu bregdan,

"When it comes to fighting, I count myself
as dangerous any day as Grendel.
So it won't be a cutting edge I'll wield
to mow him down, easily as I might.
He has no idea of the arts of war,
of shield or sword-play, although he does possess
a wild strength. No weapons, therefore,
for either this night: unarmed he shall face me
if face me he dares. And may the Divine Lord
in His wisdom grant the glory of victory
to whichever side He sees fit."

Then down the brave man lay with his bolster
under his head and his whole company
of sea-rovers at rest beside him.
None of them expected he would ever see
his homeland again or get back
to his native place and the people who reared him.
They knew too well the way it was before,
how often the Danes had fallen prey
to death in the mead-hall. But the Lord was weaving
a victory on His war-loom for the Weather-Geats.
Through the strength of one they all prevailed;
they would crush their enemy and come through
in triumph and gladness. The truth is clear:
Almighty God rules over mankind
and always has.
                        Then out of the night
came the shadow-stalker, stealthy and swift;
the hall-guards were slack, asleep at their posts,
all except one; it was widely understood
that as long as God disallowed it,
the fiend could not bear them to his shadow-bourne.

680

690

700

*The Geats await
Grendel's attack*

ac hē wæccende   wrāþum on andan
bād bolgen-mōd   beadwa geþinges.
710   Ðā cōm of mōre   under mist-hleoþum
Grendel gongan,   Godes yrre bær,
mynte se mān-scaða   manna cynnes
sumne besyrwan   in sele þām hēan.
Wōd under wolcnum,   tō þæs þe hē wīn-reced,
gold-sele gumena   gearwost wisse,
fǣttum fāhne.   Ne wæs þæt forma sīð
þæt hē Hrōþgāres   hām gesōhte.
Nǣfre hē on aldor-dagum   ǣr nē siþðan
heardran hǣle   heal-ðegnas fand.
720   Cōm þā tō recede   rinc sīðian
drēamum bedǣled.   Duru sōna onarn
fȳr-bendum fæst,   syþðan hē hire folmum gehrān:
onbrǣd þā bealo-hȳdig,   ðā hē gebolgen wæs,
recedes mūþan.   Raþe æfter þon
on fāgne flōr   fēond treddode,
ēode yrre-mōd;   him of ēagum stōd
ligge gelīcost   lēoht unfǣger.
Geseah hē in recede   rinca manige,
swefan sibbe-gedriht   samod ætgædere,
730   mago-rinca hēap.   Þā his mōd āhlōg;
mynte þæt hē gedǣlde,   ǣr þon dæg cwōme,
atol āglǣca,   ānra gehwylces
līf wið līce,   þā him ālumpen wæs
wist-fylle wēn.   Ne wæs þæt wyrd þā gēn,
þæt hē mā mōste   manna cynnes
ðicgean ofer þā niht.   Þrȳð-swȳð behēold,
mǣg Higelāces,   hū se mān-scaða
under fǣr-gripum   gefaran wolde.

One man, however, was in fighting mood,
awake and on edge, spoiling for action.

710   In off the moors, down through the mist bands

God-cursed Grendel came greedily loping.
The bane of the race of men roamed forth,
hunting for a prey in the high hall.
Under the cloud-murk he moved towards it
until it shone above him, a sheer keep
of fortified gold. Nor was that the first time
he had scouted the grounds of Hrothgar's dwelling—
although never in his life, before or since,
did he find harder fortune or hall-defenders.
720   Spurned and joyless, he journeyed on ahead
and arrived at the bawn. The iron-braced door
turned on its hinge when his hands touched it.
Then his rage boiled over, he ripped open
the mouth of the building, maddening for blood,
pacing the length of the patterned floor
with his loathsome tread, while a baleful light,
flame more than light, flared from his eyes.
He saw many men in the mansion, sleeping,
a ranked company of kinsmen and warriors
730   quartered together. And his glee was demonic,
picturing the mayhem: before morning
he would rip life from limb and devour them,
feed on their flesh; but his fate that night
was due to change, his days of ravening
had come to an end.
                Mighty and canny,
Hygelac's kinsman was keenly watching
for the first move the monster would make.
Nor did the creature keep him waiting

Grendel strikes

*A Geat warrior
perishes*

Nē þæt se āglǣca ꞁ yldan þōhte,
ac hē gefēng hraðe ꞁ forman sīðe
slǣpendne rinc, ꞁ slāt unwearnum,
bāt bān-locan, ꞁ blōd ēdrum dranc,
syn-snǣdum swealh; ꞁ sōna hæfde
unlyfigendes ꞁ eal gefeormod,
fēt ond folma. ꞁ Forð nēar ætstōp,
nam þā mid handa ꞁ hige-þīhtigne
rinc on ræste ꞁ —rǣhte ongēan
fēond mid folme; ꞁ hē onfēng hraþe
inwit-þancum ꞁ ond wið earm gesæt.
Sōna þæt onfunde ꞁ fyrena hyrde,
þæt hē ne mētte ꞁ middan-geardes,
eorþan scēatta ꞁ on elran men
mund-gripe māran; ꞁ hē on mōde wearð
forht on ferhðe; ꞁ nō þȳ ǣr fram meahte.
Hyge wæs him hin-fūs, ꞁ wolde on heolster flēon,
sēcan dēofla gedræg; ꞁ ne wæs his drohtoð þǣr,
swylce hē on ealder-dagum ꞁ ǣr gemētte.
Gemunde þā se gōda ꞁ mǣg Higelāces
ǣfen-sprǣce, ꞁ up-lang āstōd
ond him fæste wiðfēng; ꞁ fingras burston:
eoten wæs ūtweard, ꞁ eorl furþur stōp.
Mynte se mǣra, ꞁ þǣr hē meahte swā,
wīdre gewindan ꞁ ond on weg þanon
flēon on fen-hopu; ꞁ wiste his fingra geweald
on grames grāpum; ꞁ þæt wæs gēocor sīð
þæt se hearm-scaþa ꞁ tō Heorute ātēah.
Dryht-sele dynede, ꞁ Denum eallum wearð,
ceaster-būendum, ꞁ cēnra gehwylcum,
eorlum ealu-scerwen. ꞁ Yrre wǣron bēgen,
rēþe ren-weardas. ꞁ Reced hlynsode;
þā wæs wundor micel, ꞁ þæt se wīn-sele

740
750
760
770

but struck suddenly and started in;
740   he grabbed and mauled a man on his bench,
bit into his bone-lappings, bolted down his blood
and gorged on him in lumps, leaving the body
utterly lifeless, eaten up
hand and foot. Venturing closer,
his talon was raised to attack Beowulf
where he lay on the bed; he was bearing in
with open claw when the alert hero's
comeback and armlock forestalled him utterly.
The captain of evil discovered himself
750   in a handgrip harder than anything
he had ever encountered in any man
on the face of the earth. Every bone in his body
quailed and recoiled, but he could not escape.
He was desperate to flee to his den and hide
with the devil's litter, for in all his days
he had never been clamped or cornered like this.
Then Hygelac's trusty retainer recalled
his bedtime speech, sprang to his feet
and got a firm hold. Fingers were bursting,
760   the monster back-tracking, the man overpowering.
The dread of the land was desperate to escape,
to take a roundabout road and flee
to his lair in the fens. The latching power
in his fingers weakened; it was the worst trip
the terror-monger had taken to Heorot.
And now the timbers trembled and sang,
a hall-session that harrowed every Dane
inside the stockade: stumbling in fury,
the two contenders crashed through the building.
770   The hall clattered and hammered, but somehow
survived the onslaught and kept standing:

Beowulf's fight with Grendel

widðhæfde heaþo-dēorum,   þæt hē on hrūsan ne fēol,
fǣger fold-bold;   ac hē þæs fæste wæs
innan ond ūtan   īren-bendum
searo-þoncum besmiþod.   Þǣr fram sylle ābēag
medu-benc monig,   mīne gefræge,
golde geregnad,   þǣr þā graman wunnon.
Þæs ne wēndon ǣr   witan Scyldinga,
þæt hit ā mid gemete   manna ǣnig,
betlīc ond bān-fāg   tōbrecan meahte,
listum tōlūcan,   nymþe līges fæþm
swulge on swaþule.   Swēg up āstāg
nīwe geneahhe,   Norð-Denum stōd
atelīc egesa,   ānra gehwylcum
þāra þe of wealle   wōp gehȳrdon,
gryre-lēoð galan   Godes andsacan,
sige-lēasne sang,   sār wānigean
helle hæfton.   Hēold hine fæste,
sē þe manna wæs   mægene strengest
on þǣm dæge   þysses līfes.

   Nolde eorla hlēo   ǣnige þinga
þone cwealm-cuman   cwicne forlǣtan,
nē his līf-dagas   lēoda ǣnigum
nytte tealde.   Þǣr genehost brægd
eorl Bēowulfes   ealde lāfe,
wolde frēa-drihtnes   feorh ealgian,
mǣres þēodnes,   ðǣr hīe meahton swā.
Hīe þæt ne wiston,   þā hīe gewin drugon,
heard-hicgende   hilde-mecgas,
ond on healfa gehwone   hēawan þōhton,
sāwle sēcan: þone syn-scaðan
ǣnig ofer eorþan   īrenna cyst,

780

790

800

it was handsomely structured, a sturdy frame
braced with the best of blacksmith's work
inside and out. The story goes
that as the pair struggled, mead-benches were smashed
and sprung off the floor, gold fittings and all.
Before then, no Shielding elder would believe
there was any power or person upon earth
capable of wrecking their horn-rigged hall
780   unless the burning embrace of a fire
engulf it in flame. Then an extraordinary
wail arose, and bewildering fear
came over the Danes. Everyone felt it
who heard that cry as it echoed off the wall,
a God-cursed scream and strain of catastrophe,
the howl of the loser, the lament of the hell-serf
keening his wound. He was overwhelmed,
manacled tight by the man who of all men
was foremost and strongest in the days of this life.

790   But the earl-troop's leader was not inclined
to allow his caller to depart alive:
he did not consider that life of much account
to anyone anywhere. Time and again,
Beowulf's warriors worked to defend
their lord's life, laying about them
as best they could with their ancestral blades.
Stalwart in action, they kept striking out
on every side, seeking to cut
straight to the soul. When they joined the struggle
800   there was something they could not have known at the
        time,
that no blade on earth, no blacksmith's art
could ever damage their demon opponent.

*Beowulf's thanes
defend him*

gūð-billa nān   grētan nolde,
ac hē sige-wǣpnum   forsworen hæfde,
ecga gehwylcre.   Scolde his aldor-gedāl
on ðǣm dæge   þysses līfes
earmlīc wurðan,   ond se ellor-gāst
on fēonda geweald   feor sīðian.
Ðā þæt onfunde   sē þe fela ǣror
mōdes myrðe   manna cynne,
fyrene gefremede   —hē fāg wið God—
þæt him se līc-homa   lǣstan nolde,
ac hine se mōdega   mǣg Hygelāces
hæfde be honda;   wæs gehwæþer ōðrum
lifigende lāð.   Līc-sār gebād
atol ǣglǣca;   him on eaxle wearð
syn-dolh sweotol;   seonowe onsprungon,
burston bān-locan.   Bēowulfe wearð
gūð-hrēð gyfeþe;   scolde Grendel þonan
feorh-sēoc flēon   under fen-hleoðu,
sēcean wyn-lēas wīc;   wiste þē geornor,
þæt his aldres wæs   ende gegongen,
dōgera dæg-rīm.   Denum eallum wearð
æfter þām wæl-rǣse   willa gelumpen.
    Hæfde þā gefǣlsod,   sē þe ǣr feorran cōm,
snotor ond swȳð-ferhð,   sele Hrōðgāres,
genered wið nīðe.   Niht-weorce gefeh,
ellen-mǣrþum.   Hæfde Ēast-Denum
Gēat-mecga lēod   gilp gelǣsted,
swylce oncȳþðe   ealle gebētte,
inwid-sorge,   þē hīe ǣr drugon
ond for þrēa-nȳdum   þolian scoldon,
torn unlȳtel.   Þæt wæs tācen sweotol,
syþðan hilde-dēor   hond ālegde,

810

820

830

He had conjured the harm from the cutting edge
of every weapon. But his going away
out of this world and the days of his life
would be agony to him, and his alien spirit
would travel far into fiends' keeping.

Then he who had harrowed the hearts of men
with pain and affliction in former times
810   and had given offence also to God
found that his bodily powers failed him.
Hygelac's kinsman kept him helplessly
locked in a handgrip. As long as either lived,
he was hateful to the other. The monster's whole
body was in pain, a tremendous wound
appeared on his shoulder. Sinews split
and the bone-lappings burst. Beowulf was granted
the glory of winning; Grendel was driven
under the fen-banks, fatally hurt,
820   to his desolate lair. His days were numbered,
the end of his life was coming over him,
he knew it for certain; and one bloody clash
had fulfilled the dearest wishes of the Danes.
The man who had lately landed among them,
proud and sure, had purged the hall,
kept it from harm; he was happy with his nightwork
and the courage he had shown. The Geat captain
had boldly fulfilled his boast to the Danes:
he had healed and relieved a huge distress,
830   unremitting humiliations,
the hard fate they'd been forced to undergo,
no small affliction. Clear proof of this
could be seen in the hand the hero displayed
high up near the roof: the whole of Grendel's

*Grendel is defeated,
Beowulf fulfils his
boast*

earm ond eaxle   —þǣr wæs eal geador
Grendles grāpe—   under gēapne hrōf.
　　Ðā wæs on morgen,   mīne gefrǣge,
ymb þā gif-healle   gūð-rinc monig;
fērdon folc-togan   feorran ond nēan
geond wīd-wegas   wundor scēawian,
lāþes lāstas.   Nō his līf-gedāl
sārlīc þūhte   secga ǣnegum,
þāra þe tīr-lēases   trode scēawode,
hū hē wērig-mōd   on weg þanon,
nīða ofercumen,   on nicera mere,
fǣge ond geflȳmed   feorh-lāstas bær.
Ðǣr wæs on blōde   brim weallende,
atol ȳða geswing,   eal gemenged,
hāton heolfre,   heoro-drēore wēol;
dēað-fǣge dēog,   siððan drēama lēas
in fen-freoðo   feorh ālegde,
hǣþene sāwle;   þǣr him hel onfēng.
　　Þanon eft gewiton   eald-gesīðas,
swylce geong manig   of gomen-wāþe,
fram mere mōdge   mēarum rīdan,
beornas on blancum.   Ðǣr wæs Bēowulfes
mǣrðo mǣned;   monig oft gecwæð,
þætto sūð nē norð   be sǣm twēonum
ofer eormen-grund   ōþer nǣnig
under swegles begong   sēlra nǣre
rond-hæbbendra,   rīces wyrðra.
Nē hīe hūru wine-drihten   wiht ne lōgon,
glædne Hrōðgār,   ac þæt wæs gōd cyning.
　　Hwīlum heaþo-rōfe   hlēapan lēton,

shoulder and arm, his awesome grasp.

Then morning came and many a warrior
gathered, as I've heard, around the gift-hall,
clan-chiefs flocking from far and near
down wide-ranging roads, wondering greatly

840   at the monster's footprints. His fatal departure
was regretted by no-one who witnessed his trail,
the ignominious marks of his flight
where he'd skulked away, exhausted in spirit
and beaten in battle, bloodying the path,
hauling his doom to the demons' mere.
The bloodshot water wallowed and surged,
there were loathsome upthrows and overturnings
of waves and gore and wound-slurry.
With his death upon him, he had dived deep

850   into his marsh-den, drowned out his life
and his heathen soul: hell claimed him there.

Then away they rode, the old retainers
with many a young man following after,
a troop on horseback, in high spirits
on their bay steeds. Beowulf's doings
were praised over and over again.
Nowhere, they said, north or south
between the two seas or under the tall sky
on the broad earth was there anyone better

860   to raise a shield or to rule a kingdom.
Yet there was no laying of blame on their lord,
the noble Hrothgar; he was a good king.

At times the war-band broke into a gallop,
letting their chestnut horses race

on geflit faran   fealwe mēaras,
ðǣr him fold-wegas   fægere þūhton,
cystum cūðe;   hwīlum cyninges þegn,
guma gilp-hlæden,   gidda gemyndig,
sē ðe eal-fela   eald-gesegena
870   worn gemunde,   word ōþer fand
sōðe gebunden.   Secg eft ongan
sīð Bēowulfes   snyttrum styrian
ond on spēd wrecan   spel gerāde,
wordum wrixlan.   Wēl-hwylc gecwæð,
þæt hē fram Sigemunde   secgan hȳrde,
ellen-dǣdum,   uncūþes fela,
Wælsinges gewin,   wīde sīðas,
þāra þe gumena bearn   gearwe ne wiston,
fǣhðe ond fyrena,   būton Fitela mid hine,
880   þonne hē swulces hwæt   secgan wolde,
ēam his nefan,   swā hīe ā wǣron
æt nīða gehwām   nȳd-gesteallan;
hæfdon eal-fela   eotena cynnes
sweordum gesǣged.   Sigemunde gesprong
æfter dēað-dæge   dōm unlȳtel,
syþðan wīges heard   wyrm ācwealde,
hordes hyrde.   Hē under hārne stān,
æþelinges bearn,   āna genēðde
frēcne dǣde;   ne wæs him Fitela mid;
890   hwæþre him gesǣlde,   ðæt þæt swurd þurhwōd
wrǣtlīcne wyrm,   þæt hit on wealle æstōd,
dryhtlīc īren;   draca morðre swealt.
Hæfde āglǣca   elne gegongen,
þæt hē bēah-hordes   brūcan mōste

wherever they found the going good
on those well-known tracks. Meanwhile, a thane
of the king's household, a carrier of tales,
a traditional singer deeply schooled
in the lore of the past, linked a new theme
870 to a strict metre. The man started
to recite with skill, rehearsing Beowulf's
triumphs and feats in well-fashioned lines,
entwining his words.

Hrothgar's minstrel sings about Beowulf

He told what he'd heard
repeated in songs about Sigemund's exploits,
all of those many feats and marvels,
the struggles and wanderings of Waels's son,
things unknown to anyone
except to Fitela, feuds and foul doings
confided by uncle to nephew when he felt
880 the urge to speak of them: always they had been
partners in the fight, friends in need.
They killed giants, their conquering swords
had brought them down.

The tale of Sigemund, the dragon-slayer. Appropriate for Beowulf, who has defeated Grendel

After his death
Sigemund's glory   grew and grew
because of his courage   when he killed the dragon,
the guardian of the hoard.   Under grey stone
he had dared to enter   all by himself
to face the worst   without Fitela.
But it came to pass   that his sword plunged
890 *right through   those radiant scales*
and drove into the wall.   The dragon died of it.
His daring had given him   total possession
of the treasure hoard,   his to dispose of
however he liked.   He loaded a boat:

selfes dōme;   sǣ-bāt gehleōd,
bær on bearm scipes   beorhte frætwa,
Wælses eafera;   wyrm hāt gemealt.

    Sē wæs wreccena   wīde mǣrost
ofer wer-þēode,   wīgendra hlēo,
900   ellen-dǣdum   —hē þæs ǣr onðāh—
siððan Heremōdes   hild sweðrode,
eafoð ond ellen;   hē mid eotenum wearð
on fēonda geweald   forð forlācen
snūde forsended.   Hine sorh-wylmas
lemede tō lange;   hē his lēodum wearð,
eallum æþellingum   tō aldor-ceare.
Swylce oft bemearn   ǣrran mǣlum
swīð-ferhþes sīð   snotor ceorl monig,
sē þe him bealwa tō   bōte gelȳfde,
910   þæt þæt ðēodnes bearn   geþēon scolde,
fæder-æþelum onfōn,   folc gehealdan,
hord ond hlēo-burh,   hæleþa rīce,
ēðel Scyldinga.   Hē þǣr eallum wearð,
mǣg Higelāces,   manna cynne,
frēondum gefægra;   hine fyren onwōd.

    Hwīlum flītende   fealwe strǣte
mēarum mǣton.   Ðā wæs morgen-lēoht
scofen ond scynded.   Ēode scealc monig
swīð-hicgende   tō sele þām hēan,
920   searo-wundor sēon;   swylce self cyning
of brȳd-būre,   bēah-horda weard,
tryddode tīr-fæst   getrume micle,
cystum gecȳþed,   ond his cwēn mid him
medo-stigge mæt   mægþa hōse.

Waels's son   weighted her hold
with dazzling spoils.   The hot dragon melted.

Sigemund's name   was known everywhere.
He was utterly valiant   and venturesome,
a fence round his fighters   and flourished therefore
900   after King Heremod's   prowess declined
and his campaigns slowed down.   The king was betrayed,
ambushed in Jutland,   overpowered
and done away with.   The waves of his grief
had beaten him down,   made him a burden,
a source of anxiety   to his own nobles:
that expedition   was often condemned
in those earlier times   by experienced men,
men who relied   on his lordship for redress,
who presumed that the part   of a prince was to thrive
910   on his father's throne   and defend the nation,
the Shielding land   where they lived and belonged,
its holdings and strongholds.   Such was Beowulf
in the affection of his friends   and of everyone alive.
But evil entered   into Heremod.

King Heremod
remembered and
contrasted with
Beowulf

Meanwhile, the Danes kept racing their mounts
down sandy lanes. The light of day
broke and kept brightening. Bands of retainers
galloped in excitement to the gabled hall
to see the marvel; and the king himself,
920   guardian of the ring-hoard, goodness in person,
walked in majesty from the women's quarters
with a numerous train, attended by his queen
and her crowd of maidens, across to the mead-hall.

When Hrothgar arrived at the hall, he spoke,

Hrōðgār maþelode   —hē tō healle gēong,
stōd on stapole,   geseah stēapne hrōf
golde fāhne   ond Grendles hond:
"Ðisse ansȳne   Al-wealdan þanc
lungre gelimpe!   Fela ic lāþes gebād,
grynna æt Grendle;   ā mæg God wyrcan
wunder æfter wundre,   wuldres Hyrde.
Ðæt wæs ungeāra,   þæt ic ǣnigra mē
wēana ne wēnde   tō wīdan feore
bōte gebīdan,   þonne blōde fāh
hūsa sēlest   heoro-drērig stōd,
wēa wīd-scofen   witena gehwylcum
ðāra þe ne wēndon,   þæt hīe wīde-ferhð
lēoda land-geweorc   lāþum beweredon
scuccum ond scinnum.   Nū scealc hafað
þurh Drihtnes miht   dǣd gefremede,
ðe wē ealle   ǣr ne meahton
snyttrum besyrwan.   Hwæt, þæt secgan mæg
efne swā hwylc mægþa,   swā ðone magan cende
æfter gum-cynnum,   gyf hēo gȳt lyfað,
þæt hyre Eald-metod   ēste wǣre
bearn-gebyrdo.   Nū ic, Bēowulf, þec,
secg betsta,   mē for sunu wylle
frēogan on ferhþe;   heald forð tela
nīwe sibbe.   Ne bið þē nǣnigre gād
worolde wilna,   þē ic geweald hæbbe.
Ful oft ic for lǣssan   lēan teohhode,
hord-weorþunge   hnāhran rince,
sǣmran æt sæcce.   Þū þē self hafast
dǣdum gefremed,   þæt þīn dōm lyfað
āwa tō aldre.   Al-walda þec
gōde·forgylde,   swā hē nū gȳt dyde!"

standing on the steps, under the steep eaves,
gazing at the roofwork and Grendel's talon:
"First and foremost, let the Almighty Father
be thanked for this sight. I suffered a long
harrowing by Grendel. But the Heavenly Shepherd
930   can work His wonders always and everywhere.
Not long since, it seemed I would never
be granted the slightest solace or relief
from any of my burdens: the best of houses
glittered and reeked and ran with blood.
This one worry outweighed all others—
a constant distress to counsellors entrusted
with defending the people's forts from assault
by monsters and demons. But now a man,
with the Lord's assistance, has accomplished something
940   none of us could manage before now
for all our efforts. Whoever she was
who brought forth this flower of manhood,
if she is still alive, that woman can say
that in her labour the Lord of Ages
bestowed a grace on her. So now, Beowulf,
I adopt you in my heart as a dear son.
Nourish and maintain this new connection,
you noblest of men; there'll be nothing you'll want for,
no worldly goods that won't be yours.
950   I have often honoured smaller achievements,
recognized warriors not nearly as worthy,
lavished rewards on the less deserving.
But you have made yourself immortal
by your glorious action. May the God of Ages
continue to keep and requite you well."

Beowulf, son of Ecgtheow, spoke:

King Hrothgar gives
thanks for the relief
of Heorot and adopts
Beowulf "in his
heart"

Bēowulf maþelode,   bearn Ecgþēowes:
Wē þæt ellen-weorc   ēstum miclum,
feohtan fremedon,   frēcne genēðdon
eafoð uncūþes.   Ūþe ic swīþor,
þæt ðū hine selfne   gesēon mōste,
fēond on frætewum   fyl-wērigne!
Ic hine hrædlīce   heardan clammum
on wæl-bedde   wrīþan þōhte,
þæt hē for mund-gripe   mīnum scolde
licgean līf-bysig,   būtan his līc swice.
Ic hine ne mihte,   þē Metod nolde,
ganges getwǣman,   nō ic him þæs georne ætfealh,
feorh-genīðlan;   wæs tō fore-mihtig
fēond on fēþe.   Hwæþere hē his folme forlēt
tō līf-wraþe   lāst weardian,
earm ond eaxle;   nō þǣr ǣnige swā þēah
fēasceaft guma   frōfre gebohte;
nō þȳ leng leofað   lāð-getēona
synnum geswenced,   ac hyne sār hafað
in nīd-gripe   nearwe befongen,
balwon bendum;   ðǣr ābīdan sceal
maga māne fāh   miclan dōmes,
hū him scīr Metod   scrīfan wille."
Ðā wæs swīgra secg,   sunu Ecglāfes,
on gylp-sprǣce   gūð-geweorca,
siþðan æþelingas   eorles cræfte
ofer hēanne hrōf   hand scēawedon,
fēondes fingras.   Foran ǣghwylc wæs,
steda nægla gehwylc   stȳle gelīcost,
hǣþenes hand-sporu,   hilde-rinces
egl unhēoru.   Ǣghwylc gecwæð
þæt him heardra nān   hrīnan wolde

"We have gone through with a glorious endeavour
and been much favoured in this fight we dared
against the unknown. Nevertheless,

if you could have seen the monster himself
where he lay beaten, I would have been better pleased.
My plan was to pounce, pin him down
in a tight grip and grapple him to death—
have him panting for life, powerless and clasped
in my bare hands, his body in thrall.
But I couldn't stop him from slipping my hold.
The Lord allowed it, my lock on him
wasn't strong enough, he struggled fiercely
and broke and ran. Yet he bought his freedom

at a high price, for he left his hand
and arm and shoulder to show he had been here,
a cold comfort for having come among us.
And now he won't be long for this world.
He has done his worst but the wound will end him.
He is hasped and hooped and hirpling with pain,
limping and looped in it. Like a man outlawed
for wickedness, he must await
the mighty judgement of God in majesty."

There was less tampering and big talk then

from Unferth the boaster, less of his blather
as the hall-thanes eyed the awful proof
of the hero's prowess, the splayed hand
up under the eaves. Every nail,
claw-scale and spur, every spike
and welt on the hand of that heathen brute
was like barbed steel. Everybody said
there was no honed iron hard enough
to pierce him through, no time-proofed blade

Beowulf's account of the fight

The trophy: Grendel's shoulder and claw

īren ǣr-gōd, þæt ðæs āhlǣcan
blōdge beadu-folme   onberan wolde.

   Ðā wæs hāten hreþe   Heort innanweard
folmum gefrætwod;   fela þǣra wæs,
wera ond wīfa,   þe þæt wīn-reced,
gest-sele gyredon.   Gold-fāg scinon
web æfter wāgum,   wundor-sīona fela
secga gehwylcum   þāra þe on swylc starað.
Wæs þæt beorhte bold   tōbrocen swīðe,
eal inneweard   īren-bendum fæst,
heorras tōhlidene;   hrōf āna genæs
ealles ansund,   þē se āglǣca
fyren-dǣdum fāg   on flēam gewand,
aldres orwēna.   Nō þæt ȳðe byð
tō beflēonne   —fremme sē þe wille—
ac gesēcan sceal   sāwl-berendra
nȳde genȳdde,   niþða bearna,
grund-būendra   gearwe stōwe,
þǣr his līc-homa,   leger-bedde fæst,
swefeþ æfter symle.   Þā wæs sǣl ond mǣl
þæt tō healle gang   Healfdenes sunu;
wolde self cyning   symbel þicgan.
Ne gefrægen ic þā mǣgþe   māran weorode
ymb hyra sinc-gyfan   sēl gebǣran.
Bugon þā tō bence   blǣd-āgande,
fylle gefǣgon;   fægere geþǣgon
medo-ful manig   māgas þāra,
swīð-hicgende,   on sele þām hēan,
Hrōðgār ond Hroþulf.   Heorot innan wæs
frēondum āfylled;   nalles fācen-stafas

that could cut his brutal, blood-caked claw.

990   Then the order was given for all hands
to help to refurbish Heorot immediately:
men and women thronging the wine-hall,
getting it ready. Gold thread shone
in the wall-hangings, woven scenes
that attracted and held the eye's attention.
But iron-braced as the inside of it had been,
that bright room lay in ruins now.
The very doors had been dragged from their hinges.
Only the roof remained unscathed
1000   by the time the guilt-fouled fiend turned tail
in despair of his life. But death is not easily
escaped from by anyone:
all of us with souls, earth-dwellers
and children of men, must make our way
to a destination already ordained
where the body, after the banqueting,
sleeps on its deathbed.
              Then the due time arrived
for Halfdane's son to proceed to the hall.
The king himself would sit down to feast.
1010   No group ever gathered in greater numbers
or better order around their ring-giver.
The benches filled with famous men
who fell to with relish; round upon round
of mead was passed; those powerful kinsmen,
Hrothgar and Hrothulf, were in high spirits
in the raftered hall. Inside Heorot
there was nothing but friendship. The Shielding nation
was not yet familiar with feud and betrayal.

The damaged hall repaired

A victory feast

Þēod-Scyldingas   þenden fremedon.

1020   Forgeaf þā Bēowulfe   brand Healfdenes
segen gyldenne   sigores tō lēane,
hroden hilde-cumbor,   helm ond byrnan;
mǣre mādþum-sweord   manige gesāwon
beforan beorn beran.   Bēowulf geþah
ful on flette;   nō hē þǣre feoh-gyfte
for sceotendum   scamigan ðorfte.
Ne gefrægn ic frēondlīcor   fēower mādmas
golde gegyrede   gum-manna fela
in ealo-bence   ōðrum gesellan.

1030   Ymb þæs helmes hrōf   hēafod-beorge
wīrum bewunden   walu ūtan hēold,
þæt him fēla lāfe   frēcne ne meahton
scūr-heard sceþðan,   þonne scyld-freca
ongēan gramum   gangan scolde.
Heht ðā eorla hlēo   eahta mēaras
fǣted-hlēore   on flet tēon,
in under eoderas;   þāra ānum stōd
sadol swearwum fāh,   since gewurþad.
Þæt wæs hilde-setl   hēah-cyninges,

1040   ðonne sweorda gelāc   sunu Healfdenes
efnan wolde;   nǣfre on ōre læg
wīd-cūþes wīg,   ðonne walu fēollon.
Ond ðā Bēowulfe   bēga gehwæþres
eodor Ingwina   onweald getēah,
wicga ond wǣpna;   hēt hine wēl brūcan.
Swā manlīce   mǣre þēoden,
hord-weard hæleþa   heaþo-rǣsas geald
mēarum ond mādmum,   swā hȳ nǣfre man lyhð,
sē þe secgan wile   sōð æfter rihte.

1050   Ðā gȳt ǣghwylcum   eorla drihten

Then Halfdane's son presented Beowulf

with a gold standard as a victory gift,
an embroidered banner; also breast-mail
and a helmet; and a sword carried high,
that was both precious object and token of honour.
So Beowulf drank his drink, at ease;
it was hardly a shame to be showered with such gifts
in front of the hall-troops. There haven't been many
moments, I am sure, when men exchanged
four such treasures at so friendly a sitting.
An embossed ridge, a band lapped with wire

1030 arched over the helmet: head-protection
to keep the keen-ground cutting edge
from damaging it when danger threatened
and the man was battling behind his shield.
Next the king ordered eight horses
with gold bridles to be brought through the yard
into the hall. The harness of one
included a saddle of sumptuous design,
the battle-seat where the son of Halfdane
rode when he wished to join the sword-play:

1040 wherever the killing and carnage were the worst,
he would be to the fore, fighting hard.
Then the Danish prince, descendant of Ing,
handed over both the arms and the horses,
urging Beowulf to use them well.
And so their leader, the lord and guard
of coffer and strongroom, with customary grace
bestowed upon Beowulf both sets of gifts.
A fair witness can see how well each one behaved.

The chieftain went on to reward the others:
1050 each man on the bench who had sailed with Beowulf

*Victory gifts
presented to Beowulf*

*The other Geats are
rewarded*

B E O W U L F   69

þāra þe mid Bēowulfe   brim-lāde tēah,
on þǣre medu-bence   māþðum gesealde,
yrfe-lāfe,   ond þone ǣnne heht
golde forgyldan,   þone ðe Grendel ǣr
māne ācwealde,   swā hē hyra mā wolde,
nefne him wītig God   wyrd forstōde
ond ðæs mannes mōd.   Metod eallum wēold
gumena cynnes,   swā hē nū gīt dēð.
Forþan bið andgit   ǣghwǣr sēlest,
ferhðes fore-þanc.   Fela sceal gebīdan
lēofes ond lāþes,   sē þe longe hēr
on ðyssum win-dagum   worolde brūceð.
    Þǣr wæs sang ond swēg   samod ætgædere
fore Healfdenes   hilde-wīsan,
gomen-wudu grēted,   gid oft wrecen,
ðonne heal-gamen   Hrōþgāres scop
æfter medo-bence   mǣnan scolde:—
Finnes eaferum,   ðā hīe se fǣr begeat,
hæleð Healf-Dena,   Hnæf Scyldinga,
in Frēs-wæle   feallan scolde.
Nē hūru Hildeburh   herian þorfte
eotena trēowe;   unsynnum wearð
beloren lēofum   æt þām lind-plegan
bearnum ond brōðrum;   hīe on gebyrd hruron
gāre wunde;   þæt wæs geōmuru ides.

and risked the voyage received a bounty,
some treasured possession. And compensation,
a price in gold, was settled for the Geat
Grendel had cruelly killed earlier—
as he would have killed more, had not mindful God
and one man's daring prevented that doom.
Past and present, God's will prevails.
Hence, understanding is always best
and a prudent mind. Whoever remains
1060 for long here in this earthly life
will enjoy and endure more than enough.

They sang then and played to please the hero,   *Another performance*
words and music for their warrior prince,   *by the minstrel*
harp tunes and tales of adventure:
there were high times on the hall benches
and the king's poet performed his part
with the saga of Finn and his sons, unfolding
the tale of the fierce attack in Friesland
where Hnaef, king of the Danes, met death.

1070 *Hildeburh*   *Hildeburh, a Danish*
    had little cause   *princess married to*
to credit the Jutes: *the Frisian King*
     son and brother,   *Finn, loses her son*
she lost them both   *(unnamed here) and*
     on the battlefield. *her brother Hnaef in*
She, bereft   *a fight at Finn's hall*
    and blameless, they
foredoomed, cut down
    and spear-gored. She,
the woman in shock,
    waylaid by grief,

Nalles hōlinga   Hōces dohtor
meotodsceaft bemearn,   syþðan morgen cōm,
ðā hēo under swegle   gesēon meahte
morþor-bealo māga,   þǣr hēo ǣr mǣste hēold
worolde wynne.   Wīg ealle fornam
Finnes þegnas,   nemne fēaum ānum,
þæt hē ne mehte   on þǣm meðel-stede
wīg Hengeste   wiht gefeohtan,
nē þā wēa-lāfe   wīge forþringan,
þēodnes ðegne;   ac hig him geþingo budon,
þæt hīe him ōðer flet   eal gerȳmdon,
healle ond hēah-setl,   þæt hīe healfre geweald
wið eotena bearn   āgan mōston,
ond æt feoh-gyftum   Folcwaldan sunu
dōgra gehwylce   Dene weorþode,
Hengestes hēap   hringum wenede
efne swā swīðe,   sinc-gestrēonum

1080

1090

Hoc's daughter—

    how could she not

lament her fate

    when morning came

and the light broke

    on her murdered dears?

And so farewell

    delight on earth,

1080   war carried away

    Finn's troop of thanes,

all but a few.

    How then could Finn

hold the line

    or fight on

to the end with Hengest,

    how save

the rump of his force

    from that enemy chief?

So a truce was offered

    as follows: first

separate quarters

    to be cleared for the Danes,

hall and throne

    to be shared with the Frisians.

Then, second:

    every day

at the dole-out of gifts

    Finn, son of Focwald,

1090   should honour the Danes,

    bestow with an even

hand to Hengest

    and Hengest's men

the wrought-gold rings,

The Danish attack is bloody but indecisive. Hnaef is killed, Hengest takes charge and makes a truce with Finn and the Frisians

fǣttan goldes,   swā hē Frēsena cyn
on bēor-sele   byldan wolde.
Ðā hīe getruwedon   on twā healfa
fæste frioðu-wǣre.   Fin Hengeste
elne unflitme   āðum benemde
þæt hē þā wēa-lāfe   weotena dōme
ārum hēolde,   þæt ðǣr ǣnig mon
wordum nē worcum   wǣre ne brǣce,
nē þurh inwit-searo   ǣfre gemǣnden,
ðēah hīe hira bēag-gyfan   banan folgedon
ðēoden-lēase,   þā him swā geþearfod wæs;
gyf þonne Frȳsna hwylc   frēcnen sprǣce
ðæs morþor-hetes   myndgiend wǣre,
þonne hit sweordes ecg   syððan scolde.
    Āð wæs geæfned,   ond icge gold
āhæfen of horde: Here-Scyldinga

                    bounty to match
the measure he gave
                    his own Frisians—
to keep morale
                    in the beer-hall high.
Both sides then
                    sealed their agreement.
With oaths to Hengest
                    Finn swore
openly, solemnly,
                    that the battle survivors
would be guaranteed
                    honour and status.
No infringement
                    by word or deed,
no provocation
                    would be permitted.
Their own ring-giver
                    after all
was dead and gone,
                    they were leaderless,
in forced allegiance
                    to his murderer.
So if any Frisian
                    stirred up bad blood
with insinuations
                    or taunts about this,
the blade of the sword
                    would arbitrate it.
A funeral pyre
                    was then prepared,
effulgent gold
                    brought out from the hoard.

1100

The Danish
survivors to be
quartered and given
parity of treatment
with the Frisians
and their allies, the
Jutes

The bodies of the
slain burnt on the
pyre

betst beado-rinca	wæs on bæl gearu.
Æt þæm āde wæs	ēþ-gesȳne
swāt-fāh syrce,	swȳn eal-gylden,
eofer īren-heard,	æþeling manig
wundum āwyrded;	sume on wæle crungon.
Hēt ðā Hildeburh	æt Hnæfes āde
hire selfre sunu	sweoloðe befæstan,
bān-fatu bærnan	ond on bæl dōn.
Earme on eaxle	ides gnornode,
geōmrode giddum.	Gūð-rinc āstāh;
wand tō wolcnum	wæl-fȳra mæst,
hlynode for hlāwe;	hafelan multon,
bēn-geato burston,	ðonne blōd ætspranc,
lāð-bite līces.	Līg ealle forswealg,
gæsta gīfrost,	þāra ðe þær gūð fornam
bēga folces;	wæs hira blæd scacen.

The pride and prince
                    of the Shieldings lay
awaiting the flame.
                    Everywhere
there were blood-plastered
                    coats of mail.
The pyre was heaped
                    with boar-shaped helmets
forged in gold,
                    with the gashed corpses
of well-born Danes—
                    many had fallen.
Then Hildeburh
                    ordered her own
son's body
                    be burnt with Hnaef's,
the flesh on his bones
                    to sputter and blaze
beside his uncle's.
                    The woman wailed
and sang keens,
                    the warrior went up.
Carcass flame
                    swirled and fumed,
they stood round the burial
                    mound and howled
as heads melted,
                    crusted gashes
spattered and ran
                    bloody matter.
The glutton element
                    flamed and consumed
the dead of both sides.

Gewiton him ðā wīgend   wīca nēosian
frēondum befeallen,   Frȳs-land gesēon,
hāmas ond hēa-burh.   Hengest ðā gȳt
wæl-fāgne winter   wunode mid Finne
eal unhlitme;   eard gemunde,
þēah þe ne meahte   on mere drīfan
hringed-stefnan;   holm storme wēol,
won wið winde;   winter ȳþe belēac
īs-gebinde,   oþðæt ōþer cōm
gēar in geardas,   swā nū gȳt dēð,
þā ðe syngāles   sēle bewitiað,
wuldor-torhtan weder.   Ðā wæs winter scacen,
fæger foldan bearm;   fundode wrecca,
gist of geardum;   hē tō gyrn-wræce
swīðor þōhte   þonne tō sǣ-lāde,
gif hē torn-gemōt   þurhtēon mihte,
þæt hē eotena bearn   inne gemunde.

Their great days were gone.
Warriors scattered
            to homes and forts
all over Friesland,
            fewer now, feeling
loss of friends.
            Hengest stayed,
lived out that whole
            resentful, blood-sullen
1130   winter with Finn,
            homesick and helpless.
No ring-whorled prow
            could up then
and away on the sea.
            Wind and water
raged with storms,
            wave and shingle
were shackled in ice
            until another year
appeared in the yard
            as it does to this day,
the seasons constant,
            the wonder of light
coming over us.
            Then winter was gone,
earth's lap grew lovely,
            longing woke
in the cooped-up exile
            for a voyage home—
1140   but more for vengeance,
            some way of bringing
things to a head:
            his sword arm hankered

The Danes, homesick
and resentful, spend
a winter in exile

Spring comes

Swā hē ne forwyrnde   worold-rǣdenne,
þonne him Hūnlāfing   hilde-lēoman,
billa sēlest,   on bearm dyde,
þæs wǣron mid eotenum   ecge cūðe.
Swylce ferhð-frecan   Fin eft begeat
sweord-bealo slīðen   æt his selfes hām,
siþðan grimne gripe   Gūðlāf ond Ōslāf
æfter sǣ-sīðe   sorge mǣndon,
ætwiton wēana dǣl;   ne meahte wǣfre mōd
forhabban in hreþre.   Ðā wæs heal roden
fēonda fēorum,   swilce Fin slægen,
cyning on corþre,   ond sēo cwēn numen.
Scēotend Scyldinga   tō scypon feredon
eal in-gesteald   eorð-cyninges,
swylce hīe æt Finnes hām   findan meahton
sigla, searo-gimma.   Hīe on sǣ-lāde
drihtlīce wīf   tō Denum feredon,
lǣddon tō lēodum.

to greet the Jutes.
                        So he did not balk
once Hunlafing
                        placed on his lap
Dazzle-the-Duel,
                        the best sword of all,
whose edges Jutes
                        knew only too well.
Thus blood was spilled,
                        the gallant Finn
slain in his home
                        after Guthlaf and Oslaf
back from their voyage
                        made old accusation:
the brutal ambush,
                        the fate they had suffered,
all blamed on Finn.
                        The wildness in them
had to brim over.
                        The hall ran red
with blood of enemies.
                        Finn was cut down,
the queen brought away
                        and everything
the Shieldings could find
                        inside Finn's walls—
the Frisian king's
                        gold collars and gemstones—
swept off to the ship.
                        Over sea-lanes then
back to Daneland
                        the warrior troop
bore that lady home.

1150

Danish warriors spur themselves to renew the feud. Finn is killed, his stronghold looted, his widow, Hildeburh, carried back to Denmark

Lēoð wæs āsungen,

glēo-mannes gyd.   Gamen eft āstāh,
beorhtode benc-swēg,   byrelas sealdon
wīn of wunder-fatum.   Þā cwōm Wealhþēo forð
gān under gyldnum bēage,   þǣr þā gōdan twēgen
sǣton suhterge-fæderan;   þā gȳt wæs hiera sib ætgædere,
ǣghwylc ōðrum trȳwe.   Swylce þǣr Unferþ þyle
æt fōtum sæt frēan Scyldinga;   gehwylc hiora his ferhþe
    trēowde,
þæt hē hæfde mōd micel,   þēah þe hē his māgum nǣre
ār-fæst æt ecga gelācum.   Spræc ðā ides Scyldinga:
"Onfōh þissum fulle,   frēo-drihten mīn,

sinces brytta;   þū on sǣlum wes,
gold-wine gumena,   ond tō Gēatum spræc
mildum wordum,   swā sceal man dōn;
bēo wið Gēatas glæd,   geofena gemyndig,
nēan ond feorran   þū nū hafast.
Mē man sægde,   þæt þū ðē for sunu wolde
here-rinc habban.   Heorot is gefælsod,
bēah-sele beorhta;   brūc, þenden þū mōte,
manigra mēdo,   ond þīnum māgum lǣf
folc ond rīce,   þonne ðū forð scyle,

metodsceaft sēon.   Ic mīnne can
glædne Hrōþulf,   þæt hē þā geogoðe wile
ārum healdan,   gyf þū ǣr þonne hē,
wine Scildinga,   worold oflǣtest;
wēne ic þæt hē mid gōde   gyldan wille
uncran eaferan,   gif hē þæt eal gemon,
hwæt wit tō willan   ond tō worð-myndum
umbor-wesendum ǣr   ārna gefremedon."
Hwearf þā bī bence,   þǣr hyre byre wǣron,

The poem was over,
the poet had performed, a pleasant murmur
started on the benches, stewards did the rounds
with wine in splendid jugs, and Wealhtheow came to sit
in her gold crown between two good men,
uncle and nephew, each one of whom
still trusted the other; and the forthright Unferth,
admired by all for his mind and courage
although under a cloud for killing his brothers,
reclined near the king.
                    The queen spoke:
"Enjoy this drink, my most generous lord;
raise up your goblet, entertain the Geats
duly and gently, discourse with them,
be open-handed, happy and fond.
Relish their company, but recollect as well
all of the boons that have been bestowed on you.
The bright court of Heorot has been cleansed
and now the word is that you want to adopt
this warrior as a son. So, while you may,
bask in your fortune, and then bequeath
kingdom and nation to your kith and kin,
before your decease. I am certain of Hrothulf.
He is noble and will use the young ones well.
He will not let you down. Should you die before him,
he will treat our children truly and fairly.
He will honour, I am sure, our two sons,
repay them in kind when he recollects
all the good things we gave him once,
the favour and respect he found in his childhood."

She turned then to the bench where her boys sat,
Hrethric and Hrothmund, with other nobles' sons,

Hrēðrīc ond Hrōðmund,   ond hæleþa bearn,
giogoð ætgædere; þǣr se gōda sæt,
Bēowulf Gēata   be þēam gebrōðrum twǣm.

　　Him wæs ful boren   ond frēond-laþu
wordum bewægned,   ond wunden gold
ēstum geēawed,   earm-rēade twā,
hrægl ond hringas,   heals-bēaga mǣst
þāra þe ic on foldan   gefrægen hæbbe.
Nǣnigne ic under swegle   sēlran hȳrde
hord-māððum hæleþa,   syþðan Hāma ætwæg
tō þēre byrhtan byrig   Brōsinga mene,
sigle ond sinc-fæt;   searo-nīðas flēah
Eormenrīces;   gecēas ēcne rǣd.
Þone hring hæfde   Higelāc Gēata,
nefa Swertinges,   nȳhstan sīðe,
sīðþan hē under segne   sinc ealgode,
wæl-rēaf werede;   hyne wyrd fornam,
syþðan hē for wlenco   wēan āhsode,
fǣhðe tō Frȳsum.   Hē þā frætwe wæg,
eorclan-stānas   ofer ȳða ful,
rīce þēoden;   hē under rande gecranc.
Gehwearf þā in Francna fæþm   feorh cyninges,
brēost-gewǣdu   ond se bēah somod;
wyrsan wīg-frecan   wæl rēafeden
æfter gūð-sceare;   Gēata lēode
hrēa-wīc hēoldon.   Heal swēge onfēng.

　　Wealhðēo maþelode,   hēo fore þǣm werede spræc:
"Brūc ðisses bēages,   Bēowulf lēofa,
hyse, mid hǣle,   ond þisses hrægles nēot,

all the youth together; and that good man,
1190 Beowulf the Geat, sat between the brothers.

The cup was carried to him, kind words
spoken in welcome and a wealth of wrought gold
graciously bestowed: two arm bangles,
a mail-shirt and rings, and the most resplendent
torque of gold I ever heard tell of
anywhere on earth or under heaven.
There was no hoard like it since Hama snatched
the Brosings' neck-chain and bore it away
with its gems and settings to his shining fort,
1200 away from Eormenric's wiles and hatred,
and thereby ensured his eternal reward.
Hygelac the Geat, grandson of Swerting,
wore this neck-ring on his last raid;
at bay under his banner, he defended the booty,
treasure he had won. Fate swept him away
because of his proud need to provoke
a feud with the Frisians. He fell beneath his shield,
in the same gem-crusted, kingly gear
he had worn when he crossed the frothing wave-vat.
1210 So the dead king fell into Frankish hands.
They took his breast-mail, also his neck-torque,
and punier warriors plundered the slain
when the carnage ended; Geat corpses
covered the field.

Applause filled the hall.

Then Wealhtheow pronounced in the presence of the
   company:
"Take delight in this torque, dear Beowulf,
wear it for luck and wear also this mail

*Gifts presented,
including a torque:
Beowulf will present
it in due course to
King Hygelac, who
will die wearing it*

þēod-gestrēona, ond geþēoh tela;
cen þec mid cræfte, ond þyssum cnyhtum wes
lāra līðe; ic þē þæs lēan geman.
Hafast þū gefēred, þæt ðē feor ond nēah
ealne wīde-ferhþ weras ehtigað,
efne swā sīde swā sǣ bebūgeð
wind-geard, weallas. Wes, þenden þū lifige,
æþeling, ēadig! Ic þē an tela
sinc-gestrēona. Bēo þū suna mīnum
dǣdum gedēfe, drēam-healdende!
Hēr is ǣghwylc eorl ōþrum getrȳwe,
mōdes milde, man-drihtne hold;
þegnas syndon geþwǣre, þēod eal-gearo,
druncne dryht-guman dōð swā ic bidde."
    Ēode þā tō setle. Þǣr wæs symbla cyst,
druncon wīn weras; wyrd ne cūþon,
geōsceaft grimme, swā hit āgangen wearð
eorla manegum, syþðan ǣfen cwōm,
ond him Hrōþgār gewāt tō hofe sīnum,
rīce tō ræste. Reced weardode
unrīm eorla, swā hīe oft ǣr dydon;
benc-þelu beredon; hit geondbrǣded wearð
beddum ond bolstrum. Bēor-scealca sum
fūs ond fǣge flet-ræste gebēag.
Setton him tō hēafdon hilde-randas,
bord-wudu beorhtan. Þǣr on bence wæs
ofer æþelinge ȳþ-gesēne
heaþo-stēapa helm, hringed byrne,
þrec-wudu þrymlīc. Wæs þēaw hyra,
þæt hīe oft wǣron an wīg gearwe,
gē æt hām gē on herge, gē gehwæþer þāra
efne swylce mǣla, swylce hira man-dryhtne

1220

1230

1240

from our people's armoury: may you prosper in them!
Be acclaimed for strength, for kindly guidance
1220 to these two boys, and your bounty will be sure.
You have won renown: you are known to all men
far and near, now and forever.
Your sway is wide as the wind's home,
as the sea around cliffs. And so, my prince,
I wish you a lifetime's luck and blessings
to enjoy this treasure. Treat my sons
with tender care, be strong and kind.
Here each comrade is true to the other,
loyal to lord, loving in spirit.
1230 The thanes have one purpose, the people are ready:
having drunk and pledged, the ranks do as I bid."

She moved then to her place. Men were drinking wine   *Bedtime in Heorot*
at that rare feast; how could they know fate,
the grim shape of things to come,
the threat looming over many thanes
as night approached and King Hrothgar prepared
to retire to his quarters? Retainers in great numbers
were posted on guard as so often in the past.
Benches were pushed back, bedding gear and bolsters
1240 spread across the floor, and one man
lay down to his rest, already marked for death.
At their heads they placed their polished timber
battle-shields; and on the bench above them,
each man's kit was kept to hand:
a towering war-helmet, webbed mail-shirt
and great-shafted spear. It was their habit
always and everywhere to be ready for action,
at home or in the camp, in whatever case
and at whatever time the need arose

1250 þearf gesǣlde; wæs sēo þēod tilu.

Sigon þā tō slǣpe. Sum sāre angeald
æfen-ræste, swā him ful oft gelamp
siþðan gold-sele Grendel warode,
unriht æfnde, oþþæt ende becwōm,
swylt æfter synnum. Þæt gesȳne wearþ,
wīd-cūþ werum, þætte wrecend þā gȳt
lifde æfter lāþum, lange þrāge,
æfter gūð-ceare. Grendles mōdor,
ides, āglǣc-wīf yrmþe gemunde,
1260 sē þe wæter-egesan wunian scolde,
cealde strēamas, siþðan Cain wearð
tō ecg-banan āngan brēþer,
fæderen-mǣge; hē þā fāg gewāt,
morþre gemearcod, man-drēam flēon,
wēsten warode. Þanon wōc fela
geōsceaft-gāsta; wæs þǣra Grendel sum
heoro-wearh hetelīc, sē æt Heorote fand
wæccendne wer wīges bīdan.
Þǣr him āglǣca ætgrǣpe wearð;
1270 hwæþre hē gemunde mægenes strenge,
gim-fæste gife, ðe him God sealde,
ond him tō An-waldan āre gelȳfde,
frōfre ond fultum; ðȳ hē þone fēond ofercwōm,
gehnǣgde helle-gāst. Þā hē hēan gewāt,
drēame bedǣled dēaþ-wīc sēon,
man-cynnes fēond. Ond his mōdor þā gȳt
gīfre ond galg-mōd gegān wolde
sorh-fulne sīð, sunu dēoð wrecan.

Cōm þā tō Heorote, ðær Hring-Dene
1280 geond þæt sæld swǣfun. Þā ðǣr sōna wearð

to rally round their lord. They were a right people.

They went to sleep. And one paid dearly
for his night's ease, as had happened to them often,
ever since Grendel occupied the gold-hall,
committing evil until the end came,
death after his crimes. Then it became clear,
obvious to everyone once the fight was over,
that an avenger lurked and was still alive,
grimly biding time. Grendel's mother,
monstrous hell-bride, brooded on her wrongs.
She had been forced down into fearful waters,
the cold depths, after Cain had killed
his father's son, felled his own
brother with a sword. Branded an outlaw,
marked by having murdered, he moved into the wilds,
shunned company and joy. And from Cain there sprang
misbegotten spirits, among them Grendel,
the banished and accursed, due to come to grips
with that watcher in Heorot waiting to do battle.
The monster wrenched and wrestled with him
but Beowulf was mindful of his mighty strength,
the wondrous gifts God had showered on him:
He relied for help on the Lord of All,
on His care and favour. So he overcame the foe,
brought down the hell-brute. Broken and bowed,
outcast from all sweetness, the enemy of mankind
made for his death-den. But now his mother
had sallied forth on a savage journey,
grief-racked and ravenous, desperate for revenge.

She came to Heorot. There, inside the hall,
Danes lay asleep, earls who would soon endure

edhwyrft eorlum   siþðan inne fealh
Grendles mōdor.   Wæs se gryre lǣssa
efne swā micle,   swā bið mægþa cræft,
wīg-gryre wīfes,   be wǣpned-men
þonne heoru bunden,   hamere geþuren,
sweord swāte fāh   swīn ofer helme,
ecgum dyhttig,   andweard scireð.
Ðā wæs on healle   heard-ecg togen,
sweord ofer setlum,   sīd-rand manig
hafen handa fæst;   helm ne gemunde,
byrnan sīde,   þā hine se brōga angeat.

    Hēo wæs on ofste,   wolde ūt þanon,
fēore beorgan,   þā hēo onfunden wæs.
Hraðe hēo æþelinga   ānne hæfde
fæste befangen,   þā hēo tō fenne gang.
Sē wæs Hrōþgāre   hæleþa lēofost
on gesīðes hād   be sǣm twēonum,
rīce rand-wiga,   þone ðe hēo on ræste ābrēat,
blǣd-fæstne beorn.   Næs Bēowulf ðǣr,
ac wæs ōþer in   ǣr geteohhod
æfter māþðum-gife   mǣrum Gēate.
Hrēan wearð in Heorote;   hēo under heolfre genam
cūþe folme;   cearu wæs genīwod,
geworden in wīcun.   Ne wæs þæt gewrixle til,
þæt hīe on bā healfa   bicgan scoldon
frēonda fēorum.   Þā wæs frōd cyning,
hār hilde-rinc,   on hrēon mōde,
syðþan hē aldor-þegn   unlyfigendne,
þone dēorestan   dēadne wisse.

a great reversal, once Grendel's mother
attacked and entered. Her onslaught was less
only by as much as an amazon warrior's
strength is less than an armed man's
when the hefted sword, its hammered edge
and gleaming blade slathered in blood,
razes the sturdy boar-ridge off a helmet.
Then in the hall, hard-honed swords
were grabbed from the bench, many a broad shield
1290   lifted and braced; there was little thought of helmets
or woven mail when they woke in terror.

The hell-dam was in panic, desperate to get out,
in mortal terror the moment she was found.
She had pounced and taken one of the retainers
in a tight hold, then headed for the fen.
To Hrothgar, this man was the most beloved
of the friends he trusted between the two seas.
She had done away with a great warrior,
ambushed him at rest.

                            Beowulf was elsewhere.
1300   Earlier, after the award of the treasure,
the Geat had been given another lodging.
There was uproar in Heorot. She had snatched their
    trophy,
Grendel's bloodied hand. It was a fresh blow
to the afflicted bawn. The bargain was hard,
both parties having to pay
with the lives of friends. And the old lord,
the grey-haired warrior, was heartsore and weary
when he heard the news: his highest-placed adviser,
his dearest companion, was dead and gone.

Hraþe wæs tō būre   Bēowulf fetod,
sigor-ēadig secg.   Samod ǣr-dæge
ēode eorla sum,   æþele cempa,
self mid gesīðum,   þǣr se snotera bād,
hwæþre him Al-walda   ǣfre wille
æfter wēa-spelle   wyrpe gefremman.
Gang ðā æfter flōre   fyrd-wyrðe man
mid his hand-scale   —heal-wudu dynede—
þæt hē þone wīsan   wordum nǣgde,
frēan Ingwina;   frægn gif him wǣre,
æfter nēod-laðe,   niht getǣse.
    Hrōðgār maþelode,   helm Scyldinga:
"Ne frīn þū æfter sǣlum;   sorh is genīwod
Denigea lēodum.   Dēad is Æschere,
Yrmenlāfes   yldra brōþor,
mīn rūn-wita   ond mīn rǣd-bora,
eaxl-gestealla,   ðonne wē on orlege
hafelan weredon,   þonne hniton fēþan,
eoferas cnysedan.   Swylc scolde eorl wesan,
æðeling ǣr-gōd,   swylc Æschere wæs!
Wearð him on Heorote   tō hand-banan
wæl-gǣst wǣfre;   ic ne wāt hwæder
atol ǣse wlanc   eft-sīðas tēah,
fylle gefrǣgnod.   Hēo þā fǣhðe wræc,
þē þū gystran niht   Grendel cwealdest
þurh hǣstne hād   heardum clammum,
forþan hē tō lange   lēode mīne
wanode ond wyrde.   Hē æt wīge gecrang
ealdres scyldig;   ond nū ōþer cwōm
mihtig mān-scaða,   wolde hyre mǣg wrecan,
gē feor hafað   fǣhðe gestǣled,
þæs þe þincean mæg   þegne monegum,

Beowulf was quickly brought to the chamber:
the winner of fights, the arch-warrior,
came first-footing in with his fellow troops
to where the king in his wisdom waited,
still wondering whether Almighty God
would ever turn the tide of his misfortunes.
So Beowulf entered with his band in attendance
and the wooden floor-boards banged and rang
as he advanced, hurrying to address
the prince of the Ingwins, asking if he'd rested

since the urgent summons had come as a surprise.

Then Hrothgar, the Shieldings' helmet, spoke:
"Rest? What is rest? Sorrow has returned.
Alas for the Danes! Aeschere is dead.
He was Yrmenlaf's elder brother
and a soul-mate to me, a true mentor,
my right-hand man when the ranks clashed
and our boar-crests had to take a battering
in the line of action. Aeschere was everything
the world admires in a wise man and a friend.

Then this roaming killer came in a fury
and slaughtered him in Heorot. Where she is hiding,
glutting on the corpse and glorying in her escape,
I cannot tell; she has taken up the feud
because of last night, when you killed Grendel,
wrestled and racked him in ruinous combat
since for too long he had terrorized us
with his depredations. He died in battle,
paid with his life; and now this powerful
other one arrives, this force for evil

driven to avenge her kinsman's death.
Or so it seems to thanes in their grief,

*Beowulf is
summoned*

*Hrothgar laments
the death of his
counsellor. He
knows Grendel's
mother must avenge
her son*

sē þe æfter sinc-gyfan   on sefan grēoteþ,
hreþer-bealo hearde;   nū sēo hand ligeð,
sē þe ēow wēl-hwylcra   wilna dohte.

"Ic þæt lond-būend,   lēode mīne,
sele-rǣdende   secgan hȳrde,
þæt hīe gesāwon   swylce twēgen
micle mearc-stapan   mōras healdan,
ellor-gǣstas;   ðǣra ōðer wæs,
þæs þe hīe gewislīcost   gewitan meahton,
idese onlīcnes;   ōðer earm-sceapen
on weres wæstmum   wrǣc-lāstas træd,
næfne hē wæs māra   þonne ǣnig man ōðer;
þone on geār-dagum   'Grendel' nemdon
fold-būende;   nō hīe fæder cunnon,
hwæþer him ǣnig wæs   ǣr ācenned
dyrnra gāsta.   Hīe dȳgel lond
warigeað, wulf-hleoþu,   windige næssas,
frēcne fen-gelād,   ðǣr fyrgen-strēam
under næssa genipu   niþer gewīteð,
flōd under foldan.   Nis þæt feor heonon
mīl-gemearces,   þæt se mere standeð
ofer þǣm hongiað   hrinde bearwas;
wudu wyrtum fæst   wæter oferhelmað.
Þǣr mæg nihta gehwǣm   nīð-wundor sēon,
fȳr on flōde;   nō þæs frōd leofað
gumena bearna   þæt þone grund wite.
Ðēah þe hǣð-stapa   hundum geswenced,
heorot hornum trum   holt-wudu sēce,
feorran geflȳmed,   ǣr hē feorh seleð,
aldor on ōfre,   ǣr hē in wille,
hafelan hȳdan.   Nis þæt hēoru stōw;

in the anguish every thane endures
at the loss of a ring-giver, now that the hand
that bestowed so richly has been stilled in death.

"I have heard it said by my people in hall,
counsellors who live in the upland country,
that they have seen two such creatures
prowling the moors, huge marauders
from some other world. One of these things,
as far as anyone ever can discern,
looks like a woman; the other, warped
in the shape of a man, moves beyond the pale
bigger than any man, an unnatural birth
called Grendel by country people
in former days. They are fatherless creatures,
and their whole ancestry is hidden in a past
of demons and ghosts. They dwell apart
among wolves on the hills, on windswept crags
and treacherous keshes, where cold streams
pour down the mountain and disappear
under mist and moorland.

The country people's tales about the monsters

           A few miles from here
a frost-stiffened wood waits and keeps watch
above a mere; the overhanging bank
is a maze of tree-roots mirrored in its surface.
At night there, something uncanny happens:
the water burns. And the mere bottom
has never been sounded by the sons of men.
On its bank, the heather-stepper halts:
the hart in flight from pursuing hounds
will turn to face them with firm-set horns
and die in the wood rather than dive
beneath its surface. That is no good place.

The haunted mere

þonon ȳð-geblond   up āstīgeð
won tō wolcnum,   þonne wind styreþ
lāð gewidru,   oðþæt lyft ðrysmaþ,
roderas rēotað.   Nū is se rǣd gelang
eft æt þē ānum.   Eard gīt ne const,
frēcne stōwe,   ðær þū findan miht
fela-sinnigne secg;   sēc gif þū dyrre.
1380 Ic þē þā fǣhðe   fēo lēanige,
eald-gestrēonum,   swā ic ǣr dyde,
wundini golde,   gyf þȳ on weg cymest."

        Bēowulf maþelode,   bearn Ecgþēowes:
"Ne sorga, snotor guma!   Sēlre bið ǣghwǣm
þæt hē his frēond wrece,   þonne hē fela murne.
Ūre ǣghwylc sceal   ende gebīdan
worolde līfes;   wyrce sē þe mōte
dōmes ǣr dēaþe;   þæt bið driht-guman
unlifgendum   æfter sēlest.
1390 Ārīs, rīces weard,   uton hraþe fēran,
Grendles māgan   gang scēawigan!
Ic hit þē gehāte: nō hē on helm losaþ,
nē on foldan fæþm,   nē on fyrgen-holt,
nē on gyfenes grund,   gā þǣr hē wille.
Ðȳs dōgor þū   geþyld hafa
wēana gehwylces,   swā ic þē wēne tō."

        Āhlēop ðā se gomela,   Gode þancode,
mihtigan Drihtne,   þæs se man gespræc.
Þā wæs Hrōðgāre   hors gebǣted,
1400 wicg wunden-feax;   wīsa fengel
geatolīc gende;   gum-fēþa stōp
lind-hæbbendra.   Lāstas wǣron
æfter wald-swaþum   wīde gesȳne,

When wind blows up and stormy weather
makes clouds scud and the skies weep,
out of its depths a dirty surge
is pitched towards the heavens. Now help depends
again on you and on you alone.
The gap of danger where the demon waits
is still unknown to you. Seek it if you dare.
I will compensate you for settling the feud
as I did the last time with lavish wealth,
coffers of coiled gold, if you come back."

1380

Beowulf, son of Ecgtheow, spoke:
"Wise sir, do not grieve. It is always better
to avenge dear ones than to indulge in mourning.
For every one of us, living in this world
means waiting for our end. Let whoever can
win glory before death. When a warrior is gone,
that will be his best and only bulwark.
So arise, my lord, and let us immediately
set forth on the trail of this troll-dam.
I guarantee you: she will not get away,
not to dens under ground nor upland groves
nor the ocean floor. She'll have nowhere to flee to.
Endure your troubles to-day. Bear up
and be the man I expect you to be."

*Beowulf bolsters
Hrothgar's courage.
He proclaims the
heroic code that
guides their lives*

With that the old lord sprang to his feet
and praised God for Beowulf's pledge.
Then a bit and halter were brought for his horse
with the plaited mane. The wise king mounted
the royal saddle and rode out in style
with a force of shield-bearers. The forest paths
were marked all over with the monster's tracks,

*The expedition to
the mere*

gang ofer grundas,   gegnum fōr
ofer myrcan mor,   mago-þegna bær
þone sēlestan   sāwol-lēasne,
þāra þe mid Hrōðgāre   hām eahtode.
Oferēode þā   æþelinga bearn
stēap stān-hliðo,   stīge nearwe,
enge ān-paðas,   uncūð gelād,
neowle næssas,   nicor-hūsa fela.
Hē fēara sum   beforan gengde
wīsra monna,   wong scēawian;
oþþæt hē fǣringa   fyrgen-bēamas
ofer hārne stān   hleonian funde,
wyn-lēasne wudu;   wæter under stōd
drēorig on gedrēfed.   Denum eallum wæs,
winum Scyldinga,   weorce on mōde
tō geþolianne,   ðegne monegum,
oncȳð eorla gehwǣm,   syðþan Æscheres
on þām holm-clife   hafelan mētton.
    Flōd blōde wēol   —folc tō sægon—
hātan heolfre.   Horn stundum song
fūslīc fyrd-lēoð.   Fēþa eal gesæt;
gesāwon ðā æfter wætere   wyrm-cynnes fela,
sellīce sǣ-dracan   sund cunnian,
swylce on næs-hleoðum   nicras licgean,
ðā on undern-mǣl   oft bewitigað
sorh-fulne sīð   on segl-rāde,
wyrmas ond wil-dēor.   Hīe on weg hruron
bitere ond gebolgne;   bearhtm ongēaton,
gūð-horn galan.   Sumne Gēata lēod
of flān-bogan   fēores getwǣfde,
ȳð-gewinnes,   þæt him on aldre stōd
here-strǣl hearda;   hē on holme wæs

her trail on the ground wherever she had gone
across the dark moors, dragging away
the body of that thane, Hrothgar's best
counsellor and overseer of the country.
So the noble prince proceeded undismayed
up fells and screes, along narrow footpaths
1410 and ways where they were forced into single file,
ledges on cliffs above lairs of water-monsters.
He went in front with a few men,
good judges of the lie of the land,
and suddenly discovered the dismal wood,
mountain trees growing out at an angle
above grey stones: the bloodshot water
surged underneath. It was a sore blow
to all of the Danes, friends of the Shieldings,
a hurt to each and every one
1420 of that noble company when they came upon
Aeschere's head at the foot of the cliff.

Everybody gazed as the hot gore
kept wallowing up and an urgent war-horn
repeated its notes: the whole party
sat down to watch. The water was infested
with all kinds of reptiles. There were writhing sea-dragons
and monsters slouching on slopes by the cliff,
serpents and wild things such as those that often
surface at dawn to roam the sail-road
1430 and doom the voyage. Down they plunged,
lashing in anger at the loud call
of the battle-bugle. An arrow from the bow
of the Geat chief got one of them
as he surged to the surface: the seasoned shaft
stuck deep in his flank and his freedom in the water

sundes þē sǣnra,   ðē hyne swylt fornam.
Hraæþe wearð on ȳðum   mid eofer-sprēotum
heoro-hōcyhtum   hearde genearwod,
nīða genǣged   ond on næs togen
wundorlīc wǣg-bora;   weras scēawedon
gryrelīcne gist.
      Gyrede hine Bēowulf
eorl-gewǣdum,   nalles for ealdre mearn;
scolde here-byrne   hondum gebrōden,
sīd ond searo-fāh,   sund cunnian,
sēo ðe bān-cofan   beorgan cūþe,
þæt him hilde-grāp   hreþre ne mihte,
eorres inwit-feng   aldre gesceþðan;
ac se hwīta helm   hafelan werede,
sē þe mere-grundas   mengan scolde,
sēcan sund-gebland   since geweorðad,
befongen frēa-wrāsnum,   swā hine fyrn-dagum
worhte wǣpna smið,   wundrum tēode,
besette swīn-līcum,   þæt hine syðþan nō
brond nē beado-mēcas   bītan ne meahton.
Næs þæt þonne mǣtost   mægen-fultuma,
þæt him on ðearfe lāh   ðyle Hrōðgāres;
wæs þǣm hæft-mēce   Hrunting nama;
þæt wæs ān foran   eald-gestrēona;
ecg wæs īren,   āter-tānum fāh,
āhyrded heaþo-swāte;   nǣfre hit æt hilde ne swāc
manna ǣngum,   þāra þe hit mid mundum bewand,
sē ðe gryre-sīðas   gegān dorste,
folc-stede fāra.   Næs þæt forma sīð
þæt hit ellen-weorc   æfnan scolde.
 Hūru ne gemunde   mago Ecglāfes
eafoþes cræftig,   þæt hē ǣr gespræc

got less and less. It was his last swim.
He was swiftly overwhelmed in the shallows,
prodded by barbed boar-spears,
cornered, beaten, pulled up on the bank,
a strange lake-birth, a loathsome catch
men gazed at in awe.

       Beowulf got ready,
donned his war-gear, indifferent to death;
his mighty, hand-forged, fine-webbed mail
would soon meet with the menace underwater.
It would keep the bone-cage of his body safe:
no enemy's clasp could crush him in it,
no vicious armlock choke his life out.
To guard his head he had a glittering helmet
that was due to be muddied on the mere bottom
and blurred in the upswirl. It was of beaten gold,
princely headgear hooped and hasped
by a weapon-smith who had worked wonders
in days gone by and adorned it with boar shapes;
since then it had resisted every sword.
And another item lent by Unferth
at that moment of need was of no small importance:
the brehon handed him a hilted weapon,
a rare and ancient sword named Hrunting.
The iron blade with its ill-boding patterns
had been tempered in blood. It had never failed
the hand of anyone who hefted it in battle,
anyone who had fought and faced the worst
in the gap of danger. This was not the first time
it had been called to perform heroic feats.

When he lent that blade to the better swordsman,
Unferth, the strong-built son of Ecglaf,

wīne druncen, þā hē þæs wæpnes onlāh
sēlran sweord-frecan; selfa ne dorste
under ȳða gewin aldre genēþan,
drihtscype drēogan; þǣr hē dōme forlēas,
ellen-mærðum. Ne wæs þǣm ōðrum swā,
syðþan hē hine tō gūðe gegyred hæfde.

Bēowulf maþelode, bearn Ecgþēowes:
"Geþenc nū, se mǣra maga Healfdenes,
snottra fengel, nū ic eom sīðes fūs,
gold-wine gumena, hwæt wit geō sprǣcon,
gif ic æt þearfe þīnre scolde
aldre linnan, þæt ðū mē ā wǣre
forð-gewitenum on fæder stǣle.
Wes þū mund-bora mīnum mago-þegnum,
hond-gesellum, gif mec hild nime;
swylce þū ðā mādmas, þe þū mē sealdest,
Hrōðgār lēofa, Higelāce onsend.
Mæg þonne on þǣm golde ongitan Gēata dryhten,
gesēon sunu Hrǣdles, þonne hē on þæt sinc starað,
þæt ic gum-cystum gōdne funde
bēaga bryttan, brēac þonne mōste.
Ond þū Unferð lǣt ealde lāfe,
wrǣtlīc wǣg-sweord, wīd-cūðne man
heard-ecg habban; ic mē mid Hruntinge
dōm gewyrce, oþðe mec dēað nimeð."

Æfter þǣm wordum Weder-Gēata lēod
efste mid elne, nalas andsware
bīdan wolde; brim-wylm onfēng
hilde-rince. Ðā wæs hwīl dæges,
ǣr hē þone grund-wong ongytan mehte.

could hardly have remembered the ranting speech
he had made in his cups. He was not man enough
to face the turmoil of a fight under water
1470 and the risk to his life. So there he lost
fame and repute. It was different for the other
rigged out in his gear, ready to do battle.

Beowulf, son of Ecgtheow, spoke:
"Wisest of kings, now that I have come
to the point of action, I ask you to recall
what we said earlier: that you, son of Halfdane
and gold-friend to retainers, that you, if I should fall
and suffer death while serving your cause,
would act like a father to me afterwards.
1480 If this combat kills me, take care
of my young company, my comrades in arms.
And be sure also, my beloved Hrothgar,
to send Hygelac the treasures I received.
Let the lord of the Geats gaze on that gold,
let Hrethel's son take note of it and see
that I found a ring-giver of rare magnificence
and enjoyed the good of his generosity.
And Unferth is to have what I inherited:
to that far-famed man I bequeath my own
1490 sharp-honed, wave-sheened wonderblade.
With Hrunting I shall gain glory or die."

After these words, the prince of the Weather-Geats
was impatient to be away and plunged suddenly:
without more ado, he dived into the heaving
depths of the lake. It was the best part of a day
before he could see the solid bottom.

Beowulf takes his leave

Sōna þæt onfunde,   sē ðe flōda begong
heoro-gīfre behēold   hund missēra,
grim ond grǣdig,   þæt þǣr gumena sum
1500　　ǣl-wihta eard   ufan cunnode.
Grāp þā tōgēanes;   gūð-rinc gefēng
atolan clommum;   nō þȳ ǣr in gescōd
hālan līce;   hring ūtan ymb-bearh,
þæt hēo þone fyrd-hom   ðurhfōn ne mihte,
locene leoðo-syrcan   lāþan fingrum.
Bær þā sēo brim-wylf,   þā hēo tō botme cōm,
hringa þengel   tō hofe sīnum,
swā hē ne mihte,   nō hē þæs mōdig wæs,
wǣpna gewealdan;   ac hine wundra þæs fela
1510　　swencte on sunde,   sǣ-dēor monig
hilde-tūxum   here-syrcan bræc,
ēhton āglǣcan. Ðā se eorl ongeat,
þæt hē in nīð-sele   nāt-hwylcum wæs,
þǣr him nǣnig wæter   wihte ne sceþede,
nē him for hrōf-sele   hrīnan ne mehte
fǣr-gripe flōdes: fȳr-lēoht geseah,
blācne lēoman   beorhte scīnan.
　　Ongeat þā se gōda   grund-wyrgenne,
mere-wīf mihtig;   mægen-rǣs forgeaf
1520　　hilde-bille,   hond sweng ne oftēah,
þæt hire on hafelan   hring-mǣl āgōl
grǣdig gūð-lēoð. Ðā se gist onfand,
þæt se beado-lēoma   bītan nolde,
aldre sceþðan,   ac sēo ecg geswāc
ðēodne æt þearfe;   ðolode ǣr fela
hond-gemōta,   helm oft gescær,
fǣges fyrd-hrægl;   ðā wæs forma sīð
dēorum māðme,   þæt his dōm ālæg.

Quickly the one who haunted those waters,
who had scavenged and gone her gluttonous rounds
for a hundred seasons, sensed a human
observing her outlandish lair from above.
So she lunged and clutched and managed to catch him
in her brutal grip; but his body, for all that,
remained unscathed: the mesh of the chain-mail
saved him on the outside. Her savage talons
failed to rip the web of his warshirt.
Then once she touched bottom, that wolfish swimmer
carried the ring-mailed prince to her court
so that for all his courage he could never use
the weapons he carried; and a bewildering horde
came at him from the depths, droves of sea-beasts
who attacked with tusks and tore at his chain-mail
in a ghastly onslaught. The gallant man
could see he had entered some hellish turn-hole
and yet the water did not work against him
because the hall-roofing held off
the force of the current; then he saw firelight,
a gleam and flare-up, a glimmer of brightness.

The hero observed that swamp-thing from hell,
the tarn-hag in all her terrible strength,
then heaved his war-sword and swung his arm:
the decorated blade came down ringing
and singing on her head. But he soon found
his battle-torch extinguished: the shining blade
refused to bite. It spared her and failed
the man in his need. It had gone through many
hand-to-hand fights, had hewed the armour
and helmets of the doomed, but here at last
the fabulous powers of that heirloom failed.

*Beowulf is captured
by Grendel's mother*

*His sword fails to do
damage*

1500

1510

1520

Eft wæs ān-ræd,   nalas elnes læt,
1530   mærða gemyndig   mæg Hȳlāces.
Wearp ðā wunden-mæl   wrættum gebunden
yrre ōretta,   þæt hit on eorðan læg,
stīð ond stȳl-ecg;   strenge getruwode,
mund-gripe mægenes.   Swā sceal man dōn,
þonne hē æt gūðe   gegān þenceð
longsumne lof;   nā ymb his līf cearað.
Gefēng þā be eaxle   —nalas for fǣhðe mearn—
Gūð-Gēata lēod   Grendles mōdor;
brægd þā beadwe heard,   þā hē gebolgen wæs,
1540   feorh-genīðlan,   þæt hēo on flet gebēah.
Hēo him eft hraþe   andlēan forgeald
grimman grāpum,   ond him tōgēanes fēng.
Oferwearp þā wērig-mōd   wigena strengest,
fēþe-cempa,   þæt hē on fylle wearð.
Ofsæt þā þone sele-gyst   ond hyre seax getēah,
brād, brūn-ecg;   wolde hire bearn wrecan,
āngan eaferan.   Him on eaxle læg
brēost-net brōden;   þæt gebearh fēore,
wið ord ond wið ecge   ingang forstōd.
1550   Hæfde ðā forsīðod   sunu Ecgþēowes
under gynne grund,   Gēata cempa,
nemne him heaðo-byrne   helpe gefremede,
here-net hearde,   ond hālig God
gewēold wīg-sigor,   wītig Drihten,
rodera Rædend,   hit on ryht gescēd
ȳðelīce,   syþðan hē eft āstōd.
   Geseah ðā on searwum   sige-ēadig bil,
eald-sweord eotenisc   ecgum þȳhtig,
wigena weorð-mynd;   þæt wæs wǣpna cyst,
1560   būton hit wæs māre   ðonne ænig mon ōðer

Hygelac's kinsman kept thinking about
his name and fame: he never lost heart.
Then, in a fury, he flung his sword away.
The keen, inlaid, worm-loop-patterned steel
was hurled to the ground: he would have to rely
on the might of his arm. So must a man do
who intends to gain enduring glory
in a combat. Life doesn't cost him a thought.
Then the prince of War-Geats, warming to this fight
with Grendel's mother, gripped her shoulder
and laid about him in a battle frenzy:
he pitched his killer opponent to the floor
but she rose quickly and retaliated,
grappled him tightly in her grim embrace.
The sure-footed fighter felt daunted,
the strongest of warriors stumbled and fell.
So she pounced upon him and pulled out
a broad, whetted knife: now she would avenge
her only child. But the mesh of chain-mail
on Beowulf's shoulder shielded his life,
turned the edge and tip of the blade.
The son of Ecgtheow would have surely perished
and the Geats lost their warrior under the wide earth
had the strong links and locks of his war-gear
not helped to save him: holy God
decided the victory. It was easy for the Lord,
the Ruler of Heaven, to redress the balance
once Beowulf got back up on his feet.

Then he saw a blade that boded well,
a sword in her armoury, an ancient heirloom
from the days of the giants, an ideal weapon,
one that any warrior would envy,

He fights back with his bare hands

Beowulf discovers a mighty sword and slays his opponent

tō beadu-lāce   ætberan meahte,
gōd ond geatolīc,   gīganta geweorc.
Hē gefēng þā fetel-hilt,   freca Scyldinga,
hrēoh ond heoro-grim,   hring-mǣl gebrægd
aldres orwēna,   yrringa slōh,
þæt hire wið halse   heard grāpode,
bān-hringas bræc;   bil eal ðurhwōd
fǣgne flǣsc-homan;   hēo on flet gecrong,
sweord wæs swātig,   secg weorce gefeh.
1570   Līxte se lēoma,   lēoht inne stōd,
efne swā of hefene   hādre scīneð
rodores candel.   Hē æfter recede wlāt;
hwearf þā be wealle,   wǣpen hafenade
heard be hiltum   Higelāces ðegn,
yrre ond ān-rǣd.   Næs sēo ecg fracod
hilde-rince,   ac hē hraþe wolde
Grendle forgyldan   gūð-rǣsa fela,
ðāra þe hē geworhte   tō West-Denum
oftor micle   ðonne on ǣnne sīð
1580   þonne hē Hrōðgāres   heorð-genēatas
slōh on sweofote,   slǣpende frǣt
folces Denigea   fȳf-tȳne men,
ond ōðer swylc   ūt offerede,
lāðlicu lāc.   Hē him þæs lēan forgeald,
rēþe cempa,   tō ðæs þe hē on ræste geseah
gūð-wērigne   Grendel licgan,
aldor-lēasne,   swā him ǣr gescōd
hild æt Heorote.   Hrā wīde sprong,
syþðan hē æfter dēaðe   drepe þrōwade,
1590   heoro-sweng heardne,   ond hine þā hēafde becearf.
      Sōna þæt gesāwon   snottre ceorlas,

but so huge and heavy of itself
only Beowulf could wield it in a battle.
So the Shieldings' hero, hard-pressed and enraged,
took a firm hold of the hilt and swung
the blade in an arc, a resolute blow
that bit deep into her neck-bone
and severed it entirely, toppling the doomed
house of her flesh; she fell to the floor.
The sword dripped blood, the swordsman was elated.

1570 A light appeared and the place brightened
the way the sky does when heaven's candle
is shining clearly. He inspected the vault:
with sword held high, its hilt raised
to guard and threaten, Hygelac's thane
scouted by the wall in Grendel's wake.
Now the weapon was to prove its worth.
The warrior determined to take revenge
for every gross act Grendel had committed—
and not only for that one occasion
1580 when he'd come to slaughter the sleeping troops,
fifteen of Hrothgar's house-guards
surprised on their benches and ruthlessly devoured,
and as many again carried away,
a brutal plunder. Beowulf in his fury
now settled that score: he saw the monster
in his resting place, war-weary and wrecked,
a lifeless corpse, a casualty
of the battle in Heorot. The body gaped
at the stroke dealt to it after death:
1590 Beowulf cut the corpse's head off.

Immediately the counsellors keeping a lookout

*He proceeds to
behead Grendel's
corpse*

þā ðe mid Hrōðgāre   on holm wliton,
þæt wæs ȳð-geblond   eal gemenged,
brim blōde fāh.   Blonden-feaxe
gomele ymb gōdne   ongeador sprǣcon
þæt hig þæs æðelinges   eft ne wēndon,
þæt hē sige-hrēðig   sēcean cōme
mǣrne þēoden;   þā ðæs monige gewearð
þæt hine sēo brim-wylf   ābroten hæfde.

1600   Ðā cōm nōn dæges.   Næs ofgēafon
hwate Scyldingas;   gewāt him hām þonon
gold-wine gumena;   gistas sētan
mōdes sēoce,   ond on mere staredon;
wīston ond ne wēndon,   þæt hīe heora wine-drihten
selfne gesāwon.
                    Þā þæt sweord ongan
æfter heaþo-swāte   hilde-gicelum,
wīg-bil wanian.   Þæt wæs wundra sum,
þæt hit eal gemealt   īse gelīcost,
ðonne forstes bend   Fæder onlǣteð,
1610   onwindeð wæl-rāpas,   sē geweald hafað
sǣla ond mǣla;   þæt is sōð Metod.
Ne nōm hē in þǣm wīcum,   Weder-Gēata lēod,
māðm-ǣhta mā,   þēh hē þǣr monige geseah,
būton þone hafelan   ond þā hilt somod,
since fāge;   sweord ǣr gemealt,
forbarn brōden-mǣl;   wæs þæt blōd tō þæs hāt,
ǣttren ellor-gǣst,   sē þǣr inne swealt.
Sōna wæs on sunde,   sē þe ǣr æt sæcce gebād
wīg-hryre wrāðra,   wæter up þurhdeāf;
1620   wǣron ȳð-gebland   eal gefǣlsod,
ēacne eardas,   þā se ellor-gāst

with Hrothgar, watching the lake water,
saw a heave-up and surge of waves
and blood in the backwash. They bowed grey heads,
spoke in their sage, experienced way
about the good warrior, how they never again
expected to see that prince returning
in triumph to their king. It was clear to many
that the wolf of the deep had destroyed him forever.

Forebodings of those
on the shore

1600   The ninth hour of the day arrived.
The brave Shieldings abandoned the cliff-top
and the king went home; but sick at heart,
staring at the mere, the strangers held on.
They wished, without hope, to behold their lord,
Beowulf himself.
                    Meanwhile, the sword
began to wilt into gory icicles,
to slather and thaw. It was a wonderful thing,
the way it all melted as ice melts
when the Father eases the fetters off the frost
1610   and unravels the water-ropes. He who wields power
over time and tide: He is the true Lord.

The sword blade
melts

The Geat captain saw treasure in abundance
but carried no spoils from those quarters
except for the head and the inlaid hilt
embossed with jewels; its blade had melted
and the scrollwork on it burnt, so scalding was the blood
of the poisonous fiend who had perished there.
Then away he swam, the one who had survived
the fall of his enemies, flailing to the surface.
1620   The wide water, the waves and pools
were no longer infested once the wandering fiend

Beowulf returns
with the sword's hilt
and Grendel's head

oflēt līf-dagas   ond þās lǣnan gesceaft.
Cōm þā tō lande   lid-manna helm
swīð-mōd swymman,   sǣ-lāce gefeah,
mægen-byrþenne   þāra þe hē him mid hæfde.
Ēodon him þā tōgēanes,   Gode þancodon,
ðrȳðlīc þegna hēap,   þēodnes gefēgon,
þæs þe hī hyne gesundne   gesēon mōston.
Ðā wæs of þǣm hrōran   helm ond byrne
1630   lungre ālȳsed.   Lagu drūsade,
wæter under wolcnum,   wæl-drēore fāg.
Fērdon forð þonon   fēþe-lāstum,
ferhþum fægne,   fold-weg mǣton,
cūþe strǣte;   cyning-balde men
from þǣm holm-clife   hafelan bǣron
earfoðlīce   heora ǣghwæþrum
fela-mōdigra.   Fēower scoldon
on þǣm wæl-stenge   weorcum geferian
tō þǣm gold-sele   Grendles hēafod,
1640   oþðæt semninga   tō sele cōmon
frome, fyrd-hwate   fēower-tȳne
Gēata gongan;   gum-dryhten mid
mōdig on gemonge   meodo-wongas træd.
Ðā cōm in gān   ealdor ðegna,
dǣd-cēne mon   dōme gewurþad,
hæle hilde-dēor,   Hrōðgār grētan.
Þā wæs be feaxe   on flet boren
Grendles hēafod,   þǣr guman druncon,
egeslīc for eorlum   ond þǣre idese mid;
1650   wlite-sēon wrǣtlic   weras on sāwon.
Bēowulf maþelode,   bearn Ecgþēowes:

let go of her life and this unreliable world.
The seafarers' leader made for land,
resolutely swimming, delighted with his prize,
the mighty load he was lugging to the surface.
His thanes advanced in a troop to meet him,
thanking God and taking great delight
in seeing their prince back safe and sound.
Quickly the hero's helmet and mail-shirt
1630 were loosed and unlaced. The lake settled,
clouds darkened above the bloodshot depths.

With high hearts they headed away
along footpaths and trails through the fields,
roads that they knew, each of them wrestling
with the head they were carrying from the lakeside cliff,
men kingly in their courage and capable
of difficult work. It was a task for four
to hoist Grendel's head on a spear
and bear it under strain to the bright hall.
1640 But soon enough they neared the place,
fourteen Geats in fine fettle,
striding across the outlying ground
in a delighted throng around their leader.

In he came then, the thane's commander,
the arch-warrior, to address Hrothgar:
his courage was proven, his glory was secure.
Grendel's head was hauled by the hair,
dragged across the floor where the people were drinking,
a horror for both queen and company to behold.
1650 They stared in awe. It was an astonishing sight.

Beowulf, son of Ecgtheow, spoke:

He displays
Grendel's head
in Heorot

"Hwæt, wē þē þās sǣ-lāc,   sunu Healfdenes,
lēod Scyldinga,   lustum brōhton,
tīres tō tācne,   þe þū hēr tō lōcast.
Ic þæt unsōfte   ealdre gedīgde,
wigge under wætere,   weorc genēþde
earfoðlīce;   ætrihte wæs
gūð getwǣfed,   nymðe mec God scylde.
Ne meahte ic æt hilde   mid Hruntinge
1660   wiht gewyrcan,   þēah þæt wǣpen duge;
ac mē geūðe   ylda Waldend
þæt ic on wāge geseah   wlitig hangian
eald-sweord ēacen   —oftost wīsode
winigea lēasum—   þæt ic ðȳ wǣpne gebrǣd.
Ofslōh ðā æt þǣre sæcce,   þā mē sǣl āgeald,
hūses hyrdas.   Þā þæt hilde-bil
forbarn, brogden-mǣl,   swā þæt blōd gesprang,
hātost heaþo-swāta.   Ic þæt hilt þanan
fēondum ætferede,   fyren-dǣda wræc,
1670   dēað-cwealm Denigea,   swā hit gedēfe wæs.
Ic hit þē þonne gehāte,   þæt þū on Heorote mōst
sorh-lēas swefan   mid þīnra secga gedryht,
ond þegna gehwylc   þīnra lēoda,
duguðe ond iogoþe,   þæt hū him ondrǣdan ne þearft,
þēoden Scyldinga,   on þā healfe,
aldor-bealu eorlum,   swā þū ǣr dydest."
   Ðā wæs gylden hilt   gamelum rince,
hārum hild-fruman   on hand gyfen,
enta ǣr-geweorc;   hit on ǣht gehwearf
1680   æfter dēofla hryre   Denigea frēan,
wundor-smiþa geweorc;   ond þā þās worold ofgeaf
grom-heort guma,   Godes andsaca,
morðres scyldig,   ond his mōdor ēac;

"So, son of Halfdane, prince of the Shieldings,
we are glad to bring this booty from the lake.
It is a token of triumph and we tender it to you.
I barely survived the battle under water.
It was hard-fought, a desperate affair
that could have gone badly; if God had not helped me,
the outcome would have been quick and fatal.
Although Hrunting is hard-edged,
1660   I could never bring it to bear in battle.
But the Lord of Men allowed me to behold—
for He often helps the unbefriended—
an ancient sword shining on the wall,
a weapon made for giants, there for the wielding.
Then my moment came in the combat and I struck
the dwellers in that den. Next thing the damascened
sword blade melted; it bloated and it burned
in their rushing blood. I have wrested the hilt
from the enemies' hand, avenged the evil
1670   done to the Danes; it is what was due.
And this I pledge, O prince of the Shieldings:
you can sleep secure with your company of troops
in Heorot Hall. Never need you fear
for a single thane of your sept or nation,
young warriors or old, that laying waste of life
that you and your people endured of yore."

Then the gold hilt was handed over
to the old lord, a relic from long ago
for the venerable ruler. That rare smithwork
1680   was passed on to the prince of the Danes
when those devils perished; once death removed
that murdering, guilt-steeped, God-cursed fiend,
eliminating his unholy life

Beowulf presents the
sword-hilt to
Hrothgar

on geweald gehwearf   worold-cyninga
ðǣm sēlestan   be sǣm twēonum,
ðāra þe on Sceden-igge   sceattas dǣlde.

   Hrōðgār maðelode,   hylt scēawode,
ealde lāfe.   On ðǣm wæs ōr writen
fyrn-gewinnes,   syðþan flōd ofslōh,
gifen gēotende,   gīganta cyn;
frēcne gefērdon;   þæt wæs fremde þēod
ēcean Dryhtne;   him þæs ende-lēan
þurh wæteres wylm   Waldend sealde.
Swā wæs on ðǣm scennum   scīran goldes
þurh rūn-stafas   rihte gemearcod,
geseted ond gesǣd,   hwām þæt sweord geworht,
īrena cyst,   ǣrest wǣre,
wreoþen-hilt ond wyrm-fāh.   Ðā se wīsa spræc,
sunu Healfdenes   —swīgedon ealle—:
"Þæt lā mæg secgan,   sē þe sōð ond riht
fremeð on folce,   feor eal gemon,
eald ēðel-weard,   þæt ðes eorl wǣre
geboren betera!   Blǣd is ārǣred
geond wīd-wegas,   wine mīn Bēowulf,
ðīn ofer þēoda gehwylce.   Eal þū hit geþyldum healdest,
mægen mid mōdes snyttrum.   Ic þē sceal mīne gelǣstan
frēode, swā wit furðum sprǣcon.   Ðū scealt tō frōfre
   weorþan
eal lang-twīdig   lēodum þīnum
hæleðum tō helpe.

                 Ne wearð Heremōd swā
eaforum Ecgwelan,   Ār-Scyldingum;
ne gewēox hē him tō willan,   ac tō wæl-fealle
ond tō dēað-cwalum   Deniga lēodum.

and his mother's as well, it was willed to that king
who of all the lavish gift-lords of the north
was the best regarded between the two seas.

Hrothgar spoke; he examined the hilt,
that relic of old times. It was engraved all over
and showed how war first came into the world

1690   and the flood destroyed the tribe of giants.
They suffered a terrible severance from the Lord;
the Almighty made the waters rise,
drowned them in the deluge for retribution.
In pure gold inlay on the sword-guards
there were rune-markings correctly incised,
stating and recording for whom the sword
had been first made and ornamented
with its scrollworked hilt. Then everyone hushed
as the son of Halfdane spoke this wisdom.

1700   "Λ protector of his people, pledged to uphold   *Hrothgar's address*
truth and justice and to respect tradition,   *to Beowulf*
is entitled to affirm that this man
was born to distinction. Beowulf, my friend,
your fame has gone far and wide,
you are known everywhere. In all things you are even-
     tempered,
prudent and resolute. So I stand firm by the promise of
     friendship
we exchanged before. Forever you will be
your people's mainstay and your own warriors'
helping hand.
                 Heremod was different,   *He contrasts*
1710   the way he behaved to Ecgwala's sons.   *Beowulf with King*
His rise in the world brought little joy   *Heremod*
to the Danish people, only death and destruction.

Brēat bolgen-mōd   bēod-genēatas,
eaxl-gesteallan,   oþþæt hē āna hwearf,
mǣre, þēoden,   mon-drēamum from,
ðēah þe hine mihtig God   mægenes wynnum,
eafeþum stēpte,   ofer ealle men
forð gefremede.   Hwæþere him on ferhþe grēow
brēost-hord blōd-rēow;   nallas bēagas geaf
Denum æfter dōme.   Drēam-lēas gebād,
1720   þæt hē þæs gewinnes   weorc þrōwade,
lēod-bealo longsum.   Ðū þē lǣr be þon,
gum-cyste ongit!   Ic þis gid be þē
āwræc wintrum frōd.

                       Wundor is tō secganne,
hū mihtig God   manna cynne
þurh sīdne sefan   snyttru bryttað,
eard ond eorlscipe;   hē āh ealra geweald.
Hwīlum hē on lufan   lǣteð hworfan
monnes mōd-geþonc   mǣran cynnes,
1730   seleð him on ēþle   eorþan wynne
tō healdanne,   hlēo-burh wera;
gedēð him swā gewealdene   worolde dǣlas,
sīde rīce,   þæt hē his selfa ne mæg
for his unsnyttrum   ende geþencean.
Wunað hē on wiste,   nō hine wiht dweleð
ādl nē yldo,   nē him inwit-sorh
on sefan sweorceð,   nē gesacu ōhwǣr
ecg-hete ēoweð,   ac him eal worold
wendeð on willan.   Hē þæt wyrse ne con,
1740   oðþæt him on innan   ofer-hygda dǣl
weaxeð ond wrīdað,   þonne se weard swefeð,
sāwele hyrde;   bið se slǣp tō fæst,
bisgum begunden;   bona swīðe nēah,

He vented his rage on men he caroused with,
killed his own comrades, a pariah king
who cut himself off from his own kind,
even though Almighty God had made him
eminent and powerful and marked him from the start
for a happy life. But a change happened,
he grew bloodthirsty, gave no more rings
1720 to honour the Danes. He suffered in the end
for having plagued his people for so long:
his life lost happiness.

             So learn from this
and understand true values. I who tell you
have wintered into wisdom.

                  It is a great wonder
how Almighty God in His magnificence
favours our race with rank and scope
and the gift of wisdom; His sway is wide.
Sometimes He allows the mind of a man
of distinguished birth to follow its bent,
1730 grants him fulfilment and felicity on earth
and forts to command in his own country.
He permits him to lord it in many lands
until the man in his unthinkingness
forgets that it will ever end for him.
He indulges his desires; illness and old age
mean nothing to him; his mind is untroubled
by envy or malice or the thought of enemies
with their hate-honed swords. The whole world
conforms to his will, he is kept from the worst
1740 until an element of overweening
enters him and takes hold
while the soul's guard, its sentry, drowses,
grown too distracted. A killer stalks him,

Hrothgar's discourse on the dangers of power

sē þe of flān-bogan   fyrenum scēoteð.
Þonne bið on hreþre   under helm drepen
biteran strǣle —   him bebeorgan ne con —
wōm wundor-bebodum   wergan gāstes.
Þinceð him tō lȳtel   þæt hē tō lange hēold;
gȳtsað grom-hȳdig,   nallas on gylp seleð
fǣtte bēagas;   ond hē þā forð-gesceaft
forgyteð ond forgȳmeð,   þæs þe him ǣr God sealde,
wuldres Waldend,   weorð-mynda dǣl.
Hit on ende-stæf   eft gelimpeð,
þæt se līc-homa   lǣne gedrēoseð,
fǣge gefealleð;   fēhð ōþer tō,
sē þe unmurnlīce   māðmas dǣleþ
eorles ǣr-gestrēon,   egesan ne gȳmeð.
Bebeorh þē ðone bealo-nīð,   Bēowulf lēofa,
secg betsta,   ond þē þæt sēlre gecēos,
ēce rǣdas;   ofer-hȳda ne gȳm,
mǣre cempa!   Nū is þines mægnes blǣd
āne hwīle;   eft sōna bið
þæt þec ādl oððe ecg   eafoþes getwǣfeð,
oððe fȳres feng   oððe flōdes wylm
oððe gripe mēces   oððe gāres fliht
oððe atol yldo,   oððe ēagena bearhtm
forsiteð ond forsworceð;   semninga bið,
þæt ðec, dryht-guma,   dēað oferswȳðeð.
     "Swā ic Hring-Dena   hund missēra
wēold under wolcnum,   ond hig wigge belēac
manigum mǣgþa   geond þysne middan-geard,
æscum ond ecgum,   þæt ic mē ǣnigne
under swegles begong   gesacan ne tealde.
Hwæt mē þæs on ēþle   edwenden cwōm,

an archer who draws a deadly bow.
And then the man is hit in the heart,
the arrow flies beneath his defences,
the devious promptings of the demon start.
His old possessions seem paltry to him now.
He covets and resents; dishonours custom
and bestows no gold; and because of good things
that the Heavenly Powers gave him in the past
he ignores the shape of things to come.
Then finally the end arrives
when the body he was lent collapses and falls
prey to its death; ancestral possessions
and the goods he hoarded are inherited by another
who lets them go with a liberal hand.

"O flower of warriors, beware of that trap.
Choose, dear Beowulf, the better part,
eternal rewards. Do not give way to pride.
For a brief while your strength is in bloom
but it fades quickly; and soon there will follow
illness or the sword to lay you low,
or a sudden fire or surge of water
or jabbing blade or javelin from the air
or repellent age. Your piercing eye
will dim and darken; and death will arrive,
dear warrior, to sweep you away.

Beowulf is exhorted to be mindful of the fragility of life

"Just so I ruled the Ring-Danes' country
for fifty years, defended them in wartime
with spear and sword against constant assaults
by many tribes: I came to believe
my enemies had faded from the face of the earth.
Still, what happened was a hard reversal

No life is immune to danger: Hrothgar's experience proves it

gyrn æfter gomene,   seoþðan Grendel wearð,
eald-gewinna,   ingenga mīn;
ic þǣre sōcne   singāles wæg
mōd-ceare micle.   Þæs sig Metode þanc,
ēcean Dryhtne,   þæs ðe ic on aldre gebād,
þæt ic on þone hafelan   heoro-drēorigne
ofer eald gewin   ēagum starige!
Gā nū tō setle,   symbel-wynne drēoh,
wīg-geweorþad;   unc sceal worn fela
māþma gemǣnra,   siþðan morgen bið."
    Gēat wæs glæd-mōd,   gēong sōna tō,
setles nēosan,   swā se snottra heht.
Þā wæs eft swā ǣr   ellen-rōfum,
flet-sittendum   fǣgere gereorded
nīowan stefne.   Niht-helm geswearc
deorc ofer dryht-gumum.   Duguð eal ārās;
wolde blonden-feax   beddes nēosan,
gamela Scylding.   Gēat unigmetes wēl,
rōfne rand-wigan,   restan lyste.
Sōna him sele-þegn   sīðes wērgum,
feorran-cundum   forð wīsade,
sē for andrysnum   ealle beweotede
þegnes þearfe,   swylce þȳ dōgore
heaþo-līðende   habban scoldon.
    Reste hine þā rūm-heort;   reced hlīuade
gēap ond gold-fāh;   gæst inne swæf,
oþþæt hrefn blaca   heofones wynne
blīð-heort bodode.   Ðā cōm beorht scacan
scīma æfter sceadwe.   Scaþan ōnetton,
wǣron æþelingas   eft tō lēodum

from bliss to grief. Grendel struck
after lying in wait. He laid waste to the land
and from that moment my mind was in dread
of his depredations. So I praise God
in His heavenly glory that I lived to behold
this head dripping blood and that after such harrowing
I can look upon it in triumph at last.
Take your place, then, with pride and pleasure
and move to the feast. To-morrow morning
our treasure will be shared and showered upon you."

The Geat was elated and gladly obeyed
the old man's bidding; he sat on the bench.
And soon all was restored, the same as before.
Happiness came back, the hall was thronged,
and a banquet set forth; black night fell
and covered them in darkness.

Then the company rose

for the old campaigner: the grey-haired prince
was ready for bed. And a need for rest
came over the brave shield-bearing Geat.
He was a weary seafarer, far from home,
so immediately a house-guard guided him out,
one whose office entailed looking after
whatever a thane on the road in those days
might need or require. It was noble courtesy.

That great heart rested. The hall towered,
gold-shingled and gabled, and the guest slept in it
until the black raven with raucous glee
announced heaven's joy, and a hurry of brightness
overran the shadows. Warriors rose quickly,
impatient to be off: their own country

*A feast. The warriors
rest*

fūse tō farenne;   wolde feor þanon
cuma collen-ferhð   cēoles nēosan.
Heht þā se hearda   Hrunting beran
sunu Ecglāfes,   heht his sweord niman,
lēoflīc īren;   sægde him þæs lēanes þanc,
1810   cwæð, hē þone gūð-wine   gōdne tealde,
wīg-cræftigne,   nales wordum lōg
mēces ecge: þæt wæs mōdig secg.
Ond þā sīð-frome,   searwum gearwe
wīgend wǣron;   ēode weorð Denum
æþeling tō yppan,   þǣr se ōþer wæs,
hæle hilde-dēor   Hrōðgār grētte.

Bēowulf maþelode,   bearn Ecgþēowes:
"Nū wē sǣ-līðend   secgan wyllað,
feorran cumene,   þæt wē fundiaþ
1820   Higelāc sēcan.   Wǣron hēr tela,
willum bewenede;   þū ūs wēl dohtest.
Gif ic þonne on eorþan   ōwihte mæg
þīnre mōd-lufan   māran tilian,
gumena dryhten,   ðonne ic gȳt dyde,
gūð-geweorca,   ic bēo gearo sōna.
Gif ic þæt gefricge   ofer flōda begang,
þæt þec ymb-sittend   egesan þȳwað,
swā þec hetende   hwīlum dydon,
ic ðē þūsenda   þegna bringe,
1830   hæleþa tō helpe.   Ic on Higelāc wāt,
Gēata dryhten,   þēah ðe hē geong sȳ,
folces hyrde,   þæt hē mec fremman wile
wordum ond weorcum,   þæt ic þē wēl herige
ond þē tō gēoce   gār-holt bere,
mægenes fultum,   þǣr ðē bið manna þearf.
Gif him þonne Hreþric   to hofum Geata

was beckoning the nobles; and the bold voyager
longed to be aboard his distant boat.
Then that stalwart fighter ordered Hrunting
to be brought to Unferth, and bade Unferth
take the sword and thanked him for lending it.
He said he had found it a friend in battle
and a powerful help; he put no blame
on the blade's cutting edge. He was a considerate man.

And there the warriors stood in their war-gear,
eager to go, while their honoured lord
approached the platform where the other sat.
The undaunted hero addressed Hrothgar.
Beowulf, son of Ecgtheow, spoke:
"Now we who crossed the wide sea
have to inform you that we feel a desire
to return to Hygelac. Here we have been welcomed
and thoroughly entertained. You have treated us well.
If there is any favour on earth I can perform
beyond deeds of arms I have done already,
anything that would merit your affections more,
I shall act, my lord, with alacrity.
If ever I hear from across the ocean
that people on your borders are threatening battle
as attackers have done from time to time,
I shall land with a thousand thanes at my back
to help your cause. Hygelac may be young
to rule a nation, but this much I know
about the king of the Geats: he will come to my aid
and want to support me by word and action
in your hour of need, when honour dictates
that I raise a hedge of spears around you.
Then if Hrethric should think about travelling

1810

1820

1830

*Beowulf and his
band prepare to
depart*

geþingeð, þeodnes bearn,   hē mæg þær fela
frēonda findan;   feor-cȳþðe bēoð
sēlran gesōhte   þǣm þe him selfa dēah."
Hrōðgār maþelode   him on andsware:
"Þē þā word-cwydas   wigtig Drihten
on sefan sende;   ne hȳrde ic snotorlīcor
on swā geongum feore   guman þingian.
Þū eart mægenes strang   ond on mōde frōd,
wīs word-cwida.   Wēn ic talige,
gif þæt gegangeð,   þæt ðe gār nymeð,
hild heoru-grimme   Hrēþles eaferan,
ādl oþðe īren   ealdor ðīnne,
folces hyrde,   ond þū þīn feorh hafast,
þæt þē Sǣ-Gēatas   sēlran næbben
tō gecēosenne   cyning ænigne,
hord-weard hæleþa,   gyf þū healdan wylt
māga rīce.   Mē þīn mōd-sefa
līcað leng swā wēl,   lēofa Bēowulf.
Hafast þū gefēred   þæt þām folcum sceal,
Gēata lēodum   ond Gār-Denum,
sib gemǣne   ond sacu restan,
inwit-nīþas,   þē hīe ǣr drugon,
wesan, þenden ic wealde   wīdan rīces,
māþmas gemǣne,   manig ōþerne
gōdum gegrēttan   ofer ganotes bæð;
sceal hring-naca   ofer heafu bringan
lāc ond luf-tācen.   Ic þā lēode wāt
gē wið fēond gē wið frēond   fæste geworhte,
ǣghwæs untǣle   ealde wīsan."
    Ðā gīt him eorla hlēo   inne gesealde,
mago Healfdenes   māþmas twelfe,

as a king's son to the court of the Geats,
he will find many friends. Foreign places
yield more to one who is himself worth meeting."

1840   Hrothgar spoke and answered him:
"The Lord in His wisdom sent you those words
and they came from the heart. I have never heard
so young a man make truer observations.
You are strong in body and mature in mind,
impressive in speech. If it should come to pass
that Hrethel's descendant dies beneath a spear,
if deadly battle or the sword blade or disease
fells the prince who guards your people
and you are still alive, then I firmly believe
1850   the seafaring Geats won't find a man
worthier of acclaim as their king and defender
than you, if only you would undertake
the lordship of your homeland. My liking for you
deepens with time, dear Beowulf.
What you have done is to draw two peoples,
the Geat nation and us neighbouring Danes,
into shared peace and a pact of friendship
in spite of hatreds we have harboured in the past.
For as long as I rule this far-flung land
1860   treasures will change hands and each side will treat
the other with gifts; across the gannet's bath,
over the broad sea, whorled prows will bring
presents and tokens. I know your people
are beyond reproach in every respect,
steadfast in the old way with friend or foe."

Then the earls' defender furnished the hero
with twelve treasures and told him to set out,

Hrothgar declares that Beowulf is fit to be king of the Geats

Gifts presented, farewells taken

hēt hine mid þǣm lācum   lēode swǣse
sēcean on gesyntum,   snūde eft cuman.
Gecyste þā   cyning æþelum gōd,
þēoden Scyldinga   ðegn betstan
ond be healse genam;   hruron him tēaras,
blonden-feaxum.   Him wæs bēga wēn,
ealdum, infrōdum,   ōþres swīðor,
þæt hīe seoððan nā   gesēon mōston,
mōdige on meþle.   Wæs him se man tō þon lēof,
þæt hē þone brēost-wylm   forberan ne mehte;
ac him on hreþre   hyge-bendum fæst
æfter dēorum men   dyrne langað
beorn wið blōde.   Him Bēowulf þanan,
gūð-rinc gold-wlanc,   græs-moldan træd,
since hrēmig.   Sǣ-genga bād
āgend-frēan,   sē þe on ancre rād.
Þā wæs on gange   gifu Hrōðgāres
oft geæhted.   Þæt wæs ān cyning,
æghwæs orleahtre,   oþþæt hine yldo benam
mægenes wynnum   sē þe oft mangeum scōd.
    Cwōm þā tō flōde   fela-mōdigra
hæg-stealdra hēap;   hring-net bǣron,
locene leoðo-syrcan.   Land-weard onfand
eft-sīð eorla,   swā he ǣr dyde;
nō hē mid hearme   of hliðes nosan
gæstas grētte,   ac him tōgēanes rād;
cwæð þæt wil-cuman   Wedera lēodum
scaþan scīr-hame   tō scipe fōron.
Þā wæs on sande   sǣ-gēap naca
hladen here-wǣdum,   hringed-stefna
mēarum ond māðmum;   mæst hlīfade

sail with those gifts safely home
to the people he loved, but to return promptly.

1870 And so the good and grey-haired Dane,
that high-born king, kissed Beowulf
and embraced his neck, then broke down
in sudden tears. Two forebodings
disturbed him in his wisdom, but one was stronger:
nevermore would they meet each other
face to face. And such was his affection
that he could not help being overcome:
his fondness for the man was so deep-founded,
it warmed his heart and wound the heartstrings
1880 tight in his breast.
              The embrace ended
and Beowulf, glorious in his gold regalia,
stepped the green earth. Straining at anchor
and ready for boarding, his boat awaited him.
So they went on their journey, and Hrothgar's generosity
was praised repeatedly. He was a peerless king
until old age sapped his strength and did him
mortal harm, as it has done so many.

Down to the waves then, dressed in the web
of their chain-mail and warshirts the young men marched
1890 in high spirits. The coast-guard spied them,
thanes setting forth, the same as before.
His salute this time from the top of the cliff
was far from unmannerly; he galloped to meet them
and as they took ship in their shining gear,
he said how welcome they would be in Geatland.
Then the broad hull was beached on the sand
to be cargoed with treasure, horses and war-gear.
The curved prow motioned; the mast stood high

*The Geats march
back to the shore*

ofer Hrōðgāres   hord-gestrēonum.

1900 Hē þǣm bāt-wearde   bunden golde
swurd gesealde,   þæt hē syðþan wæs
on meodu-bence   māþme þȳ weorþra,
yrfe-lāfe. Gewāt him on naca,
drēfan dēop wæter,   Dena land ofgeaf.
Þā wæs be mæste   mere-hrægla sum,
segl sāle fæst;   sund-wudu þunede;
nō þǣr wēg-flotan   wind ofer ȳðum
sīðes getwǣfde. Sǣ-genga fōr,
flēat fāmig-heals   forð ofer ȳðe,
1910 bunden-stefna   ofer brim-strēamas,
þæt hīe Gēata clifu   ongitan meahton,
cūþe næssas;   cēol up geþrang
lyft-geswenced,   on lande stōd.

    Hraþe wæs æt holme   bȳð-weard geara,
sē þe ǣr lange tīd   lēofra manna
fūs æt faroðe   feor wlātode.
Sǣlde tō sande   sīd-fæþme scip
oncer-bendum fæst,   þȳ lǣs hym ȳþa ðrym
wudu wynsuman   forwrecan meahte.
1920 Hēt þā up beran   æþelinga gestrēon,
frætwe ond fǣt-gold;   næs him feor þanon
tō gesēcanne   sinces bryttan,
Higelāc Hrēþling,   þǣr æt hām wunað
selfa mid gesīðum   sǣ-wealle nēah.

    Bold wæs betlīc,   brego-rōf cyning,
hēah on healle,   Hygd swīðe geong,

above Hrothgar's riches in the loaded hold.

1900   The guard who had watched the boat was given
a sword with gold fittings and in future days
that present would make him a respected man
at his place on the mead-bench.
                            Then the keel plunged
and shook in the sea; and they sailed from Denmark.

Right away the mast was rigged with its sea-shawl; *They sail from*
sail-ropes were tightened, timbers drummed *Denmark*
and stiff winds kept the wave-crosser
skimming ahead; as she heaved forward,
her foamy neck was fleet and buoyant,
1910   a lapped prow loping over currents,
until finally the Geats caught sight of coastline
and familiar cliffs. The keel reared up,
wind lifted it home, it hit on the land.

The harbour guard came hurrying out *They arrive at*
to the rolling water: he had watched the offing *Hygelac's stronghold*
long and hard, on the lookout for those friends.
With the anchor cables, he moored their craft
right where it had beached, in case a backwash
might catch the hull and carry it away.
1920   Then he ordered the prince's treasure-trove
to be carried ashore. It was a short step
from there to where Hrethel's son and heir,
Hygelac the gold-giver, makes his home
on a secure cliff, in the company of retainers.

The building was magnificent, the king majestic,
ensconced in his hall; and although Hygd, his queen,

wīs, wēl-þungen, þēah ðe wintra lȳt
under burh-locan gebiden hæbbe,
Hæreþes dohtor; næs hīo hnāh swā þēah,
nē tō gnēað gifa Gēata lēodum
māþm-gestrēona; Mōdþrȳðo wæg
fremu folces cwēn, firen' ondrysne.
Nænig þæt dorste dēor genēþan
swæsra gesīða, nefne sin-frēa,
þæt hire an dæges ēagum starede;
ac him wæl-bende weotode tealde,
hand-gewriþene; hraþe seoþðan wæs
æfter mund-gripe mēce geþinged,
þæt hit sceāden-mæl scȳran mōste,
cwealm-bealu cȳðan. Ne bið swylc cwēnlīc þēaw
idese tō efnanne, þēah ðe hīo ænlicu sȳ,
þætte freoðu-webbe fēores onsæce
æfter lige-torne lēofne mannan.
Hūru þæt onhōhsnode Hemminges mæg.
Ealo-drincende ōðer sædan,
þæt hīo lēod-bealewa læs gefremede,
inwit-nīða, syððan ærest wearð
gyfen gold-hroden geongum cempan,
æðelum dīore, syððan hīo Offan flet
ofer fealone flōd be fæder lāre
sīðe gesōhte. Ðǣr hīo syððan well
in gum-stōle, gōde mǣre,
līf-gesceafta lifigende brēac,
hīold hēah-lufan wið hæleþa brego,
ealles mon-cynnes mīne gefrǣge
þone sēlestan bī sǣm twēonum,
eormen-cynnes. Forðām Offa wæs
geofum ond gūðum, gār-cēne man

was young, a few short years at court,
her mind was thoughtful and her manners sure.
Haereth's daughter behaved generously

1930
and stinted nothing when she distributed
bounty to the Geats.
                    Great Queen Modthryth
perpetrated terrible wrongs.
If any retainer ever made bold
to look her in the face, if an eye not her lord's
stared at her directly during daylight,
the outcome was sealed: he was kept bound
in hand-tightened shackles, racked, tortured
until doom was pronounced—death by the sword,
slash of blade, blood-gush and death qualms

1940
in an evil display. Even a queen
outstanding in beauty must not overstep like that.
A queen should weave peace, not punish the innocent
with loss of life for imagined insults.
But Hemming's kinsman put a halt to her ways
and drinkers round the table had another tale:
she was less of a bane to people's lives,
less cruel-minded, after she was married
to the brave Offa, a bride arrayed
in her gold finery, given away

1950
by a caring father, ferried to her young prince
over dim seas. In days to come
she would grace the throne and grow famous
for her good deeds and conduct of life,
her high devotion to the hero king
who was the best king, it has been said,
between the two seas or anywhere else
on the face of the earth. Offa was honoured
far and wide for his generous ways,

Queen Hygd introduced. The story of Queen Modthryth, Hygd's opposite, is told by the poet

wīde geweorðod;   wīsdōme hēold
ēðel sīnne. Þonon Ēomēr wōc
hæleðum tō helpe,   Hemminges mæg,
nefa Gārmundes,   nīða cræftig.

   Gewāt him ðā se hearda   mid his hond-scole
sylf æfter sande   sǣ-wong tredan,
wīde waroðas;   woruld-candel scān,
sigel sūðan fūs.   Hī sīð drugon,
elne geēodon,   tō ðæs ðe eorla hlēo,
bonan Ongenþēoes   burgum in innan,
geongne gūð-cyning   gōdne gefrūnon
hringas dǣlan.   Higelāce wæs
sīð Bēowulfes   snūde gecȳðed,
þæt ðǣr on worðig   wīgendra hlēo,
lind-gestealla   lifigende cwōm,
heaðo-lāces hāl   tō hofe gongan.
Hraðe wæs gerȳmed,   swā se rīca bebēad,
fēðe-gestum   flet innanweard.

   Gesæt þā wið sylfne,   sē ðā sæcce genæs,
mæg wið mæge,   syððan man-dryhten
þurh hlēoðor-cwyde   holdne gegrētte
mēaglum wordum.   Meodu-scencum
hwearf geond þæt heal-reced   Hæreðes dohtor,
lufode ðā lēode,   līð-wǣge bær
Hǣðnum tō handa.   Higelāc ongan
sīnne geseldan   in sele þām hēan
fægre fricgcean;   hyne fyrwet bræc,
hwylce Sǣ-Gēata   sīðas wǣron:
   "Hū lomp ēow on lāde,   lēofa Bīowulf,
þā ðū fǣringa   feorr gehogodest

his fighting spirit and his far-seeing

1960   defence of his homeland; from him there sprang Eomer,
Garmund's grandson, kinsman of Hemming,
his warriors' mainstay and master of the field.

Heroic Beowulf and his band of men
crossed the wide strand, striding along
the sandy foreshore; the sun shone,
the world's candle warmed them from the south
as they hastened to where, as they had heard,
the young king, Ongentheow's killer
and his people's protector, was dispensing rings

1970   inside his bawn. Beowulf's return
was reported to Hygelac as soon as possible,
news that the captain was now in the enclosure,
his battle-brother back from the fray
alive and well, walking to the hall.
Room was quickly made, on the king's orders,
and the troops filed across the cleared floor.

After Hygelac had offered greetings
to his loyal thane in lofty speech,
he and his kinsman, that hale survivor,

1980   sat face to face. Haereth's daughter
moved about with the mead-jug in her hand,
taking care of the company, filling the cups
that warriors held out. Then Hygelac began
to put courteous questions to his old comrade
in the high hall. He hankered to know
every tale the Sea-Geats had to tell.

"How did you fare on your foreign voyage,
dear Beowulf, when you abruptly decided

*Beowulf and his
troop are welcomed
in Hygelac's hall*

*Hygelac questions
Beowulf*

sæcce sēcean   ofer sealt wæter,
hilde tō Hiorote?   Ac ðū Hrōðgāre
wīd-cūðne wēan   wihte gebēttest,
mǣrum ðēodne?   Ic ðæs mōd-ceare
sorh-wylmum sēað,   sīðe ne truwode
lēofes mannes.   Ic ðē lange bæd,
þæt ðū þone wæl-gǣst   wihte ne grētte,
lēte Sūð-Dene   sylfe geweorðan
gūðe wið Grendel.   Gode ic þanc secge,
þæs ðe ic ðē gesundne   gesēon mōste."
    Bīowulf maðelode,   bearn Ecgðīoes:
"Þæt is undyrne,   dryhten Higelāc,
mǣru gemēting   monegum fīra,
hwylc orleg-hwīl   uncer Grendles
wearð on ðām wange,   þǣr hē worna fela
Sige-Scyldingum   sorge gefremede,
yrmðe tō aldre;   ic ðæt eall gewræc,
swā begylpan ne þearf   Grendeles māga
ǣnig ofer eorðan   ūht-hlem þone,
sē ðe lengest leofað   lāðan cynnes,
fācne bifongen.   Ic ðǣr furðum cwōm
tō ðām hring-sele   Hrōðgār grētan;
sōna mē se mǣra   mago Healfdenes,
syððan hē mōd-sefan   mīnne cūðe,
wið his sylfes sunu   setl getǣhte.
Weorod wæs on wynne: ne seah ic wīdan feorh
under heofones hwealf   heal-sittendra
medu-drēam māran.   Hwīlum mǣru cwēn,
friðu-sibb folca,   flet eall geondhwearf,
bǣdde byre geonge;   oft hīo bēah-wriðan
secge sealde,   ǣr hīe tō setle gēong;

1990

2000

2010

to sail away across the salt water

1990 and fight at Heorot? Did you help Hrothgar
much in the end? Could you ease the prince
of his well-known troubles? Your undertaking
cast my spirits down, I dreaded the outcome
of your expedition and pleaded with you
long and hard to leave the killer be,
let the South-Danes settle their own
blood-feud with Grendel. So God be thanked
I am granted this sight of you, safe and sound."

Beowulf, son of Ecgtheow, spoke:

2000 "What happened, Lord Hygelac, is hardly a secret
any more among men in this world—
myself and Grendel coming to grips
on the very spot where he visited destruction
on the Victory-Shieldings and violated
life and limb, losses I avenged
so no earthly offspring of Grendel's
need ever boast of that bout before dawn,
no matter how long the last of his evil
family survives.

          When I first landed

2010 I hastened to the ring-hall and saluted Hrothgar.
Once he discovered why I had come
the son of Halfdane sent me immediately
to sit with his own sons on the bench.
It was a happy gathering. In my whole life
I have never seen mead enjoyed more
in any hall on earth. Sometimes the queen
herself appeared, peace-pledge between nations,
to hearten the young ones and hand out
a torque to a warrior, then take her place.

Beowulf tells what
happened in the land
of the Danes

hwīlum for duguðe   dohtor Hrōðgāres
eorlum on ende   ealu-wǣge bær,
þā ic Frēaware   flet-sittende
nemnan hȳrde,   þǣr hīo nægled-sinc
hæleðum sealde.   Sīo gehāten is
geong, gold-hroden,   gladum suna Frōdan;
hafað þæs geworden   wine Scyldinga,
rīces hyrde,   ond þæt rǣd talað
þæt hē mid ðȳ wīfe   wæl-fǣhða dǣl,
sæcca gesette.   Oft seldan hwǣr

æfter lēod-hryre   lȳtle hwīle
bon-gār būgeð,   þēah sēo brȳd duge!
   "Mæg þæs þonne ofþyncan   ðēodne Heaðobeardna
ond þegna gehwām   þāra lēoda,
þonne hē mid fǣmnan   on flett gǣð
dryht-bearn Dena,   duguða biwenede.
On him gladiað   gomelra lāfe,
heard ond hring-mǣl   Heaðabeardna gestrēon,
þenden hīe ðam wǣpnum   wealdan mōston,
oððæt hīe forlǣddan   tō ðām lind-plegan

swǣse gesīðas   ond hyra sylfra feorh.
Þonne cwið æt bēore,   sē þe bēah gesyhð,
eald æsc-wiga,   sē ðe eall geman
gār-cwealm gumena   —him bið grim sefa—
onginneð geōmor-mōd   geongum cempan
þurh hreðra gehygd,   higes cunnian,
wīg-bealu weccean,   ond þæt word ācwyð:
   " 'Meaht ðū, mīn wine,   mēce gecnāwan,
þone þīn fæder   tō gefeohte bær
under here-grīman   hindeman sīðe,

dȳre īren,   þǣr hyne Dene slōgon,

2020	Sometimes Hrothgar's daughter distributed
	ale to older ranks, in order on the benches:
	I heard the company call her Freawaru
	as she made her rounds, presenting men
	with the gem-studded bowl, young bride-to-be
	to the gracious Ingeld, in her gold-trimmed attire.
	The friend of the Shieldings favours her betrothal:
	the guardian of the kingdom sees good in it
	and hopes this woman will heal old wounds
	and grievous feuds.
	But generally the spear
2030	is prompt to retaliate when a prince is killed,
	no matter how admirable the bride may be.

He foresees the grim consequence of a proposed marriage

"Think how the Heathobards will be bound to feel,
their lord, Ingeld, and his loyal thanes,
when he walks in with that woman to the feast:
Danes are at the table, being entertained,
honoured guests in glittering regalia,
burnished ring-mail that was their hosts' birthright,
looted when the Heathobards could no longer wield
their weapons in the shield-clash, when they went down

2040 with their beloved comrades and forfeited their lives.
Then an old spearman will speak while they are drinking,
having glimpsed some heirloom that brings alive
memories of the massacre; his mood will darken
and heart-stricken, in the stress of his emotion,
he will begin to test a young man's temper
and stir up trouble, starting like this:
'Now, my friend, don't you recognize
your father's sword, his favourite weapon,
the one he wore when he went out in his war-mask

2050 to face the Danes on that final day?

When the Danes appear at Freawaru's wedding, their hosts, the Heathobards, will be stirred to avenge an old defeat

wēoldon wæl-stōwe,   syððan Wiðergyld læg,
æfter hæleþa hryre,   hwate Scyldungas?
Nū hēr þāra banena   byre nāt-hwylces
frætwum hrēmig   on flet gǣð,
morðres gylpeð   ond þone māðþum byreð,
þone þe ðū mid rihte   rǣdan sceoldest!'
Manað swa ond myndgað   mǣla gehwylce
sārum wordum,   oððæt sǣl cymeð,
þæt se fǣmnan þegn   fore fæder dǣdum
æfter billes bite   blōd-fāg swefeð,
ealdres scyldig;   him se ōðer þonan
losað lifigende,   con him land geare.
Þonne bīoð ābrocene   on bā healfe
āð-sweorð eorla;   syððan Ingelde
weallað wæl-nīðas   ond him wīf-lufan
æfter cear-wælmum   cōlran weorðað.
Þȳ ic Heaðobeardna   hyldo ne telge,
dryht-sibbe dǣl   Denum unfǣcne,
frēondscipe fæstne.

                    Ic sceal forð sprecan,
gēn ymbe Grendel,   þæt ðū geare cunne,
sinces brytta,   tō hwan syððan wearð
hond-rǣs hæleða.   Syððan heofones gim
glād ofer grundas,   gǣst yrre cwōm,
eatol ǣfen-grom,   ūser nēosan,
ðǣr wē gesunde   sǣl weardodon.
Þǣr wæs Hondsciō   hild onsǣge,
feorh-bealu fǣgum;   hē fyrmest læg,
gyrded cempa;   him Grendel wearð,
mǣrum magu-þegne,   tō mūð-bonan,
lēofes mannes   līc eall forswealg.
Nō ðȳ ǣr ūt ðā gēn   īdel-hende

After Wethergeld died and his men were doomed
the Shieldings quickly claimed the field,
and now here's a son of one or other
of those same killers coming through our hall
overbearing us, mouthing boasts,
and rigged in armour that by right is yours.'
And so he keeps on, recalling and accusing,
working things up with bitter words
until one of the lady's retainers lies
spattered in blood, split open
on his father's account. The killer knows
the lie of the land and escapes with his life.
Then on both sides the oath-bound lords
will break the peace, a passionate hate
will build up in Ingeld and love for his bride
will falter in him as the feud rankles.
I therefore suspect the good faith of the Heathobards,
the truth of their friendship and the trustworthiness
of their alliance with the Danes.

But now, my lord,

I shall carry on with my account of Grendel,
the whole story of everything that happened
in the hand-to-hand fight.

After heaven's gem

had gone mildly to earth, that maddened spirit,
the terror of those twilights, came to attack us
where we stood guard, still safe inside the hall.
There deadly violence came down on Handscio
and he fell as fate ordained, the first to perish,
rigged out for the combat. A comrade from our ranks
had come to grief in Grendel's maw:
he ate up the entire body.
There was blood on his teeth, he was bloated and furious,

2060

2070

2080

*The tale of the fight
with Grendel
resumed*

bona blōdig-tōð   bealewa gemyndig,
of ðām gold-sele   gongan wolde,
ac hē mægnes rōf   mīn costode,
grāpode gearo-folm.   Glōf hangode
sīd ond syllīc,   searo-bendum fæst;
sīo wæs orðoncum   eall gegyrwed,
dēofles cræftum   ond dracan fellum.
Hē mec þǣr on innan   unsynnigne,
2090   dīor dǣd-fruma,   gedōn wolde
manigra sumne;   hyt ne mihte swā,
syððan ic on yrre   upp-riht āstōd.
Tō lang ys tō reccenne,   hū ic ðām lēod-sceaðan
yfla gehwylces   ondlēan forgeald,
þǣr ic, þēoden mīn,   þīne lēode
weorðode weorcum.   Hē on weg losade,
lȳtle hwīle   līf-wynna brēac;
hwæþre him sīo swīðre   swaðe weardade
hand on Hiorte,   ond hē hēan ðonan,
2100   mōdes geōmor   mere-grund gefēoll.
   "Mē þone wæl-rǣs   wine Scildunga
fǣttan golde   fela lēanode,
manegum māðmum,   syððan mergen cōm
ond wē tō symble   geseten hæfdon.
Þǣr wæs gidd ond glēo;   gomela Scilding,
fela fricgende,   feorran rehte;
hwīlum hilde-dēor   hearpan wynne,
gomen-wudu grētte,   hwīlum gyd āwræc
sōð ond sārlīc,   hwīlum syllīc spell
2110   rehte æfter rihte   rūm-heort cyning;
hwīlum eft ongan   eldo gebunden
gomel gūð-wiga   gioguðe cwīðan,

all roused up, yet still unready
to leave the hall empty-handed;
renowned for his might, he matched himself against me,
wildly reaching. He had this roomy pouch,
a strange accoutrement, intricately strung
and hung at the ready, a rare patchwork
of devilishly fitted dragon-skins.
I had done him no wrong, yet the raging demon
wanted to cram me and many another
into this bag—but it was not to be
once I got to my feet in a blind fury.
It would take too long to tell how I repaid
the terror of the land for every life he took
and so won credit for you, my king,
and for all your people. And although he got away
to enjoy life's sweetness for a while longer,
his right hand stayed behind him in Heorot,
evidence of his miserable overthrow
as he dived into murk on the mere bottom.

"I got lavish rewards from the lord of the Danes
for my part in the battle, beaten gold
and much else, once morning came
and we took our places at the banquet table.
There was singing and excitement: an old reciter,
a carrier of stories, recalled the early days.
At times some hero made the timbered harp
tremble with sweetness, or related true
and tragic happenings; at times the king
gave the proper turn to some fantastic tale,
or a battle-scarred veteran, bowed with age,
would begin to remember the martial deeds

Beowulf recalls the
feast in Heorot

hilde-strengo;   hreðer inne wēoll,
þonne hē wintrum frōd   worn gemunde.
   "Swā wē þǣr inne   andlangne dæg
nīode nāman,   oððæt niht becwōm
ōðer tō yldum.   Þā wæs eft hraðe
gearo gyrn-wræce   Grendeles mōdor,
sīðode sorh-full;   sunu dēað fornam,
wīg-hete Wedra.   Wīf unhȳre
hyre bearn gewræc,   beorn ācwealde
ellenlīce;   þǣr wæs Æschere,
frōdan fyrn-witan,   feorh ūðgenge.
Nōðer hȳ hine ne mōston,   syððan mergen cwōm,
dēað-wērigne,   Denia lēode
bronde forbærnan,   nē on bǣl hladan
lēofne mannan;   hīo þæt līc ætbær
fēondes fæðmum   under firgen-strēam.
Þæt wæs Hrōðgāre   hrēowa tornost,
þāra þe lēod-fruman   lange begēate.
Þā se ðēoden mec   ðīne līfe
healsode hrēoh-mōd,   þæt ic on holma geþring
eorlscipe efnde,   ealdre genēðde,
mǣrðo fremede;   hē mē mēde gehēt.
Ic ðā ðæs wælmes,   þē is wīde cūð,
grimne gryrelīcne   grund-hyrde fond.
Þǣr unc hwīle wæs   hand gemǣne;
holm heolfre wēoll,   ond ic hēafde becearf
in ðām gūð-sele   Grendeles mōdor
ēacnum ecgum.   Unsōfte þonan
feorh oðferede;   næs ic fǣge þā gȳt;
ac mē eorla hlēo   eft gesealde
māðma menigeo,   maga Healfdenes.

of his youth and prime and be overcome
as the past welled up in his wintry heart.

"We were happy there the whole day long
and enjoyed our time until another night
descended upon us. Then suddenly

*He tells about
Grendel's mother*

the vehement mother avenged her son
and wreaked destruction. Death had robbed her,

2120   Geats had slain Grendel, so his ghastly dam
struck back and with bare-faced defiance
laid a man low. Thus life departed
from the sage Aeschere, an elder wise in counsel.
But afterwards, on the morning following,
the Danes could not burn the dead body
nor lay the remains of the man they loved
on his funeral pyre. She had fled with the corpse
and taken refuge beneath torrents on the mountain.
It was a hard blow for Hrothgar to bear,

2130   harder than any he had undergone before.
And so the heartsore king beseeched me
in your royal name to take my chances
underwater, to win glory
and prove my worth. He promised me rewards.
Hence, as is well known, I went to my encounter
with the terror-monger at the bottom of the tarn.
For a while it was hand-to-hand between us,
then blood went curling along the currents
and I beheaded Grendel's mother in the hall

2140   with a mighty sword. I barely managed
to escape with my life; my time had not yet come.
But Halfdane's heir, the shelter of those earls,
again endowed me with gifts in abundance.

"Swā se ðēod-kyning   þēawum lyfde;
nealles ic ðām lēanum   forloren hæfde,
mægnes mēde,   ac hē mē māðmas geaf,
sunu Healfdenes,   on mīnne sylfes dōm;
ðā ic ðē, beorn-cyning,   bringan wylle,
ēstum geȳwan.   Gēn is eall æt ðē
2150   lissa gelong;   ic lȳt hafo
hēafod-māga,   nefne Hygelāc ðec!"
    Hēt ðā in beran   eafor, hēafod-segn,
heaðo-stēapne helm,   hāre byrnan,
gūð-sweord geatolīc,   gyd æfter wræc:
    "Mē ðis hilde-sceorp   Hrōðgār sealde,
snotra fengel;   sume worde hēt,
þæt ic his ǣrest ðē   ēst gesægde:
cwæð þæt hyt hæfde   Hiorogār cyning,
lēod Scyldunga,   lange hwīle.
2160   Nō ðȳ ǣr suna sīnum   syllan wolde,
hwatum Heorowearde,   þēah hē him hold wǣre,
brēost-gewǣdu.   Brūc ealles well!"
    Hȳrde ic, þæt þām frætwum   fēower mēaras,
lungre, gelīce   lāst weardode,
æppel-fealuwe;   hē him ēst getēah
mēara ond māðma.   Swā sceal mǣg dōn,
nealles inwit-net   ōðrum bregdon
dyrnum cræfte,   dēað rēnian
hond-gesteallan.   Hygelāce wæs,
2170   nīða heardum,   nefa swȳðe hold
ond gehwæðer ōðrum   hrōþra gemyndig.
    Hȳrde ic þæt hē ðone heals-bēah   Hygde gesealde,

"Thus the king acted with due custom.
I was paid and recompensed completely,
given full measure and the freedom to choose
from Hrothgar's treasures by Hrothgar himself.
These, King Hygelac, I am happy to present
to you as gifts. It is still upon your grace
that all favour depends. I have few kinsmen
who are close, my king, except for your kind self."
Then he ordered the boar-framed standard to be brought,
the battle-topping helmet, the mail-shirt grey as hoar-frost
and the precious war-sword; and proceeded with his
    speech.

*Beowulf presents
Hygelac with the
treasures he has won*

"When Hrothgar presented this war-gear to me
he instructed me, my lord, to give you some account
of why it signifies his special favour.
He said it had belonged to his older brother,
King Heorogar, who had long kept it,
but that Heorogar had never bequeathed it
to his son Heoroweard, that worthy scion,
loyal as he was.
                        Enjoy it well."

I heard four horses were handed over next.
Beowulf bestowed four bay steeds
to go with the armour, swift gallopers,
all alike. So ought a kinsman act,
instead of plotting and planning in secret
to bring people to grief, or conspiring to arrange
the death of comrades. The warrior king
was uncle to Beowulf and honoured by his nephew:
each was concerned for the other's good.

I heard he presented Hygd with a gorget,

2150

2160

2170

wrǣtlīcne wundur-māððum,   ðone þe him Wealhðēo
   geaf,
ðēodnes dohtor,   þrīo wicg somod
swancor ond sadol-beorht;   hyre syððan wæs
æfter bēah-ðege   breost geweorðod.

   Swā bealdode   bearn Ecgðēowes,
guma gūðum cūð,   gōdum dædum,
drēah æfter dōme,   nealles druncne slōg
heorð-genēatas;   næs him hrēoh sefa,
ac hē man-cynnes   mæste cræfte,
gin-fæstan gife,   þe him God sealde,
hēold hilde-dēor.   Hēan wæs lange,
swā hyne Gēata bearn   gōdne ne tealdon,
nē hyne on medo-bence   micles wyrðne
drihten Wedera   gedōn wolde;
swȳðe wēndon,   þæt hē slēac wǣre,
æðeling unfrom.   Edwenden cwōm
tīr-ēadigum menn   torna gehwylces.

   Hēt ðā eorla hlēo   in gefetian,
heaðo-rōf cyning,   Hrēðles lāfe,
golde gegyrede;   næs mid Gēatum ðā
sinc-māðþum sēlra   on sweordes hād;
þæt hē on Bīowulfes   bearm ālegde,
ond him gesealde   seofan þūsendo,
bold ond brego-stōl.   Him wæs bām samod
on ðām lēodscipe   lond gecynde,
eard, ēðel-riht,   ōðrum swīðor,
sīde rīce,   þām ðǣr sēlra wæs.

   Eft þæt geīode   ufaran dōgrum
hilde-hlæmmum,   syððan Hygelāc læg
ond Heardrēde   hilde-mēceas

the priceless torque that the prince's daughter,
Wealhtheow, had given him; and three horses,
supple creatures, brilliantly saddled.
The bright necklace would be luminous on Hygd's breast.

Thus Beowulf bore himself with valour;
he was formidable in battle yet behaved with honour

Beowulf's exemplary
life is extolled

and took no advantage; never cut down
2180 a comrade who was drunk, kept his temper
and, warrior that he was, watched and controlled
his God-sent strength and his outstanding
natural powers. He had been poorly regarded
for a long time, was taken by the Geats
for less than he was worth: and their lord too
had never much esteemed him in the mead-hall.
They firmly believed that he lacked force,
that the prince was a weakling; but presently
every affront to his deserving was reversed.

2190 The battle-famed king, bulwark of his earls,
ordered a gold-chased heirloom of Hrethel's

Hygelac presents
Beowulf with a
sword and great
tracts of land

to be brought in; it was the best example
of a gem-studded sword in the Geat treasury.
This he laid on Beowulf's lap
and then rewarded him with land as well,
seven thousand hides, and a hall and a throne.
Both owned land by birth in that country,
ancestral grounds; but the greater right
and sway were inherited by the higher born.

2200 A lot was to happen in later days
in the fury of battle. Hygelac fell

Time passes.
Beowulf rules the
Geats for fifty years

and the shelter of Heardred's shield proved useless

under bord-hrēoðan   tō bonan wurdon,
ðā hyne gesōhtan   on sige-þēode
hearde hild-frecan,   Heaðo-Scilfingas,
nīða genǣgdan   nefan Hererīces:
syððan Bēowulfe   brāde rīce
on hand gehwearf.   Hē gehēold tela
fīftig wintra—   wæs ðā frōd cyning,
eald ēþel-weard—   oððæt ān ongan
deorcum nihtum,   draca rīcsian
sē ðe on hēaum hofe   hord beweotode,
stān-beorh stēapne;   stīg under læg
eldum uncūð;   þǣr on innan gīong
niða nāt-hwylc . . . . . . gefēng
hǣðnum horde   hond . . . .
since fāhne   hē þæt syððan . . . . . .
þēah ðe hē slǣpende   besyred wurde
þēofes cræfte;   þæt sīe ðīod onfand,
bū-folc beorna,   þæt hē gebolgen wæs.

Nealles mid gewealdum   wyrm-hord ābræc,
sylfes willum,   sē ðe him sāre gesceōd,
ac for þrēa-nēdlan   þēow nāt-hwylces
hæleða bearna   hete-swengeas flēoh,
ærnes þearfa,   ond ðǣr inne fealh,
secg syn-bysig.   Sōna onfunde,
þæt . . . . . ðām gyste   gryre-brōga stōd;
hwæðre earm-sceapen . . . .
. . . . sceapen
. . . . . .   þā hyne se fǣr begeat,
sinc-fæt . . . . .   þǣr wæs swylcra fela
in ðām eorð-hūse   ǣr-gestrēona,

2210

2220

2230

against the fierce aggression of the Shylfings:
ruthless swordsmen, seasoned campaigners,
they came against him and his conquering nation,
and with cruel force cut him down
so that afterwards
                the wide kingdom
reverted to Beowulf. He ruled it well
for fifty winters, grew old and wise
2210   as warden of the land
                   until one began
to dominate the dark, a dragon on the prowl
from the steep vaults of a stone-roofed barrow
where he guarded a hoard; there was a hidden passage,
unknown to men, but someone managed
to enter by it and interfere
with the heathen trove. He had handled and removed
a gem-studded goblet; it gained him nothing,
though with a thief's wiles he had outwitted
the sleeping dragon; that drove him into rage,
2220   as the people of that country would soon discover.

The intruder who broached the dragon's treasure
and moved him to wrath had never meant to.
It was desperation on the part of a slave
fleeing the heavy hand of some master,
guilt-ridden and on the run,
going to ground. But he soon began
to shake with terror; . . . . . . in shock
the wretch . . . .
. . . . panicked and ran
2230   away with the precious . . . .
metalwork. There were many other
heirlooms heaped inside the earth-house,

A dragon awakes.
An accidental theft
provokes his wrath

swā hȳ on geār-dagum   gumena nāt-hwylc,
eormen-lāfe   æþelan cynnes,
þanc-hycgende   þǣr gehȳdde,
dēore māðmas.   Ealle hīe dēað fornam
ǣrran mǣlum,   ond se ān ðā gēn
lēoda duguðe,   sē ðǣr lengest hwearf,
weard wine-geōmor,   wēnde þæs ylcan
þæt hē lȳtel fæc   long-gestrēona
brūcan mōste.   Beorh eall-gearo
wunode on wonge   wæter-ȳðum nēah,
nīwe be næsse,   nearo-cræftum fæst.
Þǣr on innan bær   eorl-gestrēona
hringa hyrde   hord-wyrðne dǣl,
fǣttan goldes,   fēa worda cwæð:
   "Heald þū nū, hrūse,   nū hæleð ne mōstan,
eorla ǣhte!   Hwæt hyt ǣr on ðē
gōde begēaton.   Gūð-dēað fornam,
feorh-bealo frēcne,   fȳra gehwylcne
lēoda mīnra,   þāra ðe þis līf ofgeaf,
gesāwon sele-drēam;   nāh, hwā sweord wege
oððe feormie   fǣted wǣge,
drync-fæt dēore;   duguð ellor scōc.
Sceal se hearda helm,   hyrsted golde
fǣtum befeallen;   feormynd swefað,
þā ðe beado-grīman   bȳwan sceoldon;
gē swylce sēo here-pād,   sīo æt hilde gebād
ofer borda gebræc   bite īrena,
brosnað æfter beorne;   ne mæg byrnan hring
æfter wīg-fruman   wīde fēran
hæleðum be healfe.   Næs hearpan wyn,
gomen glēo-bēames,   nē gōd hafoc
geond sæl swingeð,   nē se swifta mearh

because long ago, with deliberate care,
somebody now forgotten
had buried the riches of a high-born race
in this ancient cache. Death had come
and taken them all in times gone by
and the only one left to tell their tale,
the last of their line, could look forward to nothing
2240   but the same fate for himself: he foresaw that his joy
in the treasure would be brief.
                                A newly constructed
barrow stood waiting, on a wide headland
close to the waves, its entryway secured.
Into it the keeper of the hoard had carried
all the goods and golden ware
worth preserving. His words were few:
"Now, earth, hold what earls once held
and heroes can no more; it was mined from you first
by honourable men. My own people
2250   have been ruined in war; one by one
they went down to death, looked their last
on sweet life in the hall. I am left with nobody
to bear a sword or burnish plated goblets,
put a sheen on the cup. The companies have departed.
The hard helmet, hasped with gold,
will be stripped of its hoops; and the helmet-shiner
who should polish the metal of the war-mask sleeps;
the coat of mail that came through all fights,
through shield-collapse and cut of sword,
2260   decays with the warrior. Nor may webbed mail
range far and wide on the warlord's back
beside his mustered troops. No trembling harp,
no tuned timber, no tumbling hawk
swerving through the hall, no swift horse

Long ago, a hoard
was hidden in the
earth-house by the
last survivor of a
forgotten race

burh-stede bēateð.   Bealo-cwealm hafað
fela feorh-cynna   forð onsended!"
　　Swā giōmor-mōd   giohðo mǣnde,
ān æfter eallum,   unblīðe hwearf,
dæges ond nihtes,   oððæt dēaðes wylm
hrān æt heortan.   Hord-wynne fond
eald ūht-sceaða   opene standan,
sē ðe byrnende   biorgas sēceð,
nacod nīð-draca,   nihtes flēogeð
fȳre befangen;   hyne fold-būend
swiðe ondrǣdað.   Hē gesēcean sceall
hord on hrūsan,   þǣr hē hǣðen gold
warað wintrum frōd;   ne byð him wihte ðȳ sēl.
　　Swā se ðēod-sceaða   þrēo hund wintra
hēold on hrūsan   hord-ærna sum
ēacen-cræftig,   oððæt hyne ān ābealch
mon on mōde;   man-dryhtne bær
fǣted wǣge,   frioðo-wǣre bæd
hlāford sīnne.   Ðā wæs hord rāsod,
onboren bēaga hord,   bēne getīðad
fēasceaftum men.   Frēa scēawode
fīra fyrn-geweorc   forman sīðe.
　　Þā se wyrm onwōc,   wrōht wæs genīwad;
stonc ðā æfter stāne,   stearc-heort onfand
fēondes fōt-lāst;   hē tō forð gestōp
dyrnan cræfte,   dracan hēafde nēah.
Swā mæg unfǣge   ēaðe gedīgan
wēan ond wræc-sīð,   sē ðe Waldendes
hyldo gehealdeþ.   Hord-weard sōhte
georne æfter grunde,   wolde guman findan,

pawing the courtyard. Pillage and slaughter
have emptied the earth of entire peoples."
And so he mourned as he moved about the world,
deserted and alone, lamenting his unhappiness
day and night, until death's flood
2270 brimmed up in his heart.

Then an old harrower of the dark

The dragon nests in
the barrow and
guards the gold

happened to find the hoard open,
the burning one who hunts out barrows,
the slick-skinned dragon, threatening the night sky
with streamers of fire. People on the farms
are in dread of him. He is driven to hunt out
hoards under ground, to guard heathen gold
through age-long vigils, though to little avail.
For three centuries, this scourge of the people
had stood guard on that stoutly protected
2280 underground treasury, until the intruder
unleashed its fury; he hurried to his lord
with the gold-plated cup and made his plea
to be reinstated. Then the vault was rifled,
the ring-hoard robbed, and the wretched man
had his request granted. His master gazed
on that find from the past for the first time.

When the dragon awoke, trouble flared again.
He rippled down the rock, writhing with anger

The dragon in
turmoil

when he saw the footprints of the prowler who had stolen
2290 too close to his dreaming head.
So may a man not marked by fate
easily escape exile and woe
by the grace of God.

The hoard-guardian
scorched the ground as he scoured and hunted

þone þe him on sweofote   sāre getēode;
hāt ond hrēoh-mōd   hlǣw oft ymbe-hwearf,
ealne ūtanweardne;   nē ðǣr ǣnig mon
on þǣre wēstenne;   hwæðre wīges gefeh,
beaduwe weorces;   hwīlum on beorh æthwearf,
sinc-fæt sōhte;   hē þæt sōna onfand,
ðæt hæfde gumena sum   goldes gefandod,
hēah-gestrēona.   Hord-weard onbād
earfoðlīce,   oððæt ǣfen cwōm.
Wæs ðā gebolgen   beorges hyrde,
wolde se lāða   līge forgyldan
drinc-fæt dȳre.   Þā wæs dæg sceacen
wyrme on willan;   nō on wealle læng
bīdan wolde,   ac mid bǣle fōr,
fȳre gefȳsed.   Wæs se fruma egeslīc
lēodum on lande,   swā hyt lungre wearð
on hyra sinc-gifan   sāre geendod.

    Ðā se gæst ongan   glēdum spīwan,
beorht hofu bærnan;   bryne-lēoma stōd
eldum on andan;   nō ðǣr āht cwices
lāð lyft-floga   lǣfan wolde.
Wæs þæs wyrmes wīg   wīde gesȳne,
nearo-fāges nīð   nēan ond feorran,
hū se gūð-sceaða   Geata lēode
hatode ond hȳnde.   Hord eft gescēat
dryht-sele dyrnne   ǣr dæges hwīle.
Hæfde land-wara   līge befangen,
bǣle ond bronde;   beorges getruwode,
wīges ond wealles;   him sēo wēn gelēah.
    Þā wæs Bīowulfe   brōga gecȳðed
snūde tō sōðe,   þæt his sylfes hām,

for the trespasser who had troubled his sleep.
Hot and savage, he kept circling and circling
the outside of the mound. No man appeared
in that desert waste, but he worked himself up
by imagining battle; then back in he'd go
2300 in search of the cup, only to discover
signs that someone had stumbled upon
the golden treasures. So the guardian of the mound,
the hoard-watcher, waited for the gloaming
with fierce impatience; his pent-up fury
at the loss of the vessel made him long to hit back
and lash out in flames. Then, to his delight,
the day waned and he could wait no longer
behind the wall, but hurtled forth
in a fiery blaze. The first to suffer
2310 were the people on the land, but before long
it was their treasure-giver who would come to grief.

The dragon began to belch out flames
and burn bright homesteads; there was a hot glow
that scared everyone, for the vile sky-winger
would leave nothing alive in his wake.
Everywhere the havoc he wrought was in evidence.
Far and near, the Geat nation
bore the brunt of his brutal assaults
and virulent hate. Then back to the hoard
2320 he would dart before daybreak, to hide in his den.
He had swinged the land, swathed it in flame,
in fire and burning, and now he felt secure
in the vaults of his barrow; but his trust was unavailing.

Then Beowulf was given bad news,
a hard truth: his own home,

*The dragon wreaks
havoc on the Geats*

*Beowulf's ominous
feelings about the
dragon*

bolda sēlest,   bryne-wylmum mealt,
gif-stōl Gēata.   Þæt ðām gōdan wæs
hrēow on hreðre,   hyge-sorga mǣst.
Wēnde se wīsa,   þæt hē Wealdende
ofer ealde riht,   ēcean Dryhtne,
bitre gebulge;   brēost innan wēoll
þēostrum geþoncum,   swā him geþȳwe ne wæs.
    Hæfde līg-draca   lēoda fæsten,
ēa-lond ūtan,   eorð-weard ðone
glēdum forgrunden;   him ðæs gūð-kyning,
Wedera þīoden,   wræce leornode.
Heht him þā gewyrcean   wīgendra hlēo
eall-īrenne,   eorla dryhten,
wīg-bord wrǣtlīc;   wisse hē gearwe,
þæt him holt-wudu   helþan ne meahte,
lind wið līge.   Sceolde lǣn-daga
æþeling ǣr-gōd   ende gebīdan,
worulde līfes,   ond se wyrm somod,
þēah ðe hord-welan   hēolde lange.
    Oferhogode ðā   hringa fengel,
þæt hē þone wīd-flogan   weorode gesōhte,
sīdan herge;   nō hē him þā sæcce ondrēd,
nē him þæs wyrmes wīg   for wiht dyde,
eafoð ond ellen,   forðon hē ǣr fela
nearo nēðende   nīða gedīgde,
hilde-hlemma,   syððan hē Hrōðgāres,
sigor-ēadig secg,   sele fǣlsode
ond æt gūðe forgrāp   Grendeles mǣgum
lāðan cynnes.
            Nō þæt lǣsest wæs
hond-gemōta,   þǣr mon Hygelāc slōh,
syððan Gēata cyning   gūðe rǣsum,

the best of buildings, had been burnt to a cinder,
the throne-room of the Geats. It threw the hero
into deep anguish and darkened his mood:
the wise man thought he must have thwarted
ancient ordinance of the eternal Lord,
broken His commandment. His mind was in turmoil,
unaccustomed anxiety and gloom
confused his brain; the fire-dragon
had rased the coastal region and reduced
forts and earthworks to dust and ashes,
so the war-king planned and plotted his revenge.
The warriors' protector, prince of the hall-troop,
ordered a marvellous all-iron shield
from his smithy works. He well knew
that linden boards would let him down
and timber burn. After many trials,
he was destined to face the end of his days
in this mortal world; as was the dragon,
for all his long leasehold on the treasure.

Yet the prince of the rings was too proud
to line up with a large army
against the sky-plague. He had scant regard
for the dragon as a threat, no dread at all
of its courage or strength, for he had kept going
often in the past, through perils and ordeals
of every sort, after he had purged
Hrothgar's hall, triumphed in Heorot
and beaten Grendel. He outgrappled the monster
and his evil kin.
        One of his cruellest
hand-to-hand encounters had happened
when Hygelac, king of the Geats, was killed

*Beowulf's pride and
prowess sustain him*

frēa-wine folca   Frēs-londum on,
Hrēðles eafora   hiora-dryncum swealt,
bille gebēaten.   Þonan Bīowulf cōm
sylfes cræfte,   sund-nytte drēah;
hæfde him on earme   āna þrītig
hilde-geatwa,   þā hē tō holme stāg.
Nealles Hetware   hrēmge þorfton
fēðe-wīges,   þē him foran ongēan
linde bǣron;   lȳt eft becwōm
fram þām hild-frecan   hāmes nīosan.
Oferswam ðā sioleða bigong   sunu Ecgðēowes,
earm ān-haga   eft tō lēodum;
þǣr him Hygd gebēad   hord ond rīce,
bēagas ond brego-stōl;   bearne ne truwode,
þæt hē wið æl-fylcum   ēþel-stōlas
healdan cūðe,   ðā wæs Hygelāc dēad.
Nō ðȳ ǣr fēasceafte   findan meahton
æt ðām æðelinge   ǣnige ðinga,
þæt hē Heardrēde   hlāford wǣre,
oððe þone cynedōm   cīosan wolde.
Hwæðre hē hine on folce   frēond-lārum hēold,
ēstum mid āre,   oððæt hē yldra wearð,
Weder-Gēatum wēold.   Hyne wrǣc-mæcgas
ofer sǣ sōhtan,   suna Ōhteres;
hæfdon hȳ forhealden   helm Scylfinga,
þone sēlestan   sǣ-cyninga,
þāra ðe in Swīo-rīce   sinc brytnade,
mǣrne þēoden.   Him þæt tō mearce wearð;
hē þǣr for feorme   feorh-wunde hlēat,
sweordes swengum,   sunu Hygelāces;
ond him eft gewāt   Ongenðīoes bearn

in Friesland: the people's friend and lord,
Hrethel's son, slaked a sword blade's
thirst for blood. But Beowulf's prodigious
2360   gifts as a swimmer guaranteed his safety:
he arrived at the shore, shouldering thirty
battle-dresses, the booty he had won.
There was little for the Hetware to be happy about
as they shielded their faces and fighting on the ground
began in earnest. With Beowulf against them,
few could hope to return home.

Across the wide sea, desolate and alone,
the son of Ecgtheow swam back to his people.
There Hygd offered him throne and authority
2370   as lord of the ring-hoard: with Hygelac dead,
she had no belief in her son's ability
to defend their homeland against foreign invaders.
Yet there was no way the weakened nation
could get Beowulf to give in and agree
to be elevated over Heardred as his lord
or to undertake the office of kingship.
But he did provide support for the prince,
honoured and minded him until he matured
as the ruler of Geatland.

                 Then over sea-roads
2380   exiles arrived, sons of Ohthere.
They had rebelled against the best of all
the sea-kings in Sweden, the one who held sway
in the Shylfing nation, their renowned prince,
lord of the mead-hall. That marked the end
for Hygelac's son: his hospitality
was mortally rewarded with wounds from a sword.
Heardred lay slaughtered and Onela returned

*A flashback:
Hygelac's death,
Beowulf's rearguard
action and escape
across the sea*

*Beowulf acts as
counsellor to
Hygelac's heir,
Heardred*

*Heardred is
implicated in
Swedish feuds and
slain*

hāmes nīosan,   syððan Heardrēd læg,
lēt ðone brego-stōl   Bīowulf healdan,
Gēatum wealdan;   þæt wæs gōd cyning.

Sē ðæs lēod-hryres   lēan gemunde
uferan dōgrum,   Ēadgilse wearð,
fēasceaftum frēond;   folce gestēpte
ofer sæ sīde   sunu Ōhteres,
wigum ond wæpnum;   hē gewræc syððan
cealdum cear-sīðum,   cyning ealdre binēat.

Swā hē nīða gehwane   genesen hæfde,
slīðra geslyhta,   sunu Ecgðīowes,
ellen-weorca,   oð ðone ānne dæg,
þē hē wið þām wyrme   gewegan sceolde.
Gewāt þā twelfa sum,   torne gebolgen,
dryhten Gēata   dracan scēawian.
Hæfde þā gefrūnen,   hwanan sīo fǣhð ārās,
bealo-nīð biorna;   him tō bearme cwōm
māðþum-fæt mǣre   þurh ðæs meldan hond.
Sē wæs on ðām ðrēate   þrēottēoða secg,
sē ðæs orleges   ōr onstealde,
hæft hyge-giōmor,   sceolde hēan ðonon
wong wīsian.   Hē ofer willan gīong,
tō ðæs ðe hē eorð-sele   ānne wisse,
hlǣw under hrūsan   holm-wylme nēh,
ȳð-gewinne,   sē wæs innan full
wrǣtta ond wīra.   Weard unhīore,
gearo gūð-freca   gold-māðmas hēold,
eald under eorðan;   næs þæt ȳðe cēap
tō gegangenne   gumena ǣnigum.

Gesæt ðā on næsse   nīð-heard cyning

to the land of Sweden, leaving Beowulf
to ascend the throne, to sit in majesty
2390   and rule over the Geats. He was a good king.

In days to come, he contrived to avenge
the fall of his prince; he befriended Eadgils
when Eadgils was friendless, aiding his cause
with weapons and warriors over the wide sea,
sending him men. The feud was settled
on a comfortless campaign when he killed Onela.

And so the son of Ecgtheow had survived
every extreme, excelling himself
in daring and in danger, until the day arrived
2400   when he had to come face to face with the dragon.
The lord of the Geats took eleven comrades
and went in a rage to reconnoitre.
By then he had discovered the cause of the affliction
being visited on the people. The precious cup
had come to him from the hand of the finder,
the one who had started all this strife
and was now added as a thirteenth to their number.
They press-ganged and compelled this poor creature
to be their guide. Against his will
2410   he led them to the earth-vault he alone knew,
an underground barrow near the sea-billows
and heaving waves, heaped inside
with exquisite metalwork. The one who stood guard
was dangerous and watchful, warden of that trove
buried under earth: no easy bargain
would be made in that place by any man.

The veteran king sat down on the cliff-top.

*Beowulf inherits the
kingship, settles the
feuding*

*The day of
reckoning: Beowulf
and his troop
reconnoitre*

þenden hǣlo ābēad   heorð-genēatum,
gold-wine Gēata.   Him wæs geōmor sefa,
wǣfre ond wæl-fūs,   wyrd ungemete nēah,
sē ðone gomelan   grētan sceolde,
sēcean sāwle hord,   sundur gedǣlan
līf wið līce;   nō þon lange wæs
feorh æþelinges   flǣsce bewunden.
    Bīowulf maþelade,   bearn Ecgðēowes:
"Fela ic on giogoðe   gūð-rǣsa genæs,
orleg-hwīla;   ic þæt eall gemon.
Ic wæs syfan-wintre,   þā mec sinca baldor,
frēa-wine folca   æt mīnum fæder genam.
Hēold mec ond hæfde   Hrēðel cyning,
geaf mē sinc ond symbel,   sibbe gemunde;
næs ic him tō līfe   lāðra ōwihte
beorn in burgum   þonne his bearna hwylc,
Herebeald ond Hæðcyn,   oððe Hygelāc mīn.
Wæs þām yldestan   ungedēfelīce
mǣges dǣdum   morþor-bed strēd,
syððan hyne Hæðcyn   of horn-bogan,
his frēa-wine   flāne geswencte,
miste mercelses   ond his mǣg ofscēt,
brōðor ōðerne,   blōdigan gāre.
Þæt wæs feoh-lēas gefeoht,   fyrenum gesyngad,
hreðre hyge-mēðe;   sceolde hwæðre swā þēah
æðeling unwrecen   ealdres linnan.
    "Swā bið geōmorlīc   gomelum ceorle
tō gebīdanne,   þæt his byre rīde
giong on galgan.   Þonne hē gyd wrece,
sārigne sang,   þonne his sunu hangað
hrefne tō hrōðre   ond hē him helpe ne mæg,
eald ond infrōd,   ǣnige gefremman.

He wished good luck to the Geats who had shared
his hearth and his gold. He was sad at heart,
unsettled yet ready, sensing his death.
His fate hovered near, unknowable but certain:
it would soon claim his coffered soul,
part life from limb. Before long
the prince's spirit would spin free from his body.

Beowulf, son of Ecgtheow, spoke:
"Many a skirmish I survived when I was young
and many times of war: I remember them well.
At seven, I was fostered out by my father,
left in the charge of my people's lord.
King Hrethel kept me and took care of me,
was open-handed, behaved like a kinsman.
While I was his ward, he treated me no worse
as a wean about the place than one of his own boys,
Herebeald and Haethcyn, or my own Hygelac.
For the eldest, Herebeald, an unexpected
deathbed was laid out, through a brother's doing,
when Haethcyn bent his horn-tipped bow
and loosed the arrow that destroyed his life.
He shot wide and buried a shaft
in the flesh and blood of his own brother.
That offence was beyond redress, a wrongfooting
of the heart's affections; for who could avenge
the prince's life or pay his death-price?
It was like the misery felt by an old man
who has lived to see his son's body
swing on the gallows. He begins to keen
and weep for his boy, watching the raven
gloat where he hangs: he can be of no help.
The wisdom of age is worthless to him.

*Beowulf's
forebodings*

*He recalls his early
days as a ward at
King Hrethel's court*

*An accidental killing
and its sad
consequences for
Hrethel*

*Hrethel's loss
reflected in "The
Father's Lament"*

Symble bið gemyndgad   morna gehwylce
eaforan ellor-sīð;   ōðres ne gȳmeð
tō gebīdanne   burgum in innan
yrfe-weardas,   þonne se ān hafað
þurh dēaðes nȳd   dǣda gefondad.
Gesyhð sorh-cearig   on his suna būre
wīn-sele wēstne,   wind-gereste,
rēote berofene;   rīdend swefað,
hæleð in hoðman;   nis þǣr hearpan swēg,
gomen in geardum,   swylce ðǣr iū wǣron.

   "Gewīteð þonne on sealman,   sorh-lēoð gæleð,
ān æfter ānum;   þūhte him eall tō rūm,
wongas ond wīc-stede.   Swā Wedra helm
æfter Herebealde   heortan sorge
weallinde wæg;   wihte ne meahte
on ðām feorh-bonan   fǣghðe gebētan;
nō ðȳ ǣr hē þone heaðo-rinc   hatian ne meahte
lāðum dǣdum,   þēah him lēof ne wæs.
Hē ðā mid þǣre sorhge,   sīo þe him sāre belamp,
gum-drēam ofgeaf,   Godes lēoht gecēas;
eaferum lǣfde,   swā dēð ēadig mon,
lond ond lēod-byrig,   þā hē of līfe gewāt.

   "Þā wæs synn ond sacu   Swēona ond Gēata;
ofer wīd wæter   wrōht gemǣne,
here-nīð hearda,   syððan Hrēðel swealt,
oððe him Ongenðēowes   eaferan wǣran
frome, fyrd-hwate;   frēode ne woldon
ofer heafo healdan,   ac ymb Hrēosna-beorh
eatolne inwit-scear   oft gefremedon.
Þæt mǣg-wine   mīne gewrǣcan,
fǣhðe ond fyrene,   swā hyt gefrǣge wæs,

2450 Morning after morning, he wakes to remember
that his child is gone; he has no interest
in living on until another heir
is born in the hall, now that his first-born
has entered death's dominion forever.
He gazes sorrowfully at his son's dwelling,
the banquet hall bereft of all delight,
the windswept hearthstone; the horsemen are sleeping,
the warriors under ground; what was is no more.
No tunes from the harp, no cheer raised in the yard.
2460 Alone with his longing, he lies down on his bed
and sings a lament; everything seems too large,
the steadings and the fields.
                              Such was the feeling
of loss endured by the lord of the Geats
after Herebeald's death. He was helplessly placed
to set to rights the wrong committed,
could not punish the killer in accordance with the law
of the blood-feud, although he felt no love for him.
Heartsore, wearied, he turned away
from life's joys, chose God's light
2470 and departed, leaving buildings and lands
to his sons, as a man of substance will.

"Then over the wide sea Swedes and Geats
battled and feuded and fought without quarter.
Hostilities broke out when Hrethel died.
Ongentheow's sons were unrelenting,
refusing to make peace, campaigning violently
from coast to coast, constantly setting up
terrible ambushes around Hreasnahill.
My own kith and kin avenged
2480 these evil events, as everybody knows,

*Beowulf continues
his account of wars
between the Geats
and the Swedes*

þēah ðe ōðer his   ealdre gebohte,
heardan cēape;   Hæðcynne wearð,
Gēata dryhtne,   gūð onsǣge.
Þā ic on morgne gefrægn   mǣg ōðerne
billes ecgum   on bonan stǣlan,
þǣr Ongenþēow   Eofores nīosað;
gūð-helm tōglād,   gomela Scylfing
hrēas heoro-blāc;   hond gemunde
fǣhðo genōge,   feorh-sweng ne oftēah.

2490 "Ic him þā māðmas,   þe hē mē sealde,
geald æt gūðe,   swā mē gifeðe wæs,
lēohtan sweorde;   hē mē lond forgeaf,
eard, ēðel-wyn.   Næs him ǣnig þearf,
þæt hē tō Gifðum   oððe tō Gār-Denum
oððe in Swīo-rīce   sēcean þurfe
wyrsan wīg-frecan,   weorðe gecȳpan.
Symle ic him on fēðan   beforan wolde,
āna on orde,   ond swā tō aldre sceall
sæcce fremman,   þenden þis sweord þolað,
2500 þæt mec ǣr ond sīð   oft gelǣste,
syððan ic for dugeðum   Dæghrefne wearð
tō hand-bonan,   Hūga cempan.
Nalles hē ðā frætwe   Frēs-cyninge,
brēost-weorðunge   bringan mōste,
ac in campe gecrong   cumbles hyrde,
æþeling on elne;   ne wæs ecg bona,
ac him hilde-grāp   heortan wylmas,
bān-hūs gebræc.   Nū sceall billes ecg,
hond ond heard sweord   ymb hord wīgan."

2510 Bēowulf maðelode,   bēot-wordum spræc
nīehstan sīðe: "Ic genēðde fela

but the price was high: one of them paid
with his life. Haethcyn, lord of the Geats,
met his fate there and fell in the battle.
Then, as I have heard, Hygelac's sword
was raised in the morning against Ongentheow,
his brother's killer. When Eofor cleft
the old Swede's helmet, halved it open,
he fell, death-pale: his feud-calloused hand
could not stave off the fatal stroke.

The Swedish king,
Ongentheow, dies at
the hands of Eofor,
one of Hygelac's
thanes

2490   "The treasures that Hygelac lavished on me
I paid for when I fought, as fortune allowed me,
with my glittering sword. He gave me land
and the security land brings, so he had no call
to go looking for some lesser champion,
some mercenary from among the Gifthas
or the Spear-Danes or the men of Sweden.
I marched ahead of him, always there
at the front of the line; and I shall fight like that
for as long as I live, as long as this sword
2500   shall last, which has stood me in good stead
late and soon, ever since I killed
Dayraven the Frank in front of the two armies.
He brought back no looted breastplate
to the Frisian king, but fell in battle,
their standard-bearer, high-born and brave.
No sword blade sent him to his death,
my bare hands stilled his heartbeats
and wrecked the bone-house. Now blade and hand,
sword and sword-stroke, will assay the hoard."

Beowulf recalls his
proud days in
Hygelac's retinue

2510   Beowulf spoke, made a formal boast
for the last time: "I risked my life

Beowulf's last boast

gūða on geogoðe;   gȳt ic wylle,
frōd folces weard,   fǣhðe sēcan,
mǣrðu fremman,   gif mec se mān-sceaða
of eorð-sele   ūt gesēceð!"
Gegrētte ðā   gumena gehwylcne,
hwate helm-berend   hindeman sīðe,
swǣse gesīðas: "Nolde ic sweord beran,
wǣpen tō wyrme,   gif ic wiste hū
wið ðām āglǣcean   elles meahte
gylpe wiðgrīpan,   swā ic giō wið Grendle dyde;
ac ic ðǣr heaðu-fȳres   hātes wēne,
oreðes ond attres;   forðon ic mē on hafu
bord ond byrnan.   Nelle ic beorges weard
oferflēon fōtes trem,   ac unc furður sceal
weorðan æt wealle,   swā unc wyrd getēoð
Metod manna gehwæs.   Ic eom on mōde from,
þæt ic wið þone gūð-flogan   gylp ofersitte.
Gebīde gē on beorge,   byrnum werede,
secgas on searwum,   hwæðer sēl mæge
æfter wæl-rǣse   wunde gedȳgan
uncer twēga.   Nis þæt ēower sīð,
nē gemet mannes,   nefne mīn ānes
þæt hē wið āglǣcean   eofoðo dǣle,
eorlscype efne.   Ic mid elne sceall
gold gegangan,   oððe gūð nimeð,
feorh-bealu frēcne,   frēan ēowerne!"
    Ārās ðā bī ronde   rōf ōretta,
heard under helme,   hioro-sercean bær
under stān-cleofu,   strengo getruwode
ānes mannes;   ne bið swylc earges sīð!

often when I was young. Now I am old,
but as king of the people I shall pursue this fight
for the glory of winning, if the evil one will only
abandon his earth-fort and face me in the open."

Then he addressed each dear companion
one final time, those fighters in their helmets,
resolute and high-born: "I would rather not
use a weapon if I knew another way
2520 to grapple with the dragon and make good my boast
as I did against Grendel in days gone by.
But I shall be meeting molten venom
in the fire he breathes, so I go forth
in mail-shirt and shield. I won't shift a foot
when I meet the cave-guard: what occurs on the wall
between the two of us will turn out as fate,
overseer of men, decides. I am resolved.
I scorn further words against this sky-borne foe.

"Men at arms, remain here on the barrow,
2530 safe in your armour, to see which one of us
is better in the end at bearing wounds
in a deadly fray. This fight is not yours,
nor is it up to any man except me
to measure his strength against the monster
or to prove his worth. I shall win the gold
by my courage, or else mortal combat,
doom of battle, will bear your lord away."

Then he drew himself up beside his shield.
The fabled warrior in his warshirt and helmet
2540 trusted in his own strength entirely
and went under the crag. No coward path.

Geseah ðā be wealle,   sē ðe worna fela,
gum-cystum gōd,   gūða gedīgde,
hilde-hlemma,   þonne hnitan fēðan,
stondan stān-bogan,   strēam ūt þonan
brecan of beorge;   wæs þǣre burnan wælm
heaðo-fȳrum hāt;   ne meahte horde nēah
unbyrnende   ǣnige hwīle
dēop gedȳgan   for dracan lēge.

2550   Lēt ðā of brēostum,   ðā hē gebolgen wæs,
Weder-Gēata lēod   word ūt faran,
stearc-heort styrmde;   stefn in becōm
heaðo-torht hlynnan   under hārne stān.
Hete wæs onhrēred,   hord-weard oncnīow
mannes reorde;   næs ðǣr māra fyrst
frēode tō friclan.   From ǣrest cwōm
oruð āglǣcean   ūt of stāne,
hāt hilde-swāt;   hrūse dynede.
Biorn under beorge   bord-rand onswāf
2560   wið ðām gryre-gieste,   Gēata dryhten;
ðā wæs hring-bogan   heorte gefȳsed
sæcce tō sēceanne.   Sweord ǣr gebrǣd
gōd gūð-cyning,   gomele lāfe,
ecgum ungleaw;   ǣghwæðrum wæs
bealo-hycgendra   brōga fram ōðrum.
Stīð-mōd gestōd   wið stēapne rond
winia bealdor,   ðā se wyrm gebēah
snūde tōsomne;   hē on searwum bād.
Gewāt ðā byrnende   gebogen scrīðan,
2570   tō gescipe scyndan.   Scyld wēl gebearg
līfe ond līce   lǣssan hwīle
mǣrum þēodne   þonne his myne sōhte;
ðǣr hē þȳ fyrste   forman dōgore
wealdan mōste,   swā him wyrd ne gescrāf

Hard by the rock-face that hale veteran,
a good man who had gone repeatedly
into combat and danger and come through,
saw a stone arch and a gushing stream
that burst from the barrow, blazing and wafting
a deadly heat. It would be hard to survive
unscathed near the hoard, to hold firm
against the dragon in those flaming depths.
2550 Then he gave a shout. The lord of the Geats
unburdened his breast and broke out
in a storm of anger. Under grey stone
his voice challenged and resounded clearly.
Hate was ignited. The hoard-guard recognized
a human voice, the time was over
for peace and parleying. Pouring forth
in a hot battle-fume, the breath of the monster
burst from the rock. There was a rumble under ground.
Down there in the barrow, Beowulf the warrior
2560 lifted his shield: the outlandish thing
writhed and convulsed and viciously
turned on the king, whose keen-edged sword,
an heirloom inherited by ancient right,
was already in his hand. Roused to a fury,
each antagonist struck terror in the other.
Unyielding, the lord of his people loomed
by his tall shield, sure of his ground,
while the serpent looped and unleashed itself.
Swaddled in flames, it came gliding and flexing
2570 and racing towards its fate. Yet his shield defended
the renowned leader's life and limb
for a shorter time than he meant it to:
that final day was the first time
when Beowulf fought and fate denied him

hrēð æt hilde.   Hond up ābræd
Gēata dryhten,   gryre-fāhne slōh
incge-lāfe,   þæt sīo ecg gewāc,
brūn on bāne,   bāt unswīðor
þonne his ðīod-cyning   þearfe hæfde,
bysigum gebæded.   Þā wæs beorges weard
æfter heaðu-swenge   on hrēoum mōde,
wearp wæl-fȳre,   wīde sprungon
hilde-lēoman.   Hrēð-sigora ne gealp
gold-wine Gēata;   gūð-bill geswāc,
nacod æt nīðe,   swā hyt nō sceolde,
īren ær-gōd.   Ne wæs þæt ēðe sīð,
þæt se mæra   maga Ecgðēowes
grund-wong þone   ofgyfan wolde;
sceolde ofer willan   wīc eardian
elles hwergen,   swā sceal æghwylc mon
ālǣtan lǣn-dagas.   Næs ðā long tō ðon,
þæt ða āglǣcean   hȳ eft gemētton.
Hyrte hyne hord-weard   —hreðer æðme wēoll—
nīwan stefne;   nearo ðrōwode,
fȳre befongen,   sē ðe ær folce wēold.
Nealles him on hēape   hand-gesteallan,
æðelinga bearn   ymbe gestōdon
hilde-cystum,   ac hȳ on holt bugon,
ealdre burgan.   Hiora in ānum wēoll
sefa wið sorgum.   Sibb ǣfre ne mæg
wiht onwendan   þām ðe wēl þenceð.
    Wīglāf wæs hāten,   Wēoxstānes sunu,
lēoflīc lind-wiga,   lēod Scylfinga,
mǣg Ælfheres;   geseah his mon-dryhten

glory in battle. So the king of the Geats
raised his hand and struck hard
at the enamelled scales, but scarcely cut through:
the blade flashed and slashed yet the blow
was far less powerful than the hard-pressed king
had need of at that moment. The mound-keeper
went into a spasm and spouted deadly flames:
when he felt the stroke, battle-fire
billowed and spewed. Beowulf was foiled

Beowulf's sword fails him

of a glorious victory. The glittering sword,
infallible before that day,
failed when he unsheathed it, as it never should have.
For the son of Ecgtheow, it was no easy thing
to have to give ground like that and go
unwillingly to inhabit another home
in a place beyond; so every man must yield
the leasehold of his days.

                              Before long
the fierce contenders clashed again.
The hoard-guard took heart, inhaled and swelled up
and got a new wind; he who had once ruled
was furled in fire and had to face the worst.
No help or backing was to be had then

All but one of Beowulf's band withdraw to safety

from his high-born comrades; that hand-picked troop
broke ranks and ran for their lives
to the safety of the wood. But within one heart
sorrow welled up: in a man of worth
the claims of kinship cannot be denied.

His name was Wiglaf, a son of Weohstan's,
a well-regarded Shylfing warrior
related to Aelfhere. When he saw his lord

Wiglaf stands by his lord

under here-grīman   hāt þrōwian.
Gemunde ðā ðā āre   þē hē him ǣr forgeaf,
wīc-stede weligne   Wǣgmundinga,
folc-rihta gehwylc,   swā his fæder āhte;
ne mihte ðā forhabban,   hond rond gefēng,
geolwe linde;   gomel swyrd getēah,
þæt wæs mid eldum   Ēanmundes lāf,
suna Ōhteres.   Þām æt sæcce wearð,
wrǣccan wine-lēasum,   Wēohstān bana
mēces ecgum,   ond his māgum ætbær
brūn-fāgne helm,   hringde byrnan,
eald-sweord etonisc.   Þæt him Onela forgeaf,
his gǣdelinges   gūð-gewǣdu,
fyrd-searo fūslīc;   nō ymbe ðā fǣhðe spræc,
þēah ðe hē his brōðor bearn   ābredwade.
Hē frætwe gehēold   fela missēra,
bill ond byrnan,   oððæt his byre mihte
eorlscipe efnan   swā his ǣr-fæder;
geaf him ðā mid Gēatum   gūð-gewǣda
ǣghwæs unrīm,   þā hē of ealdre gewāt,
frōd on forð-weg.   Þā wæs forma sīð
geongan cempan,   þæt hē gūðe ræs
mid his frēo-dryhtne   fremman sceolde.
Ne gemealt him se mōd-sefa,   nē his mǣges lāf
gewāc æt wīge.   Þæt se wyrm onfand,
syððan hīe tōgædre   gegān hæfdon.
Wīglāf maðelode,   word-rihta fela
sægde gesīðum   —him wæs sefa geōmor.
    "Ic ðæt mǣl geman,   þǣr wē medu þēgun,
þonne wē gehēton   ūssum hlāforde

tormented by the heat of his scalding helmet,
he remembered the bountiful gifts bestowed on him,
how well he lived among the Waegmundings,
the freehold he inherited from his father before him.
He could not hold back: one hand brandished

2610 the yellow-timbered shield, the other drew his sword—
an ancient blade that was said to have belonged
to Eanmund, the son of Ohthere, the one
Weohstan had slain when he was an exile without friends.

The deeds of
Wiglaf's father,
Weohstan, recalled

He carried the arms to the victim's kinfolk,
the burnished helmet, the webbed chain-mail
and that relic of the giants. But Onela returned
the weapons to him, rewarded Weohstan
with Eanmund's war-gear. He ignored the blood-feud,
the fact that Eanmund was his brother's son.

2620 Weohstan kept that war-gear for a lifetime,
the sword and the mail-shirt, until it was the son's turn
to follow his father and perform his part.
Then, in old age, at the end of his days
among the Weather-Geats, he bequeathed to Wiglaf
innumerable weapons.
                    And now the youth
was to enter the line of battle with his lord,
his first time to be tested as a fighter.
His spirit did not break and the ancestral blade
would keep its edge, as the dragon discovered

2630 as soon as they came together in the combat.

Sad at heart, addressing his companions,
Wiglaf spoke wise and fluent words:
"I remember that time when mead was flowing,
how we pledged loyalty to our lord in the hall,

Wiglaf's speech to
the shirkers

in bīor-sele, ðe ūs ðās bēagas geaf,
þæt wē him ðā gūð-getāwa gyldan woldon,
gif him þyslicu þearf gelumpe,
helmas ond heard sweord. Ðē hē ūsic on herge gecēas
tō ðyssum sīð-fate sylfes willum,
onmunde ūsic mærða, ond mē þās māðmas geaf,
þē hē ūsic gār-wīgend gōde tealde,
hwate helm-berend, þēah ðe hlāford ūs
þis ellen-weorc āna āðōhte
tō gefremmanne, folces hyrde,
forðām hē manna mæst mærða gefremede,
dæda dollīcra. Nū is sē dæg cumen
þæt ūre man-dryhten mægenes behōfað,
gōdra gūð-rinca; wutun gongan tō,
helpan hild-fruman, þenden hyt sȳ,
glēd-egesa grim! God wāt on mec,
þæt mē is micle lēofre, þæt mīnne līc-haman
mid mīnne gold-gyfan glēd fæðmie.
Ne þynceð mē gerysne, þæt wē rondas beren
eft tō earde, nemne wē æror mægen
fāne gefyllan, feorh ealgian
Wedra ðēodnes. Ic wāt geare,
þæt næron eald-gewyrht, þæt hē āna scyle
Gēata duguðe gnorn þrōwian,
gesīgan æt sæcce; ūrum sceal sweord ond helm,
byrne ond beadu-scrūd bām gemæne."
    Wōd þā þurh þone wæl-rēc, wīg-heafolan bær
frēan on fultum, fēa worda cwæð:
"Lēofa Bīowulf, læst eall tela,
swā ðū on geoguð-fēore geāra gecwæde,
þæt ðū ne ālæte be ðē lifigendum
dōm gedrēosan; scealt nū dædum rōf,
æðeling ān-hȳdig, ealle mægene

2640

2650

2660

promised our ring-giver we would be worth our price,
make good the gift of the war-gear,
those swords and helmets, as and when
his need required it. He picked us out
from the army deliberately, honoured us and judged us

2640   fit for this action, made me these lavish gifts—
and all because he considered us the best
of his arms-bearing thanes. And now, although
he wanted this challenge to be one he'd face
by himself alone—the shepherd of our land,
a man unequalled in the quest for glory
and a name for daring—now the day has come
when this lord we serve needs sound men
to give him their support. Let us go to him,
help our leader through the hot flame

2650   and dread of the fire. As God is my witness,
I would rather my body were robed in the same
burning blaze as my gold-giver's body
than go back home bearing arms.
That is unthinkable, unless we have first
slain the foe and defended the life
of the prince of the Weather-Geats. I well know
the things he has done for us deserve better.
Should he alone be left exposed
to fall in battle? We must bond together,

2660   shield and helmet, mail-shirt and sword."
Then he waded the dangerous reek and went
under arms to his lord, saying only:
"Go on, dear Beowulf, do everything
you said you would when you were still young
and vowed you would never let your name and fame
be dimmed while you lived. Your deeds are famous,
so stay resolute, my lord, defend your life now

*Wiglaf goes to
Beowulf's aid*

feorh ealgian;   ic ðē ful-lǣstu!"

Æfter ðām wordum   wyrm yrre cwōm,
atol inwit-gǣst,   ōðre sīðe,
fȳr-wylmum fāh,   fīonda nīosian,
lāðra manna;   līg ȳðum fōr,
born bord wið rond;   byrne ne meahte
geongum gār-wigan   gēoce gefremman;
ac se maga geonga   under his mǣgas scyld
elne geēode,   þā his āgen wæs
glēdum forgrunden.   Þā gēn gūð-cyning
mǣrða gemunde,   mægen-strengo slōh
hilde-bille,   þæt hyt on heafolan stōd
nīþe genȳded;   Nægling forbærst,
geswāc æt sæcce   sweord Bīowulfes,
gomol ond grǣg-mǣl.   Him þæt gifeðe ne wæs,
þæt him īrenna   ecge mihton
helpan æt hilde;   wæs sīo hond tō strong,
sē ðe mēca gehwane,   mīne gefrǣge,
swenge ofersōhte,   þonne hē tō sæcce bær
wǣpen wundum heard;   næs him wihte ðē sēl.

Þā wæs þēod-sceaða   þriddan sīðe,
frēcne fȳr-draca   fæhða gemyndig,
rǣsde on ðone rōfan,   þā him rūm āgeald:
hāt ond heaðo-grim,   heals ealne ymbefēng
biteran bānum;   hē geblōdegod wearð
sāwul-drīore;   swāt ȳðum wēoll.

Ðā ic æt þearfe gefrægn   þēod-cyninges
andlongne eorl   ellen cȳðan,
cræft ond cēnðu,   swā him gecynde wæs.

with the whole of your strength. I shall stand by you."

The dragon attacks again

After those words, a wildness rose
2670   in the dragon again and drove it to attack,
heaving up fire, hunting for enemies,
the humans it loathed. Flames lapped the shield,
charred it to the boss, and the body armour
on the young warrior was useless to him.
But Wiglaf did well under the wide rim
Beowulf shared with him once his own had shattered
in sparks and ashes.
                    Inspired again
by the thought of glory, the war-king threw
his whole strength behind a sword-stroke
2680   and connected with the skull. And Naegling snapped.

Another setback

Beowulf's ancient iron-grey sword
let him down in the fight. It was never his fortune
to be helped in combat by the cutting edge
of weapons made of iron. When he wielded a sword,
no matter how blooded and hard-edged the blade
his hand was too strong, the stroke he dealt
(I have heard) would ruin it. He could reap no advantage.

Then the bane of that people, the fire-breathing dragon,
was mad to attack for a third time.

The dragon's third onslaught. He draws blood

2690   When a chance came, he caught the hero
in a rush of flame and clamped sharp fangs
into his neck. Beowulf's body
ran wet with his life-blood: it came welling out.

Next thing, they say, the noble son of Weohstan
saw the king in danger at his side
and displayed his inborn bravery and strength.

Wiglaf gets past the flames and strikes

Ne hēdde hē þæs heafolan,   ac sīo hand gebarn
mōdiges mannes,   þǣr hē his mǣges healp
þæt hē þone nīð-gǣst   nioðor hwēne slōh,
secg on searum,   þæt ðæt sweord gedēaf,
fāh ond fǣted,   þæt ðæt fȳr ongon
sweðrian syððan. Þā gēn sylf cyning
gewēold his gewitte,   wæll-seaxe gebrǣd,
biter ond beadu-scearp,   þæt hē on byrnan wæg;
forwrāt Wedra helm   wyrm on middan.
Fēond gefyldan   —ferh ellen wræc—
ond hī hyne þā bēgen   ābroten hæfdon,
sib-æðelingas. Swylc sceolde secg wesan,
þegn æt ðearfe!—
                             Þæt ðām þēodne wæs
sīðast sige-hwīle   sylfes dǣdum,
worlde geweorces. Ðā sīo wund ongon,
þe him se eorð-draca   ǣr geworhte,
swelan ond swellan;   hē þæt sōna onfand,
þæt him on brēostum   bealo-nīðe wēoll
attor on innan. Ðā se æðeling gīong,
þæt hē bī wealle,   wīs-hycgende,
gesæt on sesse;   seah on enta geweorc,
hū ðā stān-bogan   stapulum fæste
ēce eorð-reced   innan healde.
Hyne þā mid handa,   heoro-drēorigne,
þēoden mǣrne,   þegn ungemete till,
wine-dryhten his   wætere gelafede,
hilde-sædne,   ond his helm onspēon.
   Bīowulf maþelode   —hē ofer benne spræc,
wunde wæl-blēate;   wisse hē gearwe,
þæt hē dæg-hwīla   gedrogen hæfde,

2700

2710

2720

He left the head alone, but his fighting hand
was burned when he came to his kinsman's aid.
He lunged at the enemy lower down
2700   so that his decorated sword sank into its belly
and the flames grew weaker.

Once again the king

*Beowulf delivers the
fatal wound*

gathered his strength and drew a stabbing knife
he carried on his belt, sharpened for battle.
He stuck it deep into the dragon's flank.
Beowulf dealt it a deadly wound.
They had killed the enemy, courage quelled his life;
that pair of kinsmen, partners in nobility,
had destroyed the foe. So every man should act,
be at hand when needed; but now, for the king,
2710   this would be the last of his many labours
and triumphs in the world.

Then the wound

dealt by the ground-burner earlier began
to scald and swell; Beowulf discovered
deadly poison suppurating inside him,
surges of nausea, and so, in his wisdom,
the prince realized his state and struggled
towards a seat on the rampart. He steadied his gaze
on those gigantic stones, saw how the earthwork
was braced with arches built over columns.
2720   And now that thane unequalled for goodness
with his own hands washed his lord's wounds,
swabbed the weary prince with water,
bathed him clean, unbuckled his helmet.

Beowulf spoke: in spite of his wounds,
mortal wounds, he still spoke
for he well knew his days in the world

*Beowulf senses that
he is near death*

eorðan wynne; ðā wæs eall sceacen
dōgor-gerīmes, dēað ungemete nēah: —
"Nū ic suna mīnum syllan wolde
gūð-gewǣdu, þǣr mē gifeðe swā
ǣnig yrfe-weard æfter wurde,
līce gelenge. Ic ðās lēode hēold
fīftig wintra; næs se folc-cyning,
ymbe-sittendra ǣnig ðāra,
þe mec gūð-winum grētan dorste,
egesan ðēon. Ic on earde bād
mǣl-gesceafta, hēold mīn tela,
ne sōhte searo-nīðas, nē mē swōr fela
āða on unriht. Ic ðæs ealles mæg,
feorh-bennum sēoc, gefēan habban;
forðām mē wītan ne ðearf Waldend fīra
morðor-bealo māga, þonne mīn sceaceð
līf of līce. Nū ðū lungre geong
hord scēawian under hārne stān,
Wīglāf lēofa, nū se wyrm ligeð,
swefeð sāre wund, since berēafod.
Bīo nū on ofoste, þæt ic ǣr-welan,
gold-ǣht ongite, gearo scēawige
swegle searo-gimmas, þæt ic ðȳ sēft mæge
æfter māððum-welan mīn ālǣtan,
līf ond lēodscipe, þone ic longe hēold."
    Ðā ic snūde gefrægn sunu Wīhstānes
æfter word-cwydum wundum dryhtne
hȳran heaðo-sīocum, hring-net beran,
brogdne beadu-sercean under beorges hrōf.
Geseah ðā sige-hrēðig, þā hē bī sesse gēong,
mago-þegn mōdig māððum-sigla fealo,

had been lived out to the end: his allotted time
was drawing to a close, death was very near.

"Now is the time when I would have wanted

He thinks back on his life

to bestow this armour on my own son,
had it been my fortune to have fathered an heir
and live on in his flesh. For fifty years
I ruled this nation. No king
of any neighbouring clan would dare
face me with troops, none had the power
to intimidate me. I took what came,
cared for and stood by things in my keeping,
never fomented quarrels, never
swore to a lie. All this consoles me,
doomed as I am and sickening for death;
because of my right ways, the Ruler of mankind
need never blame me when the breath leaves my body
for murder of kinsmen. Go now quickly,

He bids Wiglaf to inspect the hoard and return with a portion of the treasure

dearest Wiglaf, under the grey stone
where the dragon is laid out, lost to his treasure;
hurry to feast your eyes on the hoard.
Away you go: I want to examine
that ancient gold, gaze my fill
on those garnered jewels; my going will be easier
for having seen the treasure, a less troubled letting-go
of the life and lordship I have long maintained."

And so, I have heard, the son of Weohstan

Wiglaf enters the dragon's barrow

quickly obeyed the command of his languishing
war-weary lord; he went in his chain-mail
under the rock-piled roof of the barrow,
exulting in his triumph, and saw beyond the seat
a treasure-trove of astonishing richness,

gold glitinian   grunde getenge,
wundur on wealle,   ond þæs wyrmes denn,
2760   ealdes ūht-flogan,   orcas stondan,
fyrn-manna fatu,   feormend-lēase,
hyrstum behrorene.   Þær wæs helm monig,
eald ond ōmig,   earm-bēaga fela,
searwum gesǣled.   Sinc ēaðe mæg,
gold on grunde,   gum-cynnes gehwone
oferhīgian;   hŷde sē ðe wylle!
    Swylce hē siomian geseah   segn eall-gylden
hēah ofer horde,   hond-wundra mǣst,
gelocen leoðo-cræftum;   of ðām lēoma stōd,
2770   þæt hē þone grund-wong   ongitan meahte,
wrǣte giondwlītan.   Næs ðæs wyrmes þǣr
onsȳn ǣnig,   ac hyne ecg fornam.
Ðā ic on hlǣwe gefrægn   hord rēafian,
eald enta geweorc   ānne mannan,
him on bearm hladon   bunan ond discas
sylfes dōme;   segn ēac genōm,
bēacna beorhtost.   Bill ǣr gescōd
—ecg wæs īren—   eald-hlāfordes
þām ðāra māðma   mund-bora wæs
2780   longe hwīle,   līg-egesan wæg
hātne for horde,   hioro-weallende
middel-nihtum,   oðþæt hē morðre swealt.
Ār wæs on ofoste,   eft-sīðes georn,
frætwum gefyrðred;   hyne fyrwet bræc,
hwæðer collen-ferð   cwicne gemētte
in ðām wong-stede   Wedra þēoden
ellen-sīocne,   þǣr hē hine ǣr forlēt.

wall-hangings that were a wonder to behold,
glittering gold spread across the ground,
2760   the old dawn-scorching serpent's den
packed with goblets and vessels from the past,
tarnished and corroding. Rusty helmets
all eaten away. Armbands everywhere,
artfully wrought. How easily treasure
buried in the ground, gold hidden
however skilfully, can escape from any man!

And he saw too a standard, entirely of gold,
hanging high over the hoard,
a masterpiece of filigree; it glowed with light
2770   so he could make out the ground at his feet
and inspect the valuables. Of the dragon there was no
remaining sign: the sword had despatched him.
Then, the story goes, a certain man
plundered the hoard in that immemorial howe,
filled his arms with flagons and plates,
anything he wanted; and took the standard also,
most brilliant of banners.
                              Already the blade
of the old king's sharp killing-sword
had done its worst: the one who had for long
2780   minded the hoard, hovering over gold,
unleashing fire, surging forth
midnight after midnight, had been mown down.

Wiglaf went quickly, keen to get back,   *He returns with treasure*
excited by the treasure. Anxiety weighed
on his brave heart—he was hoping he would find
the leader of the Geats alive where he had left him
helpless, earlier, on the open ground.

Hē ðā mid þām māðmum   mǣrne þīoden,
dryhten sīnne   drīorigne fand,
ealdres æt ende;   hē hine eft ongon
wæteres weorpan,   oðþæt wordes ord
brēost-hord þurhbræc.   Þā se beorn gespræc,
gomel on giohðe: —gold scēawode—
    "Ic ðāra frætwa   Frēan ealles ðanc,
Wuldur-cyninge,   wordum secge,
ēcum Dryhtne,   þe ic hēr on starie,
þæs ðe ic mōste   mīnum lēodum
ǣr swylt-dæge   swylc gestrȳnan.
Nū ic on māðma hord   mīne bebohte
frōde feorh-lege,   fremmað gēna
lēoda þearfe!   Ne mæg ic hēr leng wesan.
Hātað heaðo-mǣre   hlǣw gewyrcean,
beorhtne æfter bǣle   æt brimes nosan;
sē scel tō gemyndum   mīnum lēodum
hēah hlīfian   on Hrones-næsse,
þæt hit sǣ-līðend   syððan hātan
Bīowulfes biorh,   ðā ðe brentingas
ofer flōda genipu   feorran drīfað."
    Dyde him of healse   hring gyldenne
þīoden þrīst-hȳdig,   þegne gesealde,
geongum gār-wigan,   gold-fāhne helm,
bēah ond byrnan,   hēt hyne brūcan well:
"Þū eart ende-lāf   ūsses cynnes,
Wǣgmundinga;   ealle wyrd forspēon
mīne māgas   tō meodsceafte,
eorlas on elne;   ic him æfter sceal."
    Þæt wæs þām gomelan   gingæste word

2790

2800

2810

So he came to the place, carrying the treasure,
and found his lord bleeding profusely,
2790   his life at an end; again he began
to swab his body. The beginnings of an utterance
broke out from the king's breast-cage.
The old lord gazed sadly at the gold.

"To the everlasting Lord of All,
to the King of Glory, I give thanks
that I behold this treasure here in front of me,
that I have been allowed to leave my people
so well endowed on the day I die.
Now that I have bartered my last breath
2800   to own this fortune, it is up to you
to look after their needs. I can hold out no longer.
Order my troop to construct a barrow
on a headland on the coast, after my pyre has cooled.
It will loom on the horizon at Hronesness
and be a reminder among my people—
so that in coming times crews under sail
will call it Beowulf's Barrow, as they steer
ships across the wide and shrouded waters."

*Beowulf gives thanks
and orders the
construction of a
barrow to
commemorate him*

Then the king in his great-heartedness unclasped
2810   the collar of gold from his neck and gave it
to the young thane, telling him to use
it and the warshirt and the gilded helmet well.

"You are the last of us, the only one left
of the Waegmundings. Fate swept us away,
sent my whole brave high-born clan
to their final doom. Now I must follow them."
That was the warrior's last word.

Beowulf's last words

breōst-gehygdum,   ǣr hē bǣl cure,
hāte heaðo-wylmas;   him of hwæðre gewāt
sāwol sēcean   sōð-fæstra dōm.

   Ðā wæs gegongen   guman unfrōdum
earfoðlīce,   þæt hē on eorðan geseah
þone lēofestan   līfes æt ende,
blēate gebǣran.   Bona swylce læg,
egeslīc eorð-draca,   ealdre berēafod,
bealwe gebǣded.   Bēah-hordum leng
wyrm wōh-bogen   wealdan ne mōste,
ac hine īrenna   ecga fornāmon,
hearde, heaðo-scearde,   homera lāfe,
þæt se wīd-floga   wundum stille
hrēas on hrūsan   hord-ærne nēah.
Nalles æfter lyfte   lācende hwearf
middel-nihtum,   māðm-ǣhta wlonc
ansȳn ȳwde;   ac hē eorðan gefēoll
for ðæs hild-fruman   hond-geweorce.
Hūru þæt on lande   lȳt manna ðāh,
mægen-āgendra,   mīne gefrǣge,
þēah ðe hē dǣda gehwæs   dyrstig wǣre,
þæt hē wið attor-sceaðan   oreðe geræsde,
oððe hring-sele   hondum styrede,
gif hē wæccende   weard onfunde
būon on beorge.   Bīowulfe wearð
dryht-māðma dǣl   dēaðe forgolden;
hæfde æghwæðer   ende gefēred
lǣnan līfes.

      Næs ðā lang tō ðon,

He had no more to confide. The furious heat
of the pyre would assail him. His soul fled from his breast
2820   to its destined place among the steadfast ones.

It was hard then on the young hero,
having to watch the one he held so dear
there on the ground, going through
his death agony. The dragon from underearth,
his nightmarish destroyer, lay destroyed as well,
utterly without life. No longer would his snakefolds
ply themselves to safeguard hidden gold.
Hard-edged blades, hammered out
and keenly filed, had finished him
2830   so that the sky-roamer lay there rigid,
brought low beside the treasure-lodge.

The dragon too has
been destroyed

Never again would he glitter and glide
and show himself off in midnight air,
exulting in his riches: he fell to earth
through the battle-strength in Beowulf's arm.
There were few, indeed, as far as I have heard,
big and brave as they may have been,
few who would have held out if they had had to face
the outpourings of that poison-breather
2840   or gone foraging on the ring-hall floor
and found the deep barrow-dweller
on guard and awake.
                    The treasure had been won,
bought and paid for by Beowulf's death.
Both had reached the end of the road
through the life they had been lent.

                              Before long

þæt ðā hild-latan   holt ofgēfan,
tȳdre trēow-logan,   tȳne ætsomne,
ðā ne dorston ǣr   dareðum lācan
on hyra man-dryhtnes   miclan þearfe;
ac hȳ scamiende   scyldas bǣran,
gūð-gewǣdu,   þǣr se gomela læg;
wlitan on Wīlāf.   Hē gewērgad sæt,
fēðe-cempa,   frēan eaxlum nēah;
wehte hyne wætre,   him wiht ne spēow.
Ne meahte hē on eorðan,   ðēah hē ūðe wēl,
on ðām frum-gāre   feorh gehealdan,
nē ðæs Wealdendes   wiht oncirran.
Wolde dōm Godes   dǣdum rǣdan
gumena gehwylcum,   swā hē nū gēn dēð.
    Þā wæs æt ðām geongan   grim andswaru
ēð-begēte   þām ðe ǣr his elne forlēas.
Wīglāf maðelode,   Wēohstānes sunu,
sēc sārig-ferð   —seah on unlēofe—:
"Þæt lā mæg secgan,   sē ðe wyle sōð specan,
þæt se mon-dryhten,   sē ēow ðā māðmas geaf,
ēored-geatwe,   þe gē þǣr on standað,
þonne hē on ealu-bence   oft gesealde
heal-sittendum   helm ond byrnan,
þēoden his þegnum,   swylce hē þrȳdlīcost
ōwer feor oððe nēah   findan meahte,
þæt hē gēnunga   gūð-gewǣdu
wrāðe forwurpe,   ðā hyne wīg beget.
Nealles folc-cyning   fyrd-gesteallum
gylpan þorfte;   hwæðre him God ūðe,
sigora Waldend,   þæt hē hyne sylfne gewræc,
āna mid ecge,   þā him wæs elnes þearf.

the battle-dodgers abandoned the wood,
the ones who had let down their lord earlier,
the tail-turners, ten of them together.
When he needed them most, they had made off.

The battle-dodgers
come back

2850   Now they were ashamed and came behind shields,
in their battle-outfits, to where the old man lay.
They watched Wiglaf, sitting worn out,
a comrade shoulder to shoulder with his lord,
trying in vain to bring him round with water.
Much as he wanted to, there was no way
he could preserve his lord's life on earth
or alter in the least the Almighty's will.
What God judged right would rule what happened
to every man, as it does to this day.

2860   Then a stern rebuke was bound to come
from the young warrior to the ones who had been
    cowards.

Wiglaf rebukes them

Wiglaf, son of Weohstan, spoke
disdainfully and in disappointment:
"Anyone ready to admit the truth
will surely realize that the lord of men
who showered you with gifts and gave you the armour
you are standing in—when he would distribute
helmets and mail-shirts to men on the mead-benches,
a prince treating his thanes in hall
2870   to the best he could find, far or near—
was throwing weapons uselessly away.
It would be a sad waste when the war broke out.
Beowulf had little cause to brag
about his armed guard; yet God who ordains
who wins or loses allowed him to strike
with his own blade when bravery was needed.

Ic him līf-wraðe,   lȳtyle meahte
ætgifan æt gūðe,   ond ongan swā þēah
ofer mīn gemet   mǣges helpan.
Symle wæs þȳ sǣmra,   þonne ic sweorde drep
ferhð-genīðlan,   fȳr unswīðor
wēoll of gewitte.   Wergendra tō lȳt
þrong ymbe þēoden,   þā hyne sīo þrāg becwōm.
Nū sceal sinc-þego   ond swyrd-gifu,
eall ēðel-wyn   ēowrum cynne,
lufen ālicgean;   lond-rihtes mōt
þǣre mǣg-burge   monna ǣghwylc
īdel hweorfan,   syððan æðelingas
feorran gefricgean   flēam ēowerne,
dōm-lēasan dǣd.   Dēað bið sēlla
eorla gehwylcum   þonne edwīt-līf!"
    Heht ðā þæt heaðo-weorc   tō hagan bīodan
up ofer ecg-clif,   þǣr þæt eorl-weorod
morgen-longne dæg   mōd-giōmor sæt,
bord-hæbbende,   bēga on wēnum,
ende-dōgores   ond eft-cymes
lēofes monnes.   Lȳt swīgode
nīwra spella,   sē ðe næs gerād,
ac hē sōðlīce   sægde ofer ealle:
    "Nū is wil-geofa   Wedra lēoda,
dryhten Gēata   dēað-bedde fæst,
wunað wæl-reste   wyrmes dǣdum:
him on efn ligeð   ealdor-gewinna
siex-bennum sēoc;   sweorde ne meahte
on ðām āglǣcean   ǣnige þinga
wunde gewyrcean.   Wīglāf siteð
ofer Bīowulfe,   byre Wīhstānes,

There was little I could do to protect his life
in the heat of the fray, yet I found new strength
welling up when I went to help him.
Then my sword connected and the deadly assaults
of our foe grew weaker, the fire coursed
less strongly from his head. But when the worst happened
too few rallied around the prince.

"So it is goodbye now to all you know and love
on your home ground, the open-handedness,
the giving of war-swords. Every one of you
with freeholds of land, our whole nation,
will be dispossessed, once princes from beyond
get tidings of how you turned and fled
and disgraced yourselves. A warrior will sooner
die than live a life of shame."

Then he ordered the outcome of the fight to be reported
to those camped on the ridge, that crowd of retainers
who had sat all morning, sad at heart,
shield-bearers wondering about
the man they loved: would this day be his last
or would he return? He told the truth
and did not balk, the rider who bore
news to the cliff-top. He addressed them all:
"Now the people's pride and love,
the lord of the Geats, is laid on his deathbed,
brought down by the dragon's attack.
Beside him lies the bane of his life,
dead from knife-wounds. There was no way
Beowulf could manage to get the better
of the monster with his sword. Wiglaf sits
at Beowulf's side, the son of Weohstan,

He predicts that
enemies will now
attack the Geats

A messenger tells the
people that Beowulf
is dead

eorl ofer ōðrum   unlifigendum,
healdeð hige-mǣðum   hēafod-wearde,
lēofes ond lāðes.   Nū ys lēodum wēn
orleg-hwīle,   syððan underne
Froncum ond Frȳsum   fyll cyninges
wīde weorðeð.   Wæs sīo wrōht scepen
heard wið Hūgas,   syððan Higelāc cwōm
faran flot-herge   on Frēsna land,
þǣr hyne Hetware   hilde genǣgdon,
elne geēodon   mid ofer-mægene,
þæt se byrn-wiga   būgan sceolde,
fēoll on fēðan;   nalles frætwe geaf
ealdor dugoðe.   Ūs wæs ā syððan
Merewīoingas   milts ungyfeðe.

   "Nē ic te Swēo-ðēode   sibbe oððe trēowe
wihte ne wēne;   ac wæs wīde cūð,
þætte Ongenðīo   ealdre besnyðede
Hæðcen Hrēþling   wið Hrefna-wudu,
þā for onmēdlan   ǣrest gesōhton
Gēata lēode   Gūð-Scilfingas.
Sōna him se frōda   fæder Ōhtheres,
eald ond eges-full   ondslyht āgeaf,
ābrēot brim-wīsan,   brȳd āheorde,
gomela iō-mēowlan   golde berofene,
Onelan mōdor   ond Ōhtheres;
ond ðā folgode   feorh-genīðlan,
oððæt hī oðēodon   earfoðlīce
in Hrefnes-holt   hlāford-lēase.
Besæt ðā sin-herge   sweorda lāfe
wundum wērge;   wēan oft gehēt
earmre teohhe   ondlonge niht,

the living warrior watching by the dead,
keeping weary vigil, holding a wake
for the loved and the loathed.

Now war is looming

over our nation, soon it will be known
to Franks and Frisians, far and wide,
that the king is gone. Hostility has been great
among the Franks since Hygelac sailed forth
at the head of a war-fleet into Friesland:
there the Hetware harried and attacked
and overwhelmed him with great odds.
The leader in his war-gear was laid low,
fell amongst followers; that lord did not favour
his company with spoils. The Merovingian king
has been an enemy to us ever since.

*He foresees wars
with the Franks and
the Frisians*

"Nor do I expect peace or pact-keeping
of any sort from the Swedes. Remember:
at Ravenswood, Ongentheow
slaughtered Haethcyn, Hrethel's son,
when the Geat people in their arrogance
first attacked the fierce Shylfings.
The return blow was quickly struck
by Ohthere's father. Old and terrible,
he felled the sea-king and saved his own
aged wife, the mother of Onela
and of Ohthere, bereft of her gold rings.
Then he kept hard on the heels of the foe
and drove them, leaderless, lucky to get away,
in a desperate rout into Ravenswood.
His army surrounded the weary remnant
where they nursed their wounds; all through the night
he howled threats at those huddled survivors,

*The Swedes too will
strike to avenge the
slaughter of
Ongentheow*

*Ongentheow's last
engagement at
Ravenswood: he
cornered a Geatish
force*

2910

2920

2930

cwæð hē on mergenne   mēces ecgum
gētan wolde, sum' on galg-trēowum
fuglum tō gamene.   Frōfor eft gelamp
sārig-mōdum   somod ǣr-dæge,
syððan hīe Hygelāces   horn ond bȳman,
gealdor ongēaton,   þā se gōda cōm
lēoda dugoðe   on lāst faran.
     "Wæs sīo swāt-swaðu   Swēona ond Gēata,
wæl-rǣs weora   wīde gesȳne,
hū ðā folc mid him   fǣhðe tōwehton.
Gewāt him ðā se gōda   mid his gædelingum,
frōd fela-geōmor   fæsten sēcean,
eorl Ongenþīo   ufor oncirde;
hæfde Higelāces   hilde gefrūnen,
wlonces wīg-cræft;   wiðres ne truwode,
þæt hē sǣ-mannum   onsacan mihte,
heaðo-līðendum,   hord forstandan,
bearn ond brȳde;   bēah eft þonan
eald under eorð-weall.   Þā wæs ǣht boden
Swēona lēodum,   segn Higelāces
freoðo-wong þone   forð oferēodon,
syððan Hrēðlingas   tō hagan þrungon.
Þǣr wearð Ongenðīow   ecgum sweorda,
blonden-fexa   on bid wrecen,
þæt se þēod-cyning   ðafian sceolde
Eafores ānne dōm.   Hyne yrringa
Wulf Wonrēding   wǣpne gerǣhte,
þæt him for swenge   swāt ǣdrum sprong
forð under fexe.   Næs hē forht swā ðēh,
gomela Scilfing,   ac forgeald hraðe
wyrsan wrixle   wæl-hlem þone,
syððan ðēod-cyning   þyder oncirde.

2940   promised to axe their bodies open
when dawn broke, dangle them from gallows
to feed the birds. But at first light
when their spirits were lowest, relief arrived.
They heard the sound of Hygelac's horn,
his trumpet calling as he came to find them,
the hero in pursuit, at hand with troops.

Hygelac relieved the besieged Geats

"The bloody swathe that Swedes and Geats
cut through each other was everywhere.
No one could miss their murderous feuding.
Then the old man made his move,
2950   pulled back, barred his people in:
Ongentheow withdrew to higher ground.

Ongentheow withdrew

Hygelac's pride and prowess as a fighter
were known to the earl; he had no confidence
that he could hold out against that horde of seamen,
defend wife and the ones he loved
from the shock of the attack. He retreated for shelter
behind the earthwall. Then Hygelac swooped
on the Swedes at bay, his banners swarmed
into their refuge, his Geat forces
2960   drove forward to destroy the camp.
There in his grey hairs, Ongentheow
was cornered, ringed around with swords.

The Swedish king fought for his life. He survived a blow from Wulf, hit back, but was killed by Wulf's brother, Eofor

And it came to pass that the king's fate
was in Eofor's hands, and in his alone.
Wulf, son of Wonred, went for him in anger,
split him open so that blood came spurting
from under his hair. The old hero
still did not flinch, but parried fast,
hit back with a harder stroke:
2970   the king turned and took him on.

Ne meahte se snella   sunu Wonrēdes
ealdum ceorle   ondslyht giofan,
ac hē him on hēafde   helm ǣr gescer,
þæt hē blōde fāh   būgan sceolde,
fēoll on foldan;   næs hē fǣge þā gīt,
ac hē hyne gewyrpte,   þēah ðe him wund hrine.
Lēt se hearda   Higelāces þegn
brādne mēce,   þā his brōðor læg,
eald-sweord eotonisc,   entiscne helm
2980   brecan ofer bord-weal;   ðā gebēah cyning,
folces hyrde,   wæs in feorh dropen.
Ðā wǣron monige,   þe his mǣg wriðon,
ricone ārǣrdon,   ðā him gerȳmed wearð,
þæt hīe wæl-stōwe   wealdan mōston.
Þenden rēafode   rinc ōðerne,
nam on Ongenðīo   īren-byrnan,
heard swyrd hilted   ond his helm somod;
hāres hyrste   Higelāce bær.
Hē ðām frætwum fēng   ond him fægre gehēt
2990   lēana mid lēodum,   ond gelǣste swā;
geald þone gūð-rǣs   Gēata dryhten,
Hrēðles eafora,   þā hē tō hām becōm,
Iofore ond Wulfe   mid ofer-māðmum;
sealde hiora gehwæðrum   hund þūsenda
landes ond locenra bēaga   —ne ðorfte him ðā lēan
    oðwītan
mon on middan-gearde—   syððan hīe ðā mǣrða
    geslōgon;
ond ðā Iofore forgeaf   āngan dohtor,
hām-weorðunge,   hyldo tō wedde.
    "Þæt ys sīo fǣhðo   ond se fēondscipe,
3000   wæl-nīð wera,   ðæs ðe ic wēn hafo,

Then Wonred's son, the brave Wulf,
could land no blow against the aged lord.
Ongentheow divided his helmet
so that he buckled and bowed his bloodied head
and dropped to the ground. But his doom held off.
Though he was cut deep, he recovered again.

"With his brother down, the undaunted Eofor,
Hygelac's thane, hefted his sword
and smashed murderously at the massive helmet

2980   past the lifted shield. And the king collapsed,
The shepherd of people was sheared of life.

"Many then hurried to help Wulf,
bandaged and lifted him, now that they were left
masters of the blood-soaked battleground.
One warrior stripped the other,
looted Ongentheow's iron mail-coat,
his hard sword-hilt, his helmet too,
and carried the graith to King Hygelac;
he accepted the prize, promised fairly   *The victorious Geats*

2990   that reward would come, and kept his word.   *returned home*
For their bravery in action, when they arrived home
Eofor and Wulf were overloaded
by Hrethel's son, Hygelac the Geat,
with gifts of land and linked rings
that were worth a fortune. They had won glory,
so there was no gainsaying his generosity.
And he gave Eofor his only daughter
to bide at home with him, an honour and a bond.

"So this bad blood between us and the Swedes,

3000   this vicious feud, I am convinced,

þē ūs sēceað tō   Swēona lēoda,
syððan hīe gefricgeað   frēan ūserne
ealdor-lēasne,   þone ðe ǣr gehēold
wið hettendum   hord ond rīce
æfter hæleða hryre,   hwate Scildingas,
folc-rēd fremede   oððe furður gēn
eorlscipe efnde.

                Nū is ofost betost,
þæt wē þēod-cyning   þǣr scēawian
ond þone gebringan,   þe ūs bēagas geaf,
3010   on ād-fære.   Ne scel ānes hwæt
meltan mid þām mōdigan,   ac þǣr is māðma hord,
gold unrīme,   grimme gecēapod;
ond nū æt sīðestan   sylfes fēore
bēagas gebohte: þā sceall brond fretan,
ǣlad þeccean,   nalles eorl wegan
māððum tō gemyndum,   nē mægð scȳne
habban on healse   hring-weorðunge,
ac sceal geōmor-mōd,   golde berēafod,
oft, nalles ǣne,   elland tredan,
3020   nū se here-wīsa   hleahtor ālegde,
gamen ond glēo-drēam.   Forðon sceall gār wesan
monig morgen-ceald   mundum bewunden,
hæfen on handa,   nalles hearpan swēg
wīgend weccean,   ac se wonna hrefn
fūs ofer fǣgum   fela reordian,
earne secgan,   hū him æt ǣte spēow,
þenden hē wið wulf   wæl rēafode."

    Swā se secg hwata   secggende wæs
lāðra spella;   hē ne lēag fela
3030   wyrda nē worda.   Weorod eall ārās,

is bound to revive; they will cross our borders
and attack in force when they find out
that Beowulf is dead. In days gone by
when our warriors fell and we were undefended
he kept our coffers and our kingdom safe.
He worked for the people, but as well as that
he behaved like a hero.

                                        We must hurry now
to take a last look at the king
and launch him, lord and lavisher of rings,
on the funeral road. His royal pyre
will melt no small amount of gold:
heaped there in a hoard, it was bought at heavy cost,
and that pile of rings he paid for at the end
with his own life will go up with the flame,
be furled in fire: treasure no follower
will wear in his memory, nor lovely woman
link and attach as a torque around her neck—
but often, repeatedly, in the path of exile
they shall walk bereft, bowed under woe,
now that their leader's laugh is silenced,
high spirits quenched. Many a spear
dawn-cold to the touch will be taken down
and waved on high; the swept harp
won't waken warriors, but the raven winging
darkly over the doomed will have news,
tidings for the eagle of how he hoked and ate,
how the wolf and he made short work of the dead."

Such was the drift of the dire report
that gallant man delivered. He got little wrong
in what he told and predicted.
                                        The whole troop

*The messenger
predicts that the
Swedes will soon
retaliate*

3010

3020

3030

ēodon unblīðe   under Earna-næs,
wollen-teāre,   wundur scēawian.
Fundon ðā on sande   sāwul-lēasne
hlim-bed healdan,   þone þe him hringas geaf
ǣrran mǣlum;   þā wæs ende-dæg
gōdum gegongen,   þæt se gūð-cyning,
Wedra þēoden,   wundor-dēaðe swealt.
Ǣr hī þǣr gesēgan   syllīcran wiht,
wyrm on wonge   wiðer-ræhtes þǣr,
lāðne licgean: wæs se lēg-draca,
grimlīc gryre-fāh,   glēdum beswǣled.
Sē wæs fīftiges   fōt-gemearces
lang on legere;   lyft-wynne hēold
nihtes hwīlum,   nyðer eft gewāt
dennes nīosian;   wæs ðā dēaðe fæst,
hæfde eorð-scrafa   ende genyttod.
Him big stōdan   bunan ond orcas,
discas lāgon   ond dȳre swyrd,
ōmige, þurhetone,   swā hīe wið eorðan fæðm
þūsend wintra   þǣr eardodon.
Þonne wæs þæt yrfe   ēacen-cræftig,
iū-monna gold,   galdre bewunden,
þæt ðām hring-sele   hrīnan ne mōste
gumena ǣnig,   nefne God sylfa,
sigora Sōð-cyning,   sealde þām ðe hē wolde
—hē is manna gehyld—   hord openian,
efne swā hwylcum manna,   swā him gemet ðūhte.
   Þā wæs gesȳne,   þæt se sīð ne ðāh
þām ðe unrihte   inne gehȳdde
wrǣte under wealle;   weard ǣr ofslōh
fēara sumne;   þā sīo fǣhð gewearð

3040

3050

3060

rose in tears, then took their way
to the uncanny scene under Earnaness.
There, on the sand, where his soul had left him,
they found him at rest, their ring-giver
from days gone by. The great man
had breathed his last. Beowulf the king
had indeed met with a marvellous death.

But what they saw first was far stranger:
the serpent on the ground, gruesome and vile,
lying facing him. The fire-dragon
was scaresomely burnt, scorched all colours.
From head to tail, his entire length
was fifty feet. He had shimmered forth
on the night air once, then winged back
down to his den; but death owned him now,
he would never enter his earth-gallery again.
Beside him stood pitchers and piled-up dishes,
silent flagons, precious swords
eaten through with rust, ranged as they had been
while they waited their thousand winters under ground.
That huge cache, gold inherited
from an ancient race, was under a spell—
which meant no one was ever permitted
to enter the ring-hall unless God Himself,
mankind's Keeper, True King of Triumphs,
allowed some person pleasing to Him—
and in His eyes worthy—to open the hoard.

What came about brought to nothing
the hopes of the one who had wrongly hidden
riches under the rock-face. First the dragon slew
that man among men, who in turn made fierce amends

3040

3050

3060

gewrecen wrāðlīce.   Wundur hwār þonne
eorl ellen-rōf   ende gefēre
līf-gesceafta,   þonne leng ne mæg
mon mid his māgum   medu-seld būan.
Swā wæs Bīowulfe,   þā hē biorges weard
sōhte, searo-nīðas;   seofa ne cūðe
þurh hwæt his worulde-gedāl   weorðan sceolde;
swā hit oð dōmes dæg   dīope benemdon
þēodnas mære,   þā ðæt þær dydon,
þæt se secg wǣre   synnum scildig,
hergum geheaðerod,   hell-bendum fæst,
wommum gewītnad,   sē ðone wong strude;
næs hē gold-hwǣte   gearwor hæfde
āgendes ēst   ǣr gescēawod.
     Wīglāf maðelode,   Wīhstānes sunu:
"Oft sceall eorl monig   ānes willan
wrǣc ādrēogan,   swā ūs geworden is.
Ne meahton wē gelǣran   lēofne þēoden.
rīces hyrde   rǣd ǣnigne,
þæt hē ne grētte   gold-weard þone,
lēte hyne licgean   þǣr hē longe wæs,
wīcum wunian   oð woruld-ende;
hēold on hēah-gesceap.   Hord ys gescēawod,
grimme gegongen;   wæs þæt gifeðe tō swīð.
þē ðone þēod-cyning   þyder ontyhte.
Ic wæs þǣr inne   ond þæt eall geondseh,
recedes geatwa,   þā mē gerȳmed wæs,
nealles swǣslīce   sīð ālȳfed
inn under eorð-weall.   Ic on ofoste gefēng
micle mid mundum   mægen-byrðenne
hord-gestrēona,   hider ūt ætbær
cyninge mīnum: cwico wæs þā gēna,

3070

3080

3090

and settled the feud. Famous for his deeds
a warrior may be, but it remains a mystery
where his life will end, when he may no longer
dwell in the mead-hall among his own.
So it was with Beowulf, when he faced the cruelty
and cunning of the mound-guard. He himself was ignorant
of how his departure from the world would happen.
The high-born chiefs who had buried the treasure
3070   declared it until doomsday so accursed
that whoever robbed it would be guilty of wrong
and grimly punished for their transgression,
hasped in hell-bonds in heathen shrines.
Yet Beowulf's gaze at the gold treasure
when he first saw it had not been selfish.

Wiglaf, son of Weohstan, spoke: *Wiglaf ponders*
"Often when one man follows his own will   *Beowulf's fate*
many are hurt. This happened to us.
Nothing we advised could ever convince
3080   the prince we loved, our land's guardian,
not to vex the custodian of the gold,
let him lie where he was long accustomed,
lurk there under earth until the end of the world.
He held to his high destiny. The hoard is laid bare,
but at a grave cost; it was too cruel a fate
that forced the king to that encounter.
I have been inside and seen everything
amassed in the vault. I managed to enter
although no great welcome awaited me
3090   under the earthwall. I quickly gathered up
a huge pile of the priceless treasures
handpicked from the hoard and carried them here
where the king could see them. He was still himself,

wīs ond gewittig.   Worn eall gespræc
gomol on gehðo   ond ēowic grētan hēt,
bæd þæt gē geworhton   æfter wines dǣdum
in bǣl-stede   beorh þone hēan,
micelne ond mǣrne,   swā hē manna wæs
wīgend weorð-fullost   wīde geond eorðan,
þenden hē burh-welan   brūcan mōste.
Uton nū efstan   ōðre sīðe
sēon ond sēcean   searo-gimma geþræc,
wundur under wealle;   ic ēow wīsige,
þæt gē genōge   nēon scēawiað
bēagas ond brād gold.   Sīe sīo bǣr gearo,
ǣdre geæfned,   þonne wē ūt cymen,
ond þonne geferian   frēan ūserne,
lēofne mannan,   þǣr hē longe sceal
on ðæs Waldendes   wǣre geþolian.”

Hēt ðā gebēodan   byre Wīhstānes,
hæle hilde-dīor,   hæleða monegum,
bold-āgendra,   þæt hīe bǣl-wudu
feorran feredon,   folc-āgende,
gōdum tōgēnes: “Nū sceal glēd fretan,
—weaxan wonna lēg—   wigena strengel,
þone ðe oft gebād   īsern-scūre,
þonne strǣla storm   strengum gebǣded
scōc ofer scild-weall,   sceft nytte hēold,
fæðer-gearwum fūs,   flāne fullēode.”

Hūru se snotra   sunu Wīhstānes
ācīgde of corðre   cyniges þegnas,
syfone ætsomne,   þā sēlestan,
ēode eahta sum   under inwit-hrōf

alive, aware, and in spite of his weakness
he had many requests. He wanted me to greet you
and order the building of a barrow that would crown
the site of his pyre, serve as his memorial,
in a commanding position, since of all men
to have lived and thrived and lorded it on earth
3100 his worth and due as a warrior were the greatest.
Now let us again go quickly
and feast our eyes on that amazing fortune
heaped under the wall. I will show the way
and take you close to those coffers packed with rings
and bars of gold. Let a bier be made
and got ready quickly when we come out
and then let us bring the body of our lord,
the man we loved, to where he will lodge
for a long time in the care of the Almighty."

3110 Then Weohstan's son, stalwart to the end,
had orders given to owners of dwellings,
many people of importance in the land,
to fetch wood from far and wide
for the good man's pyre.
                              "Now shall flame consume
our leader in battle, the blaze darken
round him who stood his ground in the steel-hail,
when the arrow-storm shot from bowstrings
pelted the shield-wall. The shaft hit home.
Feather-fledged, it finned the barb in flight."

3120 Next the wise son of Weohstan
called from among the king's thanes
a group of seven: he selected the best
and entered with them, the eighth of their number,

He reports Beowulf's
last wishes

Wiglaf gives orders
for the building of a
funeral pyre

He goes with seven
thanes to remove the
treasure from the
hoard

hilde-rinca;   sum on handa bær
æled-lēoman,   sē ðe on orde gēong.
Næs ðā on hlytme,   hwā þæt hord strude,
syððan orwearde,   ænigne dæl,
secgas gesēgon   on sele wunian,
læne licgan;   lȳt ænig mearn,
3130   þæt hī ofostlīce   ūt geferedon
dȳre māðmas;   dracan ēc scufun,
wyrm ofer weall-clif,   lēton wēg niman,
flōd fæðmian   frætwa hyrde.
Þā wæs wunden gold   on wæn hladen,
æghwæs unrīm,   æþelingc boren,
hār hilde-rinc   tō Hrones-næsse.
   Him ðā gegiredan   Gēata lēode
ād on eorðan   unwāclīcne,
helmum behongen,   hilde-bordum,
3140   beorhtum byrnum,   swā hē bēna wæs;
ālegdon ðā tōmiddes   mærne þēoden
hæleð hīofende,   hlāford lēofne.
Ongunnon þā on beorge   bæl-fȳra mæst
wīgend weccan: wudu-rēc āstāh
sweart ofer swioðole,   swōgende lēg,
wōpe bewunden   —wind-blond gelæg—
oðþæt hē ðā bān-hūs   gebrocen hæfde,
hāt on hreðre.   Higum unrōte
mōd-ceare mændon,   mon-dryhtnes cwealm;
3150   swylce giōmor-gyd   Gēatisc mēowle
. . . .   bunden-heorde
song sorg-cearig.   Sæde geneahhe,
þæt hīo hyre here-geongas   hearde ondrēde
wæl-fylla worn,   werudes egesan,
hȳnðo ond hæft-nȳd.   Heofon rēce swealg.

under the God-cursed roof; one raised
a lighted torch and led the way.
No lots were cast for who should loot the hoard
for it was obvious to them that every bit of it
lay unprotected within the vault,
there for the taking. It was no trouble
to hurry to work and haul out
the priceless store. They pitched the dragon
over the clifftop, let tide's flow
and backwash take the treasure-minder.
Then coiled gold was loaded on a cart
in great abundance, and the grey-haired leader,
the prince on his bier, borne to Hronesness.

The Geat people built a pyre for Beowulf,
stacked and decked it until it stood four-square,
hung with helmets, heavy war-shields
and shining armour, just as he had ordered.
Then his warriors laid him in the middle of it,
mourning a lord far-famed and beloved.
On a height they kindled the hugest of all
funeral fires; fumes of woodsmoke
billowed darkly up, the blaze roared
and drowned out their weeping, wind died down
and flames wrought havoc in the hot bone-house,
burning it to the core. They were disconsolate
and wailed aloud for their lord's decease.
A Geat woman too sang out in grief;
with hair bound up, she unburdened herself
of her worst fears, a wild litany
of nightmare and lament: her nation invaded,
enemies on the rampage, bodies in piles,
slavery and abasement. Heaven swallowed the smoke.

3130

3140

3150

Beowulf's funeral

A Geat woman's dread

Geworhton ðā   Wedra lēode
hlēo on hōe,   sē wæs hēah ond brād,
wēg-līðendum   wīde gesȳne,
ond betimbredon   on tȳn dagum
beadu-rōfes bēcn;   bronda lāfe
wealle beworhton,   swā hyt weorðlīcost
fore-snotre men   findan mihton.
Hī on beorg dydon   bēg ond siglu,
eall swylce hyrsta,   swylce on horde ǣr
nīð-hēdige men   genumen hæfdon;
forlēton eorla gestrēon   eorðan healdan,
gold on grēote,   þǣr hit nū gēn lifað
eldum swā unnyt,   swa hit ǣror wæs.
Þā ymbe hlǣw riodan   hilde-dēore,
æþelinga bearn,   ealra twelfe,
woldon ceare cwīðan,   kyning mǣnan,
word-gyd wrecan   ond ymb wer sprecan:
eahtodan eorlscipe   ond his elle-weorc;
duguðum dēmdon,   swā hit gedēfe bið
þæt mon his wine-dryhten   wordum herge,
ferhðum frēoge,   þonne hē forð scile
of līc-haman   lǣded weorðan.
Swā begnornodon   Gēata lēode
hlāfordes hryre,   heorð-genēatas;
cwǣdon þæt hē wǣre   wyruld-cyninga,
manna mildust   ond mon-ðwǣrust,
lēodum līðost   ond lof-geornost.

3160
3170
3180

Then the Geat people began to construct *Beowulf's barrow*
a mound on a headland, high and imposing,
a marker that sailors could see from far away,
and in ten days they had done the work.
3160   It was their hero's memorial; what remained from the fire
they housed inside it, behind a wall
as worthy of him as their workmanship could make it.
And they buried torques in the barrow, and jewels
and a trove of such things as trespassing men
had once dared to drag from the hoard.
They let the ground keep that ancestral treasure,
gold under gravel, gone to earth,
as useless to men now as it ever was.
Then twelve warriors rode around the tomb,
3170   chieftain's sons, champions in battle,
all of them distraught, chanting in dirges,   *His people lament*
mourning his loss as a man and a king.
They extolled his heroic nature and exploits
and gave thanks for his greatness; which was the proper
      thing,
for a man should praise a prince whom he holds dear
and cherish his memory when that moment comes
when he has to be convoyed from his bodily home.
So the Geat people, his hearth companions,
sorrowed for the lord who had been laid low.
3180   They said that of all the kings upon the earth
he was the man most gracious and fair-minded,
kindest to his people and keenest to win fame.

Family Trees

Acknowledgements

Family Trees

Family trees of the Danish, Swedish, and Geatish dynasties.
Names given here are the ones used in this translation.

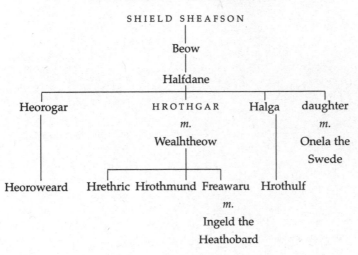

THE DANES or THE SHIELDINGS

SHIELD SHEAFSON
|
Beow
|
Halfdane

Heorogar   HROTHGAR   Halga   daughter
                        m.   *m.*
                  Wealhtheow   Onela the
                                                          Swede

Heoroweard   Hrethric Hrothmund Freawaru   Hrothulf
                                              m.
                                         Ingeld the
                                         Heathobard

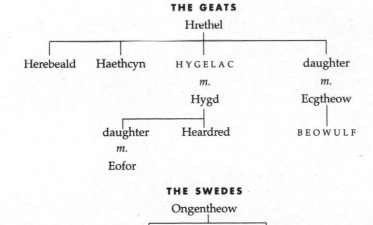

THE GEATS

Hrethel

Herebeald   Haethcyn   HYGELAC   daughter
                              m.   *m.*
                              Hygd   Ecgtheow

                daughter   Heardred   BEOWULF
                   m.
                 Eofor

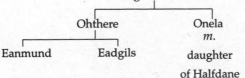

THE SWEDES

Ongentheow

            Ohthere   Onela
                                   m.
Eanmund   Eadgils   daughter
                              of Halfdane

Acknowledgements

The proposal that I should translate *Beowulf* came in the early 1980s from the editors of *The Norton Anthology of English Literature*, so my first thanks go to M. H. Abrams and Jon Stallworthy, who encouraged the late John Benedict to commission some preliminary passages. Then, when I got going in earnest four years ago, Norton appointed Professor Alfred David to keep a learned eye on what I was making of the original, and without his annotations on the first draft and his many queries and suggested alternatives as the manuscript advanced towards completion, this translation would have been a weaker and a wobblier thing. Al's responses were informed by scholarship and by a lifetime's experience of teaching the poem, so they were invaluable. Nevertheless, I was often reluctant to follow his advice and persisted many times in what we both knew were erroneous ways, so he is not to be held responsible for any failures here in the construing of the original or for the different directions in which it is occasionally skewed.

I am also grateful to W. W. Norton & Co. for allowing the translation to be published by Faber and Faber in London and Farrar, Straus and Giroux in New York.

At Faber's, I benefited greatly from Christopher Reid's editorial pencil on the first draft and Paul Keegan's on the second. I also had important encouragement and instruction in the latter stages of the work from colleagues at Harvard, who now include by happy coincidence the present Associate General Editor of *The Norton Anthology*, Professor Stephen Greenblatt. I remember with special pleasure a medievalists' seminar where I finally recanted on the use of the word "gilly" in the presence of Professors Larry Benson, Dan Donoghue, Joseph Harris, and Derek Pearsall. Professor John D. Niles happened to attend that seminar and I was lucky to enjoy another, too brief discussion with him in Berkeley, worrying about word choices and wondering about the prejudice in favour of Anglo-Saxon over Latinate diction in translations of the poem.

Helen Vendler's reading helped, as ever, in many points of detail, and I received other particular and important comments from Professors Mary Clayton and Peter Sacks.

Extracts from the first hundred lines of the translation appeared in *The Haw Lantern* (1987) and *Causley at 70* (1987). Excerpts from the more recent work were published in *Agni, The Sunday Times, The Threepenny Review, The Times Literary Supplement*; also in *A Parcel of Poems: For Ted Hughes on His Sixty-fifth Birthday* and *The Literary Man, Essays Presented to Donald W. Hannah*. Lines 88–98 were printed in January 1999 by Bow & Arrow Press as a tribute to Professor William Alfred, himself a translator of the poem and, while he lived, one of the great teachers of it. Bits of the introduction first appeared in *The Sunday Times* and in an article entitled "Further Language" (*Studies in the Literary Imagination*, vol. XXX, no. 2). The epigraph to the introduction is from my poem "The Settle Bed" (*Seeing Things*, 1991). The broken lines on p. 151 indicate lacunae in the original text.

S.H.